The Future Agenda Internationalization

The internationalization of higher education is a worldwide phenomenon, subject to multiple interpretations at national, institutional, and individual levels. Still, much of the mainstream literature on this topic is concentrated on a small number of countries and a narrow range of key topics.

To address this gap, *The Future Agenda for Internationalization in Higher Education* offers a broader set of perspectives from outside the dominant English-speaking and Western European paradigms, while simultaneously focusing on dimensions of internationalization that are known to be under-researched. Additionally, the editors give primacy to next generation perspectives, not only to amplify our current understanding of key issues around the world, but also to shine a light on possible future agendas for this important aspect of contemporary higher education.

The notions of new modes, new topics, and new contexts frame the analysis, providing new pathways for exploring and understanding distinct aspects of this crucially important phenomenon in higher education around the world. Key topics covered include:

- the current state of research and analysis on the internationalization of higher education
- aspects of internationalization and international activities which have not previously been explored or have limited current exposure
- how research into internationalization is conducted, showcasing innovative methodological practices
- a synthesis of common themes and differences in relation to the future agenda of topics, modes, and contexts for internationalization
- an identification of key areas for future research.

A thoughtful guide for considering the many possible directions ahead for internationalization in higher education, *The Future Agenda for Internationalization in Higher Education* is essential reading for academic researchers and graduate students, as well as international education practitioners and leaders keen to make sense of evolving trends in this field.

Douglas Proctor is Director of International Affairs at University College Dublin, Ireland, and has previously held academic and senior managerial positions at universities in France, New Caledonia, and Australia.

Laura E. Rumbley is Assistant Professor of the Practice and Associate Director of the Boston College Center for International Higher Education, USA, and was previously Deputy Director of the Academic Cooperation Association, Belgium.

Internationalization in Higher Education

This series addresses key themes in the development of internationalization within Higher Education. Up to the minute and international in both appeal and scope, books in the series focus on delivering contributions from a wide range of contexts and provide both theoretical perspectives and practical examples. Written by some of the leading experts in the field, they are vital guides that discuss and build upon evidence-based practice and provide a clear evaluation of outcomes.

Series Editor: Elspeth Jones, Emerita Professor, Leeds Beckett University, UK

Titles in the series:

Comprehensive Internationalization
Institutional pathways to success
John Hudzik

Internationalizing the Curriculum
Betty Leask

The Globalization of Internationalization
Emerging voice and perspectives
Hans de Wit, Jocelyne Gacel-Ávila, Elspeth Jones and Nico Jooste

Intercultural Competence in Higher Education
International approaches, assessment and application
Darla K. Deardorff and Lily A. Arasaratnam-Smith

Intercultural Interventions in Study Abroad
Jane Jackson and Susan Oguro

The Future Agenda for Internationalization in Higher Education
Next generation insights into research, policy, and practice
Douglas Proctor and Laura E. Rumbley

For more information about this series, please visit: www.routledge.com/
Internationalization-in-Higher-Education-Series/book-series/INTHE

The Future Agenda for Internationalization in Higher Education

Next Generation Insights into Research, Policy, and Practice

Edited by Douglas Proctor and Laura E. Rumbley

Routledge
Taylor & Francis Group

LONDON AND NEW YORK

First published 2018
by Routledge
2 Park Square, Milton Park, Abingdon, Oxon OX14 4RN

and by Routledge
711 Third Avenue, New York, NY 10017

Routledge is an imprint of the Taylor & Francis Group, an informa business

British Library Cataloguing-in-Publication Data
A catalogue record for this book is available from the British Library

Library of Congress Cataloging-in-Publication Data
A catalog record has been requested for this book

ISBN: 978-1-138-28978-9 (hbk)
ISBN: 978-1-138-28979-6 (pbk)
ISBN: 978-1-315-26690-9 (ebk)

Typeset in Galliard
by Swales & Willis Ltd, Exeter, Devon, UK

Contents

Contributors

Chelsea Blackburn Cohen is a doctoral candidate in the Department of Educational Leadership and Policy Analysis at the University of Wisconsin-Madison. Blackburn Cohen's research interests center on academic freedom and the effects of globalization on higher education, society, and knowledge production. Her dissertation examines the forced displacement of academics worldwide and the experiences of those scholars with ongoing appointments at colleges and universities in the United States.

Daniela Crăciun is a Yehuda Elkana Fellow at the Central European University (Hungary), where she is pursuing a Ph.D. Recently, Daniela has been a visiting scholar at the Center for International Higher Education at Boston College (USA) and the Federal University of São Carlos (Brazil). Previously, she received a bachelor's degree in Marketing and Media from Canterbury Christ Church University (England) and a master's degree in Global Studies from Leipzig University (Germany), Jawaharlal Nehru University (India) and Wroclaw University (Poland). Daniela's research interests lie in the areas of methodology and education policy, specifically higher education internationalization and international student mobility.

Hans de Wit is Director of the Boston College (BC) Center for International Higher Education and a professor in BC's Lynch School of Education. He is the founding Director of the Centre for Higher Education Internationalisation of the Università Cattolica del Sacro Cuore in Milan, Italy; the founding editor of the *Journal of Studies in International Education*; and a founding member and past president of the European Association for International Education. A former Fulbright New Century Scholar, Hans de Wit has served as a consultant for a wide range of national ministries and international organizations – such as the OECD, the World Bank, and the European Commission. He also serves on international advisory boards for universities in Colombia, Germany, the Netherlands, and Russia.

Susanne Feiertag is senior policy officer at Nuffic. Currently she coordinates Internationalization for All, an agenda for continuous internationalization from primary to higher education. She has broad experience in internationalization in education acquired through a number of positions, including coordinating a national program aimed at the retention of international students, and programs on professional recognition related to countries' EU accession. She was posted at the Ministry of Education, Culture and Science. Susanne graduated from the Amsterdam School of the Arts in Teacher in Dance (BA) and holds a master's in Slavonic Languages (cum laude) from the University of Amsterdam.

Andrea Ferrer holds a master's degree (2017) in French and International Education from the University of Wisconsin-Madison's Professional French Master's Program. After completing an 11-month internship at IES Abroad's Paris French Studies Center, she is now internship program coordinator and program assistant at IES. In this role, she guides incoming international university students through the internship application process, while securing internship positions in the greater Paris area. In addition, she facilitates cross-cultural communication and understanding between the students and host companies during their internships.

Richard Garrett is Chief Research Officer at Eduventures, a higher education research firm based in Boston, USA, which is part of the National Research Center for College & University Admissions (NRCCUA). Richard is also Director of the Observatory on Borderless Higher Education, a think tank on online learning, transnational education, and new providers around the world. The Observatory is part of i-graduate and Tribal Group.

Thomas Greenaway is a doctoral candidate at the University or Warwick researching teamwork in higher education and intercultural competence. His research interest in refugee education began through volunteering with refugees in Calais, France. He subsequently worked as a volunteer researcher in Kiron Open Higher Education. He has since organized refugee education related events in the United Kingdom. Alongside his passion for improving the situations of refugees, Thomas has a keen interest in the relationship between culture and working in diverse teams, which is the focus of his doctoral research and aims to contribute new insights into how students negotiate and achieve group tasks in a university setting.

Jermain Griffin is a Professorial Lecturer in the American University School of Education. He is also a research consultant with the American Council on Education. His research focuses on the internationalization of higher education in the USA, Mexico, and Central America. Griffin's professional experience also includes managing an International Studies academic program and doing international development work in Central America and Africa. He holds a Ph.D. in Education and Human Resource Studies from Colorado State University.

Robin Matross Helms is Director of the American Council on Education's Center for Internationalization and Global Engagement, where her work focuses on internationalization of U.S. institutions and global higher education issues. Her previous experience includes international program management for the Institute of International Education, EF Education, and CET Academic Programs, and faculty development program management at the University of Minnesota. Helms has also worked as a consultant to a number of organizations in the international and higher education fields, including the World Bank, the Institute for Higher Education Policy, and Harvard University's Collaborative on Academic Careers in Higher Education.

Kiyomi Horiuchi is a graduate student of the Graduate School of Education at Hiroshima University in Japan. After having served as a journalist at the Japan Broadcasting Corporation (NHK), he worked as an administrative staff member at the International Exchange Center of Aoyama Gakuin University (2005–2010) and the Institutional Research and Planning Section of Tokyo International University (2011–2016). He obtained a Master's of Higher Education Administration at J. F. Oberlin University, an MBA from Tama University, and a BA in Comparative Culture from Sophia University. His primary research interests lie in the development of English-taught programs at Japanese universities and their impact on institutional management.

Fiona Hunter is based in Italy, where she is Associate Director at the Centre for Higher Education Internationalisation (CHEI) at the Università Cattolica del Sacro Cuore in Milan. She also works as a global higher education consultant helping universities to think more strategically, either for organizational improvement in general or with a specific focus on internationalization. She is co-editor of the *Journal of Studies in International Education* (JSIE), holds a Doctor of Business Administration (DBA) in Higher Education Management from the University of Bath in the UK, and is past President of the European Association for International Education.

Mark S. Johnson is a senior specialist in the International Division and a senior lecturer in the School of Education at the University of Wisconsin-Madison, as well as senior consultant at the Eurasia Foundation in Washington, DC. He has worked as an associate professor of history at Colorado College, and a guest professor at the Institute of Education, National Research University Higher School of Economics in Moscow. His research and teaching interests include global higher education policies, innovation in university teaching and learning, and the role of higher education in global sustainability.

Jane Knight, of the Ontario Institute for Studies in Education, University of Toronto, has worked in over 70 countries with universities, governments, and United Nations Agencies, which helps to bring a comparative, development, and international perspective to her research, teaching, and policy work. She is the author of numerous publications on internationalization, is the co-founder of the African Network for the Internationalization of Education (ANIE), and sits on the advisory boards of international organizations, universities, and journals. The awards she has received include honorary doctorates from the University of Exeter (UK) and Symbiosis International University (India), the Outstanding Researcher award from EAIR, and the Gilbert Medal from Universitas 21.

Sonja Knutson is the Director of the Internationalization Office at Memorial University of Newfoundland. She is responsible for leading the Internationalization Office to implement the actions of the Strategic Internationalization Plan 2020 at Memorial, and contributes frequently to international education conferences on the Canadian context of internationalization. She served for six years on the board of directors of the Canadian Bureau for International Education, and is chair of the NAFSA International Education Leadership Knowledge Community.

Li Mengyang is a Ph.D. candidate in the Faculty of Education at the University of Hong Kong. Her core research interests are in international academic relations, internationalization of the humanities and social sciences, and China's global engagement in higher education. Her dissertation project examines internationalization of the humanities and social sciences in China by looking at China's English-language academic journals in these areas.

Charles Mathies is an Academy of Finland Research Fellow based at the Finnish Institute for Educational Research in the University of Jyväskylä (Finland). He previously held multiple university management positions in Europe and the United States primarily in strategic planning and institutional research. Dr. Mathies' research focuses on international student migration and mobility; data usage, analytics, and its management in higher education; and institutional strategic planning.

Bryan McAllister-Grande received his EdD in Higher Education in 2017 from the Harvard Graduate School of Education, where he was also a Spencer Foundation Early Career Scholar. He is currently a program associate with the Harvard Civic and Moral Education Initiative. Bryan's work examines the moral and ethical aspects of internationalization, as well as the history of modern universities and their relationship to politics and society. His work is interdisciplinary, crossing the boundaries of religious, social, and intellectual inquiry. He also earned an M.Ed. from Harvard and a BA from the University of Massachusetts-Amherst.

Rachael Merola is Senior Researcher at the Observatory on Borderless Higher Education. She has worked in international affairs at universities in Seoul, South Korea and Barcelona, Spain, and has extensive experience in both research and practice in transnational education. She holds a BSc from Tufts University, an EdM in International Education Policy from Harvard, and is a Ph.D. candidate in International Higher Education at the University of Groningen.

Ana Luisa Muñoz-García is a Doctor in Educational Culture, Policy and Society. She is an Assistant Professor in the School of Education at the Pontifical Catholic University of Chile, was trained as a teacher of history and geography and holds a master's degree in Curriculum Studies. Her research areas have included educational research and practice in poverty areas and construction of knowledge in academia within the framework of internationalization policies. Today, she is working on a project focused on first-generation indigenous students in the university and policies of research in education.

Jackline Nyerere is a Senior Lecturer and Researcher in the Department of Educational Management, Policy and Curriculum Studies at Kenyatta University (Kenya). She has over 15 years' experience working in higher education, in teaching, research, and administrative positions. Her research projects have concentrated on open and flexible learning, university partnerships, internationalization of education, as well as sustainability. Jackline holds a Ph.D. in planning and economics of education from Kenyatta University, and a professional training in Higher Education Leadership and Management from Carl von Ossietzky University of Oldenburg (Germany).

Milton Obamba is currently Academic Fellow in International Education Policy and Management at the School of Education, University of Leeds (UK). He was previously a Carnegie Centenary Fellow at Leeds Beckett University, where he received his Ph.D. in international higher education in 2011. Over the last decade, Obamba has led and participated in several research and engagement projects in higher education across various countries. Some of his recent publications have appeared in *Higher Education Policy*, *Journal of International and Comparative Education*, and the *Sage Handbook of International Higher Education*. His latest co-authored book, *The Transnationally Partnered University* (2014), is published in Palgrave Macmillan's International and Development Education series.

Hiroshi Ota is Professor of the Center for Global Education at Hitotsubashi University (HU) and Director of the Hitotsubashi University Global Education Program. Before his current position, he worked for the Office for the Promotion of International Relations at HU, the HU School of Commerce and Management (as an International Student Advisor), the Office of International Education at SUNY-Buffalo (USA), and at Toyo University (Japan). His research primarily focuses on higher education policies and practices related to internationalization and international student mobility from a comparative perspective. From SUNY-Buffalo, Ota received both his EdM and Ph.D. in Comparative and Global Studies in Education.

Douglas Proctor is Director of International Affairs at University College Dublin (Ireland), where he has management responsibility for the international office and provides leadership to the broader university community on internationalization and international engagement. Douglas won the Tony

Adams Award for Doctoral Studies in International Education in 2014 and completed a Ph.D. in international higher education at the University of Melbourne (Australia) in late 2016. Douglas has authored papers and reports in relation to his doctoral research, focusing on the international dimensions of academic work and the international engagement of academic staff, as well as on the global landscape of international education research.

Susanne Ress is a postdoctoral researcher at the Center for Comparative and International Education, Humboldt-Universität Berlin. In 2015, she completed her joint degree in the Department of Educational Policy Studies and Development Studies Program at the University of Wisconsin-Madison. Contributing to postcolonial and critical race studies, she explores international education discourses, especially as international development policies, changing economic pressures, and new climate dynamics reshape young people's lives. In 2016, her dissertation won the Gail P. Kelly Outstanding Dissertation Award from the U.S.-based Comparative and International Education Society (CIES). Her current work focuses on employability and sustainability discourses.

Laura E. Rumbley, Ph.D., is Assistant Professor of the practice and Associate Director at the Boston College Center for International Higher Education (CIHE), where she coordinates the MA program in International Higher Education. Her research and teaching focus largely on internationalization of U.S. and European higher education. Formerly Deputy Director of the Brussels-based Academic Cooperation Association (ACA), she serves as a co-editor of the *Journal of Studies in International Education*; the Boston College quarterly, *International Higher Education*; and the series *International Briefs for Higher Education Leaders*, co-published by CIHE and the American Council on Education. Since 2013, she has been Publications Committee chair for the European Association for International Education (EAIE).

Hiro Saito is Assistant Professor of Sociology at Singapore Management University. Given his broad interest in intersections between power and knowledge, he studies how interactions between government and citizens shape public policy by focusing on the role of experts. The bulk of research he has done so far on this topic resulted in *The History Problem: The Politics of War Commemoration in East Asia* (University of Hawaii Press, 2016). Currently, he is working on multiple research projects to examine various effects of globalization on higher education institutions as producers of public goods and focal points of the public sphere.

Neil Sparnon is an independent consultant and trainer in higher education management and systems with extensive experience in public, private, and faith-based institutions. He specializes in academic and administrative systems, project management, quality assurance, online learning, and strategic planning. In the last 27 years, he has worked in Europe, Africa, the Middle East,

Asia, and latterly North America. His most recent role was Chief Academic Officer to the "Jesuit Commons: Higher Education at the Margins" project, which has brought accredited online higher education provision to refugees in Malawi, Jordan, Kenya, Sri Lanka, the Philippines, Afghanistan, Myanmar, and Thailand.

Dina Uzhegova is a Program Officer and advanced Ph.D. student at the Melbourne Centre for the Study of Higher Education, the University of Melbourne. Her research is focused on internationalization of higher education in Russia; more specifically, she is interested in internationalization process in regional universities in Siberia and the Far East. Prior to commencing her Ph.D., Dina worked in the Institute for International Studies at Lock Haven University and International Student Services at Ashland University in the USA. She also completed an internship at the Institute of International Education office in Budapest.

Adinda van Gaalen is senior policy officer at Nuffic and part time Ph.D. candidate at Ghent University. She is particularly interested in internationalization strategies and policy. Adinda has worked on the development of quality assurance tools for internationalization. She has conducted studies on internationalization in higher education and (co-)authored several publications. She works as an advisor and trainer. Her main focus is on higher education, although she is also involved in the internationalization of secondary education. Previously, Adinda worked at the Amsterdam University of Applied Sciences. She also served as an elected member on the General Council of the European Association for International Education (EAIE) from 2014 to 2016.

Louise Michelle Vital is a faculty member in the Global Studies and International Relations program at Northeastern University. Her interests include higher education in crisis and conflict; global student access and success in higher education; scholar/practitioner preparation for international engagement; and critical reflective practice in research and the classroom. She is also the senior instructional advisor for the Global Citizens' Initiative-sponsored "Fundamentals of Global Citizen Leadership" course. Dr. Vital earned her Ph.D. in higher, adult, and lifelong education (with a specialization in Latin American and Caribbean studies) and graduate certificate in international development from Michigan State University in 2015.

Leasa Weimer, Ph.D., is the Knowledge Development Adviser for the European Association for International Education and a researcher at the University of Jyväskylä, Finland. She has over 20 years of experience in higher education and has been active in the field of international education as a Fulbright scholar, president of the Erasmus Mundus Association, and an expert consultant for numerous European projects. Her work bridges research with the practice of international higher education; she has authored several conference papers, book chapters, and policy papers on the topics of national policies and international student mobility, alumni relations, and joint degrees.

Linda Hui Yang has a Ph.D. in intercultural studies from Durham University. She is currently a postdoctoral researcher for a project titled "Internationalisation of Irish Higher Education" at the School of Education, University College Dublin. The project, funded by the Irish Research Council, aims to inform sector thinking with reference to a holistic approach to internationalization, as well as supporting internationalization of higher education. This is the first nationwide study involving all of the Irish universities and institutes of technology in the Republic of Ireland. Linda's research interests include internationalization of higher education, intercultural education, acculturation, and second/foreign language teaching and learning.

Christina W. Yao, Ph.D., is an Assistant Professor of Higher Education in the Department of Educational Administration at the University of Nebraska-Lincoln. She is a qualitative researcher who primarily studies student engagement and learning in higher education. She operationalizes her research focus through three connected topical areas: international/comparative education, teaching and learning, and graduate education. Some current projects include a collaborative study on doctoral students' international research development, teaching and learning in Vietnam, and the college transition process for international students of color. Christina completed her D.Phil. in higher, adult, and lifelong education at Michigan State University.

Acknowledgments

The editors are keen to thank the many contributors to this book for their time, energy, and responsiveness to our feedback. We have also been privileged to draw on the guidance and support of some of the leading scholars in the field, notably Jane Knight and Hans de Wit, who agreed to co-author the Preface, and Elspeth Jones, Routledge Series Editor and frequent source of moral and intellectual support. We must also thank our families for their patience and support, when we were reviewing draft chapters in the evenings and on weekends, and teleconferencing at odd times of day and night. The preparation of this book has been truly international, as it has been edited from nearly every continent. Indeed, we regularly made efficient use of our travel plans – remarkably, even a completely serendipitous meet-up in Charles de Gaulle airport in Paris en route to different destinations – to find convenient time zones for teleconferences or face-to-face meetings. This project saw us meet up in many different contexts, communicate via multiple modes, and cover an enormous array of topics on the road to the finish line. We are grateful for all of the people and the privileging factors that made it possible for us to complete this work.

Douglas Proctor, Dublin (Ireland)
Laura E. Rumbley, Chestnut Hill (United States)
October 2017

Foreword to the series
Internationalization in Higher Education

This series addresses the rapidly changing and highly topical field of internationalization in higher education. Increasingly visible in institutional strategies as well as national and international agendas since the latter part of the 20th century, internationalization has been informed by diverse disciplines, including anthropology, languages and communication, business and marketing, pedagogy and environmental studies. In part its rise can be seen as a response to globalization and growing competition among higher education institutions. However, it also responds to the recognition that students must be prepared for changing local and global environments in both personal and professional life.

The diverse and complex dimensions of contemporary internationalization require institutions to adjust and define the concept for their own purposes, adding to the richness of our understanding. Insights from countries where institutional and curricular internationalization is a more recent development will enhance our awareness of the benefits and challenges of internationalization practice over the coming years.

There are compelling drivers for university leaders to adopt an integrated rather than a unidimensional approach to internationalization. Intensifying competition for talent, changes in global student flows, international branch campuses and growing complexity in cross-border activity, along with the rising influence of institutional rankings, all provide economic impetus and reputational consequences of success or failure. Meanwhile added incentive is provided by the awareness that the intercultural competence required for global contexts is equally important for living and working in today's increasingly diverse multicultural societies. Rising employer and student demand reflects growing interest in international and intercultural experiences and competencies. Internationalization thus has both global and more local intercultural interests at its heart.

Internationalization as a powerful force for change is an underlying theme of this series, in contrast to economic or brand-enhancing aspects of international engagement. It seeks to address these complex topics as internationalization matures into its next phase. It aims to reflect contemporary concerns, with volumes geared to the major questions of our time. Written or edited by leading thinkers and authors from around the world, while giving a voice to emerging researchers, the series offers theoretical perspectives with practical applications, examining some of the critical issues in this developing field for higher education leaders and practitioners alike.

This volume in the series allows the reader to hear from scholars who, building on the foundations of internationalization in recent years, are exploring and framing its future direction through research and practice. At its heart are aspects of next generation internationalization that the editors identify as under-researched to date and which frame their approach to this book. The issues and insights offered by authors are organized around three themes – new topics, new modes, and new contexts for higher education internationalization.

The editors are keenly aware of the complexity of this topic in today's world. Thus they have assembled a group of authors who take global, regional, and local dimensions into account by reflecting on major international factors common to all, while also noting local and regional differences in the concerns and future course for internationalization. Significant breadth of perspective is presented, as a result of contributions from all six continents. Some of the ensuing chapters help the reader to consider familiar themes in different ways, while others bring into focus aspects of internationalization which we may have failed to take into account so far. This timely and interesting volume will be of value to everyone involved in the field.

Elspeth Jones, Series Editor
Emerita Professor of the Internationalisation of
Higher Education, Leeds Beckett University, UK

Preface

Internationalization of higher education: where have we come from and where are we going?

Jane Knight and Hans de Wit

Over the past 25 years, internationalization has evolved from a marginal and minor component to a global, strategic, and mainstream factor in higher education. We have been active participants and analysts in that evolution, and in the context of this collection of contributions about new perspectives on higher education internationalization it seems appropriate to ask ourselves the question: where have we come from and where are we going? In no way intending to ignore other researchers' contributions to the analysis of internationalization, we have opted explore this question by reflecting on our own publications (Knight & de Wit, 1995, 1997, 1999) to help frame the underpinnings of the "next generation" contributions contained in this new volume.

In 1995, we co-wrote "Strategies for internationalisation of higher education: historical and conceptual perspectives" as the introductory chapter of what can be considered the first comparative international study on internationalization strategies (de Wit, 1995), building on a small number of previous studies emanating primarily from American and European sources. Since then, while the meanings, rationales, and approaches to internationalization have evolved, as has the context in which it is taking place, the foundation for the study of internationalization has not substantively changed. As we stated then, with reference to the Association of Universities and Colleges of Canada (AUCC),"there is no simple, unique or all encompassing definition of internationalisation of the university," nor is it "helpful for internationalisation to become a 'catch-all' phrase for everything and anything international" (Knight & de Wit, 1995, p. 16). That notion is probably even truer now than it was two decades ago. Internationalization has become a very broad and varied concept, including many new rationales, approaches, and strategies in different and constantly changing contexts. It is revealing to see how the terminology used to describe the international dimension of higher education has evolved over the past five decades. Table 0.1 illustrates how the new developments, trends, issues, and some unintended consequences of internationalization are reflected in the evolution of the terminology over the years.

Who would have guessed in the 1960s – when the emphasis was on scholarships for foreign students, international development projects, and area studies – that we would today be discussing new developments such as branding, international

Table 0.1 Evolution of international education terminology

Recent terms Last 15 years	New terms Last 25 years	Existing terms Last 35 years	Traditional terms Last 50 years
Generic terms			
• regionalization • glocalization • global citizenship • education hubs • edu-glomerates • global rankings • academic cities • international program and provider mobility	• globalization • borderless education • cross-border education • transnational education • virtual education • internationalization 'abroad' • internationalization "at home" • comprehensive internationalization	• internationalization • multicultural education • intercultural education • global education • distance education • offshore or overseas education	• international education • international development cooperation • comparative education • correspondence education
Specific elements			
• MOOCs • international competencies • degree mills • visa factories • joint, double, multiple degrees • branding, status-building • international joint/co-founded universities	• education providers • corporate universities • liberalization of educational services • networks • virtual universities • branch campus • twinning and franchise programs • internationalization of the curriculum • international, intercultural, and global competences	• international students • study abroad • institution agreements • partnership projects • area studies • binational cooperation	• foreign students • student exchange • development projects • cultural agreements • language study

Source: adapted from Knight (2017).

program and provider mobility, global citizenship, internationalization at home, MOOCs, global rankings, knowledge diplomacy, world-class universities, cultural homogenization, franchising, and joint and double degree programs. "International education" has been a term used commonly throughout the years – and is still preferred in many countries. However, the processes of internationalization, globalization, regionalization, and now planetization, are actively debated concepts and central to understanding, promoting, and sustaining the international dimension of higher education (Knight, 2015a).

Rereading our 1995 chapter, it is striking that the current anti-global, anti-immigration, and inward-looking political climate in different parts of the world, was already announcing itself at that time: "The danger of isolationalism, racism and monoculturalism is a threatening cloud hanging over the present interest in internationalisation of higher education" (Knight & de Wit, 1995, p. 29). That cloud has only become bigger and more threatening since, and may define present and future challenges of internationalization more than ever (Altbach & de Wit, 2017). We also referred to Clark Kerr's analysis of the "partial convergence" of the cosmopolitan university. Has the 20th century indeed become, as he stated, more universal? It may seem so, but the international dimensions of higher education today may have become too disconnected from the local context. One of the main challenges for higher education and its international dimensions is to emphasize the connection between the global and the local (de Wit, Gacel-Avila, Jones, & Jooste, 2017).

In the discourse and study of internationalization, a great deal of attention has been paid to all modes of international academic mobility – people, programs, providers, policies, and projects – but not enough attention has been paid to the internationalization of graduate education and research, including international co-authorship and other international research benchmarks. Research has become more complex in recent years. It both requires and is distinguished by more international collaboration than in the past, and it is increasingly competitive in nature. National and institutional needs to acquire academic talent are urgent and processes around issues such as the awarding of patents and knowledge transfer require more support than ever. Long-term planning for research infrastructure, increased research capacity, development of new research platforms, and better coordination between research units, all require a more strategic focus on capacity development and international research policies and systems. Growth in international research funding, patents, publications, and citations requires the development of internationalized, or globalized, research teams. Bibliometric analysis yields evidence of increasing scientific collaboration within the international scientific community (de Wit, forthcoming).

The generation of new knowledge through the production and application of research has introduced the notion of international education and research as a form of soft power. The use of knowledge as power is a development requiring serious reflection because soft power is characterized by competitiveness, dominance, and self-interest. An alternative to the power paradigm is the framework of diplomacy. Diplomacy focuses on strategies, such as negotiation, mediation, collaboration, compromise, and facilitation. These are very different tactics and concepts than those usually attached to power. Does this suggest that diplomacy is a more appropriate structure to frame the role of higher education and research in international relations than a power paradigm? Knowledge diplomacy involves the contribution that education and knowledge creation, sharing, and use makes to international relations and engagement. But, knowledge diplomacy should be seen as a reciprocal process. Knowledge diplomacy contributes to international relations, and conversely, international engagement brings added value to the development of knowledge and its contribution to society. One serves the other. Mutual benefits and a two-way exchange are therefore essential to the concept of international education and research as a tool of knowledge diplomacy. In short, knowledge sharing and mutual benefits are fundamental to the understanding and operationalization of knowledge diplomacy (Knight, 2015b).

There is no doubt that internationalization has come of age. No longer is it an ad hoc or marginalized part of the higher education landscape. University strategic plans, national policy statements, regionalization initiatives, international declarations, and academic articles all indicate the centrality of internationalization in the world of higher education. The popularity of the phrase "comprehensive internationalization" does not reflect widespread reality, however: For most institutions around the world, internationalization is still characterized by a collection of fragmented and unrelated activities. Meanwhile, the increasing commodification of higher education remains primarily oriented towards reaching targets without a debate on potential risks and ethical consequences. However, there is increased awareness that the notion of "internationalization" not only touches on relations between nations, but even more so on the relations between cultures and between realities at the global and local levels (de Wit, 2013).

It is prudent to take a close look at the policies, plans, and priorities of key actors, such as universities, government ministries, national/ regional/international academic associations, and international organizations and agencies. These documents reveal that internationalization of higher education and research is closely linked with economic competitiveness and innovation, the great brain race, the quest for world-class status, and soft power. Economic and political rationales are increasingly the key drivers for national policies related to the internationalization of higher education, while academic and social/cultural motivations are not increasing in importance at the same rate. Because of the more interdependent and connected world in which we live, this imbalance must be addressed and re-calibrated (Knight, 2015a).

It may behoove us to look back at the last 20 or 30 years of internationalization and ask ourselves some questions. Has international higher education lived up to our expectations and its potential? What have been the values that have guided it through the information and communication revolution; the unprecedented mobility of people, ideas, and technology; the clash of cultures; and the periods of economic booms and busts? What have we learned from the past that will guide us into the future? Is the strong appeal for internationalization of the curriculum, international and intercultural learning outcomes, and global citizenship to be perceived as a return to the former days of cooperation and exchange, or a call for a more responsible process of internationalization in reaction to the current political climate and the increased commercialization of internationalization? Who could have forecasted that internationalization would transform from what has been traditionally considered a process based on values of cooperation, partnership, exchange, mutual benefits, and capacity building to one that is increasingly characterized by competition, commercialization, self-interest, and status building (Knight, 2015b)?

As we look backwards and forwards, it is thus important to ask one question. What are the core principles and values underpinning internationalization of higher education that 10 or 20 years from now will make us look back and be proud of the track record and contribution that international higher education has made to the more interdependent world we live in, the next generation of citizens, and the bottom billion people living in poverty on our planet?

The contributions included in this book strive to take this conversation forward in new and meaningful ways. Undertaking this work is impossible without clearly understanding where we have come from, and developing innovative insights into the future of internationalization is impossible without providing opportunities for a new generation of scholars to advance their best guesses as to where we may be headed next. Who would have guessed 25 years ago that so many angles on internationalization of higher education would have been explored, so many developments would have unfolded, and so many new questions and concerns would have emerged to engage us for the very long haul ahead?

References

Altbach, P. G., & de Wit, H. (2017). The new nationalism and internationalisation of HE. *University World News* (September 15), 474.

de Wit, H. (Ed.). (1995). *Strategies for Internationalisation of Higher Education, A Comparative Study of Australia, Canada, Europe and the United States of America.* Amsterdam: EAIE in cooperation with IMHE/OECD and AIEA.

de Wit, H. (2013). Rethinking the concept of internationalisation. In M. Stiasny & T. Gore (Eds.), *Going Global: Identifying Trends and Drivers of International Education* (pp. 213–218). London: Emerald Group Publishing.

de Wit, H. (forthcoming). Internationalization of research and knowledge development. In P. Teixeira & J. Shin (Eds.), *Springer Encyclopedia of Higher Education Systems and Institutions.* Dordrecht: Springer.

de Wit, H., Gacel-Avila, J, Jones, E., & Jooste, N. (Eds.). (2017). *The Globalization of Internationalization: Emerging Voices and Perspectives* (Internationalization in Higher Education Series). New York: Routledge.

Knight, J. (2015a). Meaning, rationales and tensions in internationalization of higher education. In S. McGrath & Q. Gu (Eds.), *Routledge Handbook on International Education and Development* (pp. 325–339). London, UK: Routledge.

Knight, J. (2015b). The potential of knowledge diplomacy: higher education and international relations. In L. Weimer (Ed.), *A Wealth of Nations* (pp. 37–45). Amsterdam: EAIE.

Knight. J. (2017). The international university: models and muddles. In R. Barnett & M. Peters (Eds.), *The Idea of the University*, vol. 2, *Contemporary Perspectives*. New York: Peter Lang Publishing.

Knight, J., & de Wit, H. (1995). Strategies for internationalisation of higher education: historical and conceptual perspectives. In de Wit, H. (Ed.), *Strategies for Internationalisation of Higher Education, A Comparative Study of Australia, Canada, Europe and the United States of America*. Amsterdam: EAIE in cooperation with IMHE/OECD and AIEA.

Knight, J., & de Wit, H. (Eds.). (1997). *Strategies for Internationalisation of Higher Education in Asia Pacific countries*. Amsterdam: EAIE in co-operation with IMHE/OECD and IDP-Education Australia.

Knight, J., & de Wit, H. (Eds.). (1999). *Quality and Internationalisation of Higher Education*. Paris: OECD.

Introduction

New voices, new ideas, and new approaches in the internationalization of higher education

Douglas Proctor and Laura E. Rumbley

The Future Agenda for Internationalization in Higher Education responds to two distinct needs: first, it seeks to focus specifically on dimensions of internationalization that are known to be under-researched; and second, it aims to give voice to a new generation of researchers and analysts, thereby framing 'next generation' perspectives on the phenomenon of internationalization. In so doing, this volume endeavors to present perspectives on new contexts shaping the internationalization of higher education, new modes for exploring and understanding distinct aspects of the phenomenon, and new topics relevant to its development and implementation.

Why a 'next generation,' and why now?

But, why does such an exploration of emerging perspectives on internationalization of higher education matter at this particular moment in time? There are several reasons driving this conversation currently. One argument rests on a purely 'human resources' observation; that is, that there is a new group of internationalization specialists emerging from behind the relatively small contingent of cutting-edge scholars and analysts who opened the door on the contemporary study of internationalization (particularly from the mid-1980s and early 1990s onward). That small vanguard of researchers and policymakers laid the early – and crucially important – foundation for the field. By initiating the study of internationalization in higher education over the last two decades, they have had a profound influence and continue to inform internationalization research and analysis in substantive ways. By way of example, the definitions proposed and reworked by Knight and de Wit (de Wit, 2011; de Wit, Hunter, Howard, & Egron-Polak, 2015; Knight, 2014, 2015a) have had a significant impact on the field. In seeking to reflect institutional practice, these definitions have subsequently served to shape and guide the internationalization strategies adopted by institutions and governments around the world (Maringe, 2010). However, a new generation of researchers and analysts is coming to the fore. Unquestionably, the early pioneers in the field have influenced the perspectives of those who have come after, but this emerging group also brings new questions, concerns, and insights to bear on the examination of the phenomenon of internationalization in higher education.

As the community of researchers focused on internationalization is evolving, so too is the focus and content of the research itself, as is the context in which we work. For example, mid- to late 20th-century conversations focused heavily on the individual student mobility experience (nearly always reported in highly positive terms) and, to a lesser extent, on the serendipitous side effects of expected soft power benefits for the nations involved in the sending and receiving of students and academics. In the 21st century, space is being given to increasingly expansive and critical understandings of deeper and more complex trends and issues at play – many with profound economic, social, political, and educational implications. The concept of knowledge diplomacy as an alternative approach to soft power (Knight, 2015b) is an example of these kinds of conceptual developments, as is the evolving consideration of how regionalization fits into our understanding of internationalization dynamics – not only in the famed context of the European Union, but also more recently in Africa (Knight & Woldegiorgis, 2017) and Asia (Knight, 2017; Kuroda, 2017).

As a result, we understand today, much more clearly than ever before, that the internationalization of higher education is a worldwide phenomenon, and that it is subject to multiple interpretations at national, regional, institutional, and individual levels. We recognize that internationalization is a relatively recent development and, as such, it presents new challenges, opportunities, and imperatives for institutions and systems of higher education that, in many instances, have been operating for decades (if not centuries) with highly localized frames of reference and without the need to consider matters of global engagement in significant ways. We appreciate that internationalization is a phenomenon that demands and exerts change, while simultaneously responding and adapting to shifting contextual realities.

Our increasingly refined awareness about the complex and multi-dimensional nature of internationalization is playing out against a global backdrop of rapid change and, on balance, profoundly worrisome environmental, economic, social, and political realities. The key questions of the day (including: How can we improve the human condition in the face of profoundly entrenched inequities? How do we assure peace and security in the face of deeply embedded and long-standing mistrust? How will our species adapt to climate change?) are notable not only for their scope and gravity, but also because of the way in which they connect to both immediate, intimate, local concerns and to massive regional, international, and global dynamics. Higher education institutions – as creators of new knowledge; repositories of historical insights and artifacts; educators of the next generation of citizens, artists, politicians, scientists, entrepreneurs, bureaucrats, and more – stand on the front lines of many of the key issues of our time. The ability of these institutions to understand, engage, and contribute meaningfully to 'the world,' near and far, is a matter of particular urgency in the current context. Internationalization of higher education – coherently conceived, contextually nuanced, and thoughtfully executed – offers an important avenue for societies around the world to enhance the ability of their higher education institutions and systems to enable these same societies to respond to the challenges and opportunities of our time. It is therefore crucial to identify and cultivate a new generation of experts that can advance our understanding of internationalization in consequential and innovative terms.

The importance of who, what, and how

There has been a veritable explosion in attention paid to the internationalization of higher education in recent years, particularly in terms of policy and practice. Evidence for this includes the robust growth in numbers of attendees at the annual conferences and other meetings of professional organizations, such as the International Education Association of South Africa (IEASA), NAFSA: Association of International Educators in the United States, the International Education Association of Australia (IEAA), the European Association for International Education (EAIE), the Asia-Pacific Association for International Education (APAIE), and the African Network for the Internationalization of Education (ANIE), among others. Publications and media outlets that focus on the international dimensions of higher education have proliferated, while a wide array of relevant training modules and graduate programs have also emerged or expanded to meet increasing demand.

The expansion of the field has been impressive, but has brought with it some concerns about quality versus quantity, untested assumptions guiding policy, and a range of imbalances embedded in the field. At the level of an individual institution, such imbalances may be made manifest by the lack of representation of diverse stakeholders in internationalization activities or agenda development. On a global scale, concerns in this vein have prompted moves to heighten awareness about inequities inherent in many international "partnerships" and programs, guided by the notion that internationalization should ideally "be based on mutual benefit and development for entities and individuals in the developed, emerging and developing countries" (*Nelson Mandela Bay Global Dialogue Declaration on the Future of Internationalisation of Higher Education*, 2014, p. 1).

Similar trends are in evidence in relation to research in the field. Indeed, although research into the internationalization of higher education is conducted around the world (Rumbley et al., 2014), recent analysis of global trends in research highlights a concentration of focus on a small number of countries and a narrow range of key topics (Proctor, 2016). Based on an analysis of data from the IDP Database of Research on International Education,[1] over 50 percent of all international education research published between 2011 and 2014 centered on English-speaking countries, with a predominant focus on the higher/post-secondary education sector. Students and their international mobility were the most common topics of this research, rather than the faculty who teach them, the broader internationalization agendas of their institutions or countries, or the communities in which they live and subsequently work (Proctor, 2015).

Given the predominance of the Anglophone world in international education research, new works – such as the edited collection *The Globalization of*

Internationalization (de Wit, Gacel-Avila, Jones, & Jooste, 2017) – are seeking to address a broader set of perspectives on internationalization from outside the dominant English-speaking and Western European paradigms. Similarly, a range of other reports and articles in recent years has documented and mapped relevant research, either through bibliometric analysis or through the compilation of detailed catalogues (Bedenlier, Kondakci, & Zawacki-Richter, 2017; Kosmützky & Krücken, 2014; Kosmützky & Putty, 2015; Kuzhabekova, Hendel, & Chapman, 2015). These efforts to illuminate the wider base of scholarship and analysis emerging in relation to internationalization are important and timely. As internationalization becomes increasingly relevant for strategic decision-making by institutions, and with respect to policymaking and resource allocation activities by governmental entities and other key decision-makers, it is vital that diverse perspectives – grounded in critical, high-quality scholarship – are taken into account.

Our contribution: new voices, new ideas, new approaches

This volume aims to expand the scholarly discussions about internationalization by bringing the voices of a 'next generation' of scholars and analysts to the fore, not only to amplify our current understanding of key issues related to internationalization around the world, but also to shine a light on possible future agendas for this important aspect of contemporary higher education. For the purposes of this volume, the editors have principally defined 'next generation' perspectives as those from early career individuals with fewer than 10 years of post-Ph.D. or professional experience or from advanced doctoral students. However, some contributions have been made by individuals who, although more established in their careers, have a particularly 'forward-thinking' perspective to share on the future of internationalization.

To anchor the contribution of 'generation' scholars, the volume features invited contributions from recognized expert authors in each of its principal sections. To further highlight the 'intergenerational dimensions' of this work, the Preface is authored by Jane Knight and Hans de Wit, who help us reflect on where the field of internationalization has come from and where it may be headed. Given the difficult changes and challenging scenarios ahead, our starting point for this volume is that it is crucial to look out across the horizon and understand the deep complexity of internationalization in higher education, as well as to clear a path for new ideas and new voices to join in this conversation to encourage both new questions and new solutions.

Structure and contents

This volume aims to highlight the thoughtful consideration of *new contexts* shaping the internationalization of higher education, *new modes* for exploring and understanding distinct aspects of the phenomenon, and *new topics* relevant to its development and implementation. Our premise is that it is vitally important to further develop these dimensions of the study of internationalization in order to understand the complex web of factors that will shape its future, as well as our ability to leverage the phenomenon to enhance both the quality of higher education and the many services that the sector provides to society.

New contexts

Internationalization has long been recognized as a key feature of particular types of institutions or in particular national or regional contexts. For example, in the United States, prestigious liberal arts institutions have historically sent high numbers of students to study abroad, while the top U.S. research universities have successfully attracted large numbers of international students and scholars. Globally, cities, as opposed to rural areas, are often seen as key centers for internationalized higher education activity. Wealthy enclaves (à la Singapore or the Emirates in the Middle East) have given us the now well-known configuration of the international education 'hub.' The peaceful, prosperous European Union of the late 20th century – featuring a dynamic policy agenda valuing regional engagement and multiculturalism, along with attendant funding – has been a global 'poster child,' of sorts, for internationalization in a regional context. Meanwhile, some fields and disciplines have been historically more predisposed to embrace internationalization than others.

Our exploration of new contexts for internationalization – with chapters from contributors based in Africa, Asia, Australia, Europe, and North America – pushes the boundaries on these well-known settings for the phenomenon in a variety of ways. For example, the lead chapter for this section, authored by Hiroshi Ota and Kiyomi Horiuchi, presents us with the complex situation of economically and educationally strong Japan finding it difficult to gain traction in its internationalization efforts in relation to English medium instruction. Cultural, political, and educational forces at play complicate this effort on several fronts, highlighting the challenging dynamic between aspirational policy formulation and real-world practical implementation. Across the world in Ireland, Linda Hui Yang's chapter on that country's evolving discussions about an internationalization policy in the face of economic austerity gives additional insight into political and policymaking dynamics, this time in moments of deep national uncertainty. Meanwhile, Sonja Knutson explores ways in which theory and practice in relation to the phenomenon of indigenization of higher education in Canada could provide a model for the field of internationalization to find firmer philosophical and epistemological footing as a transformational force for good in a highly unequal world.

Geography is another key consideration when it comes to context, and several of our authors present unique perspectives on matters of place. Dina Uzhegova's consideration of the particular challenges facing higher education institutions in Siberia offers a stark reinforcement of the classic real estate mantra: location,

location, location. Creativity, persistence, and a dogged determination to tell the real story of what Siberian higher education institutions are all about offers a compelling lesson for other institutions situated in remote or less well-known locations. Meanwhile, Jermain Griffin and Robin Matross Helms take us not south of the border but actually to the U.S.–Mexican border, to shed light on "the borderland context," a place where "boundaries, bridges, and barriers" abound, and internationalization can both flourish and languish.

These and other contributions featured in this section provide us with a rich look at several new contexts for internationalization and new ways of contextualizing our frames of reference about the phenomenon.

New modes

The new modes section of our analysis offers several fascinating approaches to understanding internationalization that reach well beyond the classic case study or small-scale survey. Using i-graduate's International Student Barometer as a key example, Richard Garrett and Rachael Merola ask us in their lead chapter to consider the ways in which large-scale data can provide individual institutions with new ways to understand what internationally mobile students think about a range of issues that are fundamental to their decision-making and, ultimately, their satisfaction with their educational experience abroad. Data collection methods for the future are also considered. Data are also important to author Daniela Crăciun, who proposes a highly innovative approach, known as computer-assisted topic modeling, to make sense of vast amounts of written text. This can be helpful to policymakers and policy analysts who, faced with massive and growing numbers of policy documents referencing internationalization, struggle to make sense of recurring trends, issues, and themes, or the absence thereof.

The new modes section also asks us – courtesy of Charles Mathies and Leasa Weimer on the one hand, and Bryan McAllister-Grande on the other – to both look forward and to consider looking back at history for new insights into internationalization. For Mathies and Weimer, the populist/nationalist movements unfolding in the United States and Europe present a fundamental challenge to the future of the economic narrative that has framed international education (particularly student mobility aspects) in the West for some time. Tracking discourse developments against student mobility numbers over time may offer insights into these "shifting" narratives while, moving forward, institutions and systems of higher education have choices to make when it comes to matters of "exclusive" or "inclusive" internationalization. For McAllister-Grande, looking back at the "Anglo-Protestant, capitalist spirit" gives new insight into U.S. and Western engagement with internationalization since the Cold War era, which in turn leads the author to advocate for "a more humanistic internationalization." Finally, from China, we see a perspective on how the internationalization of Chinese humanities and social sciences research may be explored through an analysis of English-language academic journals in China. Here, we come to understand internationalization as a complex process of achieving greater cultural self-awareness while fostering meaningful international and intercultural engagement.

The standpoints of the authors of this section – who are currently based in the United States, Hungary, Chile, Finland, and Hong Kong – are diverse and multifaceted. Together, they indicate that there is wide range for thinking in new and innovative ways about the 'how?' and the 'how do we know?' in relation to the internationalization of higher education as the phenomenon evolves around the world.

New topics

The 'new topics' section provides us with an opportunity to turn to the question of the concrete subjects and issues that can be the focus of research in connection with internationalization, and which may not yet have been explored to any significant extent. For their part, the lead authors in this section – Fiona Hunter and Neil Sparnon – acknowledge that, indeed, internationalization has only recently emerged from 'second tier' status among institutional priorities. Still, by unabashedly placing it at the service of institutional strategic planning, there is hope to attend to the chronically overlooked, fundamental work of "bridging the gap between [the] rhetoric and [the] reality . . . of internationalization." In their eyes, "getting real about internationalization" means understanding it as a key pillar within institutional strategic plans and, ultimately, having it serve as an engine of change for institutional growth and renewal and not a stand-alone star of the show.

Other topics of note identified by our contributors include Louise Michelle Vital and Christina W. Yao's consideration of new ways to think about doctoral research training for young scholars of international higher education; innovative approaches to educating refugee students at the post-secondary level, as explored by Thomas Greenaway; how, according to Susanne Ress, internationalization of higher education in Brazil has contributed to a unique process of national identity construction in that country; and Hiro Saito's perception of a critical need – in the face of negative, commercial, and highly competitive aspects of internationalization – for "rearticulating the publicness" of universities, both as providers of public goods and as loci of public spheres, at global, national, and local levels. Adinda van Gaalen and Susanne Feiertag even expand the discussion beyond the level of post-secondary education, with their quest to understand the synergies in relation to internationalization between secondary and higher education.

With affiliations spanning Belgium, Germany, Italy, the Netherlands, Singapore, the United States, and United Kingdom, the authors showcased in this section offer up a wide panorama of insights into lesser known aspects of the topic at hand: internationalization of higher education.

Caveats and kudos

In the shaping of this volume across the three dimensions of new contexts, new modes, and new topics, the placement of individual chapters in a given section was ultimately more art than science. Arguments could be made that one or more of the chapters we opted to classify as an example of a 'new mode' or a 'new context' analysis could have instead been understood as a representation of a 'new topic,' etc. Our aim with the organization of the volume into sections, and the designation of content into each section (which was done in consultation with the authors), was not to force an artificial framework for the content onto readers, but rather to provide a workable organizing principle for what is, arguably, a set of quite distinct and highly individualized analyses of a fundamentally complex topic.

From our perspective, the end result provides a thoughtful roadmap for considering the many possible dimensions of the internationalization of higher education of the future, as perceived by a most impressive cohort of next generation researchers and analysts.

Note

1 www.idp.com/researchdatabase

References

Bedenlier, S., Kondakci, Y., & Zawacki-Richter, O. (2017). Two decades of research into the internationalization of higher education: major themes in the *Journal of Studies in International Education* (1997–2016). *Journal of Studies in International Education*. doi:10.1177/1028315317710093

de Wit, H. (2011, October 23). Naming internationalisation will not revive it. *University World News*. Retrieved from www.universityworldnews.com/article.php?story=20111021215849411

de Wit, H., Gacel-Avila, J., Jones, E., & Jooste, N. (Eds.). (2017). *The Globalization of Internationalization: Emerging Voices and Perspectives*. New York: Routledge.

de Wit, H., Hunter, F., Howard, L., & Egron-Polak, E. (2015). *Internationalisation of Higher Education*. European Parliament, Committee on Culture and Education. Retrieved from www.europarl.europa.eu/RegData/etudes/STUD/2015/540370/IPOL_STU%282015%29540370_EN.pdf

Knight, J. (2014). Is internationalization of higher education having an identity crisis? In A. Maldonado-Maldonado & R. Bassett (Eds.), *The Forefront of International Higher Education: A Festschrift in Honor of Phil G. Altbach*. (pp. 75–88). Dordrecht: Springer.

Knight, J. (2015a). Meaning, rationales and tensions in internationalization of higher education. In S. McGrath & Q. Gu (Eds.), *Routledge Handbook on International Education and Development* (pp. 325–339). London: Taylor & Francis.

Knight, J. (2015b). The potential of knowledge diplomacy. Higher education and international relations. In J. Weimer (Ed.), *A Wealth of Nations* (pp. 37–45). Amsterdam: EAIE.

Knight, J. (2017). Regionalization of higher education in Asia: functional, organizational, and political approaches. In C. S. Collins, M. N. N. Lee, J. N. Hawkins, & D. E. Neubauer (Eds.), *The Palgrave Handbook of Asia Pacific Higher Education* (pp. 113–128). Basingstoke, UK/New York: Palgrave Macmillan.

Knight, J., & Woldegiorgis, E. T. (Eds.). (2017). *Regionalization of African Higher Education: Progress and Prospects*. Dordrecht: Springer.

Kosmützky, A., & Krücken, G. (2014). Growth or steady state? A bibliometric focus on international comparative higher education research. *Higher Education*, *67*(4), 457–472. Retrieved from https://doi.org/10.1007/s10734-013-9694-9

Kosmützky, A., & Putty, R. (2015). Transcending borders and traversing boundaries: a systematic review of the literature on transnational, offshore, cross-border, and borderless higher education. *Journal of Studies in International Education*, *11*, 290–305. doi:1028315315604719.

Kuroda, K. (2017). Regionalization of higher education in Asia. In C. S. Collins, M. N. N. Lee, J. N., Hawkins, & D. E. Neubauer (Eds.), *The Palgrave Handbook of Asia Pacific Higher Education* (pp. 141–156). Basingstoke, UK /New York: Palgrave Macmillan.

Kuzhabekova, A., Hendel, D. D., & Chapman, D. W. (2015). Mapping global research on international higher education. *Research in Higher Education*, *56*(8), 861–882. doi:10.1007/s11162-015-9371-1

Maringe, F. (2010). The meanings of globalization and internationalization in HE: findings from a world survey. In F. Maringe & N. Foskett (Eds.), *Globalization and Internationalization in Higher Education: Theoretical, Strategic and Management Perspectives* (pp. 17–34). New York: Continuum International Publishing Group.

Nelson Mandela Bay Global Dialogue Declaration on the Future of Internationalisation of Higher Education. (2014). Retrieved from www.ieaa.org.au/documents/item/208

Proctor, D. (2015). *Key Trends in International Education Research 2011–14: What Does the Data Tell Us?* International Education Association of Australia. Retrieved from www.ieaa.org.au/iern/key-trends

Proctor, D. (2016). The changing landscape of international education research. *International Higher Education*, *84*(Winter 2016), 19–21.

Rumbley, L. E., Altbach, P. G., Stanfield, D. A., Shimmi, Y., De Gayardon, A., & Chan, R. Y. (2014). *Higher Education: A Worldwide Inventory of Research Centers, Academic Programs, and Journals and Publications* (3rd ed.). Chestnut Hill, MA: Boston College Center for International Higher Education.

Part I

New contexts

Chapter 2

Internationalization through English-medium instruction in Japan
Challenging a contemporary Dejima

Hiroshi Ota and Kiyomi Horiuchi

EMI: an international trend

"A high-walled, fan-shaped artificial island, some two hundred paces along its outer curve, . . . by eighty paces deep, and erected, like much of Amsterdam, on sunken piles" (Mitchell, 2010, p. 16). This is the portrait of *Dejima* appearing in British novelist David Mitchell's *The Thousand Autumns of Jacob de Zoet*. Literally translated as 'Exit Island,' *Dejima* was a man-made island off the coast of Nagasaki in southwestern Japan, constructed in 1636 as home to Dutch merchants. During the Edo period in Japanese history, when Japan had put in place a national isolation policy limiting interactions with other countries, trade and exchange with other countries took place exclusively on this small island. The aim was to protect Japan from foreign influences, while simultaneously importing necessary resources, such as foreign goods and Western knowledge. *Dejima* functioned as the sole gateway to the outside world, and it seems to mirror current efforts for the internationalization of Japanese higher education through English-medium instruction (commonly referred to as "EMI").

The growth in number of EMI programs offered by higher education institutions in non-English speaking countries has recently become a remarkable phenomenon (Dearden, 2015). One of the factors behind this development is the advance of globalization, accompanied by the rapid movement of people, goods, services, money, and information across national borders; the internet has also played an important role in cementing English as the language of international communication. Academic research is not exempt from this trend. A cyclical system has been constructed in which a university rises up the global university rankings if a paper written in English by one of its researchers appears in a prominent journal, leading in turn to an improvement in its reputation. As such, for both higher education institutions and individual researchers, English acts as an indispensable tool for participation in international academic networks. This trend is also influencing university education. For universities in non-English-speaking countries, it is understood that the implementation of EMI advances the internationalization of the institution and demonstrates a sense of meaningful existence in a globalized world.

Another major factor behind the establishment of EMI in non-English-speaking countries is the growth of the international student market (Wilkinson, 2013). According to the statistics compiled by the Organisation for Economic Co-operation and Development (OECD, 2015), the number of international students globally has grown steadily from 0.8 million in 1975, to 1.7 million in 1995, to 3 million in 2005, reaching nearly 4.5 million by 2012. Driven by economic development, population growth, and insufficient domestic provision of higher education in the emerging nations of Asia and elsewhere, studying abroad has undergone massive popularization, moving from a government-backed program for the elite to self-funded overseas study for self-actualization. This has resulted in a far larger body of internationally mobile students. EMI is seen as a potentially effective means of realizing strategies for participating in this enormous market and securing high-quality international students. In countries such as Japan, where the official language is one with low global currency, making the attainment of this national language a requirement for entry to higher education programs acts as a major obstacle in the acquisition of academically superior international students.

The origins of the spread of EMI can be found in Europe in the latter half of the 1980s. Accompanying the advance of the ERASMUS plan, which aimed to foster student exchange within Europe, EMI courses were established to cater to international students, enabling them to earn credits through classes taught in English.[1] According to a large-scale survey of EMI courses offered in Europe (involving 28 countries), around 27% of the higher education institutions had put in place degree programs in English by 2014, and the number of such programs had climbed to 8,089 (Wächter & Maiworm, 2014). Meanwhile, in Asia, in addition to EMI developments in Singapore and Hong Kong (countries that derive their higher education models from the United Kingdom), EMI is currently promoted as a part of higher education internationalization policy in countries such as China, Malaysia, Thailand, and South Korea. Moreover, at the same time, Asian countries have been successful in attracting foreign universities to their shores. Universities from English-speaking countries such as the United States, the United Kingdom, and Australia have set up branch campuses or offshore programs in the region, acting as a driving force behind the global expansion of transnational education (TNE) offered in English.

Phillipson (1992) set out a theory of "linguistic imperialism," in which the world is made up of "centers" and "peripheries," and language is positioned as a tool for hegemonic domination by the center. As such, the Anglo-Saxon countries, the United States and the United Kingdom, are criticized for spreading their language, English, in order to impose their will on and strengthen their domination of non-English-speaking countries. However, rapid globalization, the increasing accessibility of higher education to the general population, the dissemination of English as a lingua franca, and the economic development of emerging nations, have subsequently interacted in complex ways: EMI has gone beyond the relationship of dependence between centers and peripheries to become increasingly prominent as one of the diverse types of higher education programs demanded by the market.

The development of EMI in Japan

EMI was first noted in Japanese higher education in 1949, when a bachelor's program was established at Sophia University (a private Catholic university). Other small-scale EMI bachelor's programs were subsequently opened at private universities. However, they were targeted at foreigners living in Japan, international students, and returnees from overseas; since they were rare exceptions from the standpoint of Japanese higher education as a whole, it was impossible for them to influence mainstream higher education. Changes to this trend were seen at the start of the 21st century. This coincided with a time when Japanese companies, which were struggling with an ongoing recession since the early 1990s and a shrinking domestic market caused by population decline, sought to expand overseas and began to proclaim the need for global personnel fit for this task. In order to respond to this business trend and the attendant demands of the labor market, in the early 2000s some private universities began offering EMI undergraduate programs aimed not simply at international students but also at Japanese students.

According to the Ministry of Education, Culture, Sports, Science and Technology (MEXT, 2017), there are 780 universities in Japan, of which the private sector accounts for 77.4%. Unlike the public sector, which can rely on a steady flow of operating funds from the national or local government, the private sector has a high degree of financial dependency on student tuition fees, making the securing of students an issue of vital operational importance. For this reason, the private sector is adept at rapidly responding to changes in the market and reflecting these in curricula and student services. Therefore, private universities were also the first to introduce EMI.

Within the Japanese higher education community, there were initially many skeptics of universities' moves to set up new EMI undergraduate programs aimed mainly at Japanese students. However, Akita International University and Ritsumeikan Asia Pacific University, new institutions whose founding mission was the provision of EMI undergraduate programs, attracted a large number of both Japanese and international students, and many of their graduates went on to employment at Japan's top companies. These success stories were extensively covered by the mass media, transforming the reputation of EMI.

In response to these changes, the Japanese government also committed to policies promoting EMI. In 2008, the government adopted the 300,000 International Students Plan, which aimed to more than double the number of international students in Japan (to a total of 300,000) by 2020. In addition to increasing the international competitiveness of Japanese universities, this policy reflected an intention to compensate for the contraction of the domestic population of 18-year-olds by attracting international students. This plan laid out as goals the construction of a system that would make studying in Japan more accessible for international students – for instance, through improved admissions processes (i.e., selection methods) – and the wider provision of degree programs in English (MEXT, 2008). In 2009, MEXT launched a competitive funding program, the Global 30 Project, as part of the 300,000 International Students Plan. This project was to provide annual internationalization grants of between 200 million and 400 million yen (USD 1.8 million–3.6 million) over a period of five years to each selected university, which was then required to put in place at least one undergraduate and one graduate EMI degree program (MEXT, 2009). The original plan was to select 30 universities but, influenced by budget cuts accompanying a change of government, the project did not expand beyond the 13 universities initially chosen. However, since these 13 universities (7 national and 6 private) were all leading comprehensive universities with long-established traditions, the project served to instill the idea among the university sector and society that the establishment of EMI degree programs was a necessary condition for joining the ranks of the top universities in Japan. Moreover, the Global 30 Project led to a turning point by introducing EMI undergraduate programs into the national university sector, whereas previously they had been developed primarily at private universities.

While the main policy goal of the Global 30 Project was to attract international students, a policy project aiming to increase study abroad among Japanese students was also put in place. This was the Go Global Japan Project, launched in 2012. This project, which sought to reverse a decline in the number of Japanese students going abroad and to develop global personnel through study abroad experience, provided grants of between 120 million and 260 million yen (USD 1.0 million–2.3 million) annually over a five-year period to each university selected. The performance indicators for the project included not only the number of Japanese students undertaking study abroad, but also the achievement of target scores on English language tests such as TOEFL. As a result, of the 42 universities selected, almost all introduced EMI courses as a part of the curriculum, with the aim of improving the English proficiency of Japanese students.

In 2014, these earlier policy initiatives were followed by the larger and longer-term Top Global University Project. This promotes comprehensive initiatives for university internationalization, including the expansion of both inbound and outbound mobility, and the improvement of English proficiency among Japanese students. MEXT provides annual grants of between 200 million and 500 million yen (USD 1.8 million–4.5 million) to each of 37 selected universities (from among 140 applicant universities) over a 10-year period, beginning in 2014. These 37 universities were divided into two categories, Type A and Type B. There are 13 Type A universities and these focus on world-class research, with the goal of enabling them to aim for a place among the top 100 in world university rankings. There are 24 Type B universities, which are required to undertake institution-wide internationalization initiatives, becoming a driving force behind the globalization of Japanese society. Both types of universities are required to set numerical targets for 18 performance indicators, including numbers of international students, Japanese students studying abroad, foreign academics, and EMI courses and degree programs.

Clark (1983) proposed a triangle model, in which three actors – the state, academics, and the market – influence one another to shape higher education trends. If we view EMI trends in Japan in terms of these three actors, we find that the business community (the market) first made the case for the need for globally minded personnel (with skills including English ability) from the second half of the 1990s. Next, from the early 2000s, the voluntary introduction of EMI became more widespread among private universities, which were quick to respond to market demands. Then, following these moves by the market and by private universities, from 2009 onwards the national government began to promote EMI through policy incentives. According to a survey by MEXT (2016), 37.1% of Japanese universities teach a part of the undergraduate curriculum using EMI, while 33.2% do so at the graduate level, representing respective increases of 10.6 percentage points and 5.0 percentage points on the figures from the survey five years earlier. On the other hand, there are still only 3.3% of universities offering programs in which an undergraduate degree can be obtained solely via EMI courses, and 14.3% offering such graduate degree programs. It can therefore be said that many universities are taking a cautious approach towards conducting EMI degree programs (where all courses are in English).

Divisions and tensions: the current situation of EMI in Japanese higher education

Due in part to the influence of national policy incentives, EMI is gradually on the rise in Japan, with two main identifiable approaches. One targets Japanese students, with the aim of improving their English language ability or developing a globally minded workforce; the other principally targets international students (Shimauchi, 2016). We focus here on the latter type, discussing the divisions and tensions that have arisen within Japanese universities. The reason for doing so is that, while EMI for Japanese students can be classed as an extension of existing English language education, the introduction of EMI degree programs – which presuppose the enrollment of non-Japanese-speaking international students – presents a new challenge for Japanese universities, where education, research, and university management have traditionally been conducted in Japanese. The term 'English divide' is used to represent a division within society between those with English language ability and those without; at Japanese universities, divisions around EMI are occurring at the institutional level.

Student divide

The most common format for setting up an EMI degree program targeted at international students is to tack a program taught entirely in English onto an existing department. Since this method permits the launch of an EMI program without making any drastic changes to the existing educational structure, it is one that can readily be adopted by Japanese universities, with their bureaucratic and vertical organizational structures. In fact, almost all the universities selected for the Global 30 Project chose this method. However, these programs are designed simply as add-ons, and it appears that care has been taken to minimize their broader impact on existing departments. This is also clear from the admission quotas for EMI degree programs: at many universities, including the ones selected for the Global 30 Project, places are limited to between 10 and 30 students. For example, in the case of one department with an overall admission quota of 250 students, 20 places have been set aside for students on the EMI program, while the remaining 230 places are used (as they always have been) to recruit Japanese students, who are taught in Japanese.

As a result, divisions are now arising on the ground between Japanese students and international students on EMI degree programs. Even though students are enrolled in the same department, different curricula are used throughout the four years for the Japanese and EMI programs, meaning that there are hardly any opportunities for Japanese and international students to take the same classes. Moreover, since almost all events and the provision of day-to-day information at Japanese universities take place in Japanese, international students on EMI programs, who lack sufficient Japanese language ability, have limited access to university information, giving rise to a situation that could be called a 'Japanese divide.' For these reasons, the international students on EMI programs risk ending up spending their four years at university marooned on a small 'English island' within the institution.

The current reality is that EMI degree programs, which have a small number of students, appear as 'irregular' entities when seen from the perspective of the university as a whole, making it hard for universities to build an institution-wide commitment to them. Some even argue that EMI programs have perhaps deliberately been kept small-scale from the outset in order to avoid friction with the academics teaching the university's existing programs in Japanese (Brown, 2014). Moreover, while the introduction of EMI was aimed at widening the field for recruiting and securing international students, looking at the low admission quotas for many EMI degree programs, they have not led to a significant growth in the number of international students. A broad chasm can therefore be seen between policy intentions and the ways in which policies are actually put into practice by universities.

Faculty divide

The majority of academic staff at universities in Japan studied for their master's and doctoral degrees at Japanese universities. In developing countries, where domestic higher education provision is not yet sufficiently mature, many personnel have obtained their doctorates abroad before returning home to become academics.

In Japan, because the provision of education in Japanese became established from an early stage of the country's modern higher education development, academics who have obtained degrees abroad remain in the minority. Thus, a large number of academics have received their education in Japanese and have only taught in this language. As such, there is a shortage of academics able to teach in English. When setting up an EMI program, the choice is often made to employ foreign academics hired specifically for these EMI courses in fixed-term roles, rather than in new tenure-track positions. In order to hire additional tenured staff, it is necessary to reduce the number of non-English-speaking academics already employed. In Japan, though, employment practices make it hard to dismiss staff. It is extremely difficult to lay off tenured academics due to their lack of teaching skills in English. On the other hand, academics on fixed-term contracts can be employed using funding from the government over a specified period for projects such as the Top Global University Project.

However, there are concerns that where EMI programs are run mostly by academics on fixed-term contracts, it can prove difficult to amass educational knowhow, interfering with stable program administration (Brown & Iyobe, 2014). In addition, since faculty meetings and internal communications are essentially conducted in Japanese, access to internal information by foreign academics with a low level of Japanese language ability is restricted and the opportunities for their opinions to be reflected within the university are limited. There is a risk that academics on temporary contracts employed to teach in EMI programs may become isolated, cut off from the university mainstream by a language barrier just like the international students enrolled in these programs.

Certainly, there are cases in which Japanese academics already working at the university assume responsibility for EMI courses. However, when Japanese academics teach classes in English, it is said that class preparation takes four to five times as long as for an equivalent class in Japanese, placing an additional burden on them (Tsuneyoshi, 2005). Despite this, it is rare for this extra burden to be reflected in salaries, and so most Japanese academics are uninterested in EMI. Furthermore, where EMI programs target international students, there is an expectation that classes will not be one-way lectures in the Japanese style, but rather American-style interactive classes. Japanese academics responsible for EMI classes can therefore be exposed to the risk of rejection on the basis of their traditional teaching methods. As a result, besides non-tenured foreign faculty, EMI is inevitably underpinned by voluntarism on the part of a relatively small number of Japanese academics (Tsuneyoshi, 2005).

Staff divide

Similar challenges exist among the administrative staff who support EMI programs. Universities use fixed-term contracts to recruit staff who are able to deal in English with international students and EMI program academics. This situation also has its roots in Japanese employment practices. When new graduates are employed by Japanese organizations (not only companies but also universities) as permanent staff, they are expected to become generalists, with all staff changing position or division every three to four years. The aim is to promote them to management positions after they have gained broad operational experience in multiple divisions of the organization. Since this long-term staff development method is based on a lifetime employment model and focuses on developing generalists, it is difficult to develop specialists. For this reason, in an attempt to prevent changes to the existing Japanese personnel system, temporary staff are put in positions that require particular skills, such as the ability to deal with students and academics in English and to communicate with overseas universities. Even though the temporary staff responsible for EMI programs possess high-level international communication skills, their status is generally impermanent, regardless of how great a contribution they make through their work, nor are they given any opportunity to become involved with the decision-making process (Poole, 2016). There is also a tendency for them to be isolated from the community of permanent staff.

Insularity versus globalization

The format of contemporary Japanese universities dates to the late 19th century under the imported models of universities from the West, where foreign (Western) academics hired by the Japanese government taught their classes in foreign languages (Ota, 2014). Soon after this initial stage of Japanese higher education, however, universities shifted to absorb Western culture and knowledge through translation into Japanese. Thereafter, Japanese universities progressed to maturity with Japanese as the sole language of instruction.

The internationalization approach currently taken by Japan's universities, of which the spread of EMI is one important aspect, represents the government's attempt to open Japanese universities to the wider world through policy initiatives. Nevertheless, it appears that, contrary to the intention behind the policy, each university is taking great pains to find a way to introduce EMI with minimal changes to the existing organizational culture and system. This situation is producing internal tensions between the forces (such as the government) that stress the need to introduce EMI and promote globalization in order to triumph in the global competition among universities, and those forces (with vested interests) that are trying to hold on to the conventional structures and identities of Japanese universities.

The management of EMI within Japan's higher education appears to be replicating the Edo period in Japanese history: foreign students, academics, and administrative staff who use English (and cannot use Japanese) seem to be confined to a small *Dejima* within the university. Indeed, universities are constructing a small *Dejima* for EMI and using this as a means (or some form of 'window dressing') to demonstrate a certain degree of legitimacy to the government and business community, which are pushing for globalization. At the same time, it can be argued that universities are skillfully protecting their traditional, internal organization and university management, which use the Japanese language.

The influence of English and its opposing force in Japan

It is not solely within higher education that moves to resist or avoid globalization have emerged in direct proportion to the strength of the voices advocating for it. It is possible to think of the existence of EMI in higher education in the same way as the moves to give English a more prominent role in Japanese society. In recent years, the introduction of English as the official language of various Japanese companies has attracted attention. Since certain leading companies have switched to English, moves to make a particular English language test score a condition for new employee recruitment or staff promotion have spread among other major companies and megabanks, and in 2015, the automotive manufacturer Honda announced that it was aiming to make English its official language in 2020. However, in the face of such moves by companies to place a greater emphasis on English, voices cautioning against an 'English divide' have also become more firmly entrenched, with concerns raised about an ever-widening economic gap between those who can speak English and those who cannot, and a resulting split among the population. These voices argue that if opportunities to play an active role in the workplace are taken away from employees simply because they have a low level of English, many of those who have sustained Japan's national strength until now will be unable to participate fully in society, leading to national decline (Se, 2015). In fact, although the societal impact of the switch to English by some companies has been great, the few companies who have taken the bold step of making English their official language company-wide are still very much in the minority. Furthermore, it appears that the majority of companies have preferred to maintain their public image as 'global corporations' by raising the English ability of only a portion of their employees, while at the same time trying to minimize the impact on existing organizational management.

How do young people, who have spent their university years and begun their working lives in a society that proclaims the need to respond to globalization stridently, experience this situation? The results of a survey into the overseas orientation of recent graduates show interesting implications (Sanno Institute of Management, 2015). When asked "Would you feel resistant to having a foreigner as your boss?" 19.7% replied, "I would feel resistant," while 31.4% replied, "On balance, I would feel resistant," showing resistance from more than half of respondents. Furthermore, in response to the question "Do you want to work overseas?" 63.7% replied, "I do not want to work overseas," the highest percentage since the survey was first administered in 2001. On the other hand, when asked "Should Japanese companies move ahead with globalization?" the majority of respondents (73.4%) gave an affirmative response: "They should move ahead" (24.5%) or "On balance, they should move ahead" (48.9%). Moreover, in response to the question "What are the abilities which you consider necessary in order to play an active role overseas?" 80.4% of respondents chose "Linguistic and communicative abilities."

These survey results reveal the dilemma of young Japanese people, who are aware of the need for a response to globalization by Japanese companies and for improved English language ability, but have a pessimistic attitude towards the globalization of their workplace and overseas postings due to a sense that they are poor at English. In other words, while they understand the necessity of responding to globalization, as ordinary citizens and workers, their discomfort with and resistance to the English language and foreigners remains strong. In order to overcome this sense among young people that they are poor at English, MEXT has decided to make English language education (currently beginning in the fifth grade of elementary school) a compulsory subject from the third grade by 2020. In addition, in secondary education, the government has set a goal of promoting the adoption of the International Baccalaureate Programme (IBP), greatly increasing the number of Japanese schools offering the program from the current 39 to 200 by 2018. However, only 70 IBPs had been established by August 2017 and 33 candidates are expected to be authorized in the near future.

Globalization, English, and 'third opening'

In Japan, there are many voices proclaiming the need for globalization, with the switch to English as one of its axes. There is heightened interest from society, but opposition to this change is also strong, and the current reality is that only peripheral initiatives have been taken. Underlying this situation is the strong sense of pride felt by Japanese people in their great economic and academic achievements using their mother tongue. In Japan, the civilization and enlightenment promoted by the *Meiji* government around the middle of the 19th century, after the end of more than two centuries of national isolation, is referred to as 'the first opening up of the country.' The democratization and reform resulting from occupation policy after the loss of World War II are known as 'the second opening up of the country.'

During both of these periods of transition, Japan assimilated concentrated doses of Western civilization through translation. The translation that took place in these cases was not a simple mechanical task of transferring information from foreign languages into Japanese, as the concepts and vocabulary needed to express Western knowledge, science, and technology did not truly exist in Japan at that time. For this reason, the intellectuals of the day often made full use of their imaginative powers to create new Japanese words corresponding to the concepts expressed in foreign languages. As one part of Japan's modernization, they constructed the schema of academic Japanese in various intellectual fields. Japan is known as a country that has succeeded in modernizing and developing economically at phenomenal speed in the modern era, based on European and American models; translation can be said to have been one of the important factors enabling this growth to take place (Sakakibara, 2010).

As a result of the maturation of Japanese into a rich language, the concepts, knowledge, and vocabulary needed to understand each and every academic subject through Japanese are all in place. It is also possible to study in virtually any field in Japanese at the higher education level, a rare phenomenon outside of the Western world. Moreover, Japan produces Nobel laureates almost every year. As such, it has been pointed out that nurturing such excellent 'home-grown' scientists has a meritorious effect on the educational and research environment, permitting a deep understanding of science in the mother tongue (Matsuo, 2015).

On the other hand, there are disadvantages produced by a history of over-dependence on translation into Japanese, such as the one-way communication of culture and the failure to foster two-way international communication skills. One-way absorption of culture also means isolation within international society (Maruyama & Kato, 1998). In Japan, which has benefited from the richness of the Japanese language and the culture of translation, opportunities to interact directly with foreign languages and to use these foreign languages have been limited, and so it is still the case that many people feel what is often termed an 'allergy,' an instinctive aversion towards using English and other foreign languages. Whenever a debate arises about enhancing English language education or making English a second official language, zero-sum counterarguments – that "It is more important to study Japanese than English", or that "If English is made an official language, it will be the end of Japanese" – erupt as a near-automatic reflex (Funabashi, 2000).

However, as a result of globalization and changes in the environment, with the use of English as a lingua franca at the forefront, Japan is now facing a 'third opening up of the country.' A globalized society requires not simply the one-way absorption of foreign knowledge through translation; it becomes crucial to disseminate Japan's culture, history, and society, as well as Japanese scholarship, and science and technology, in English, and to ensure two-way communication. If the majority of Japanese people overcome their 'allergy' towards English and come to have a shared understanding of globalization, this will surely lead to the third opening up of the society to the outer world. Only then will Japan's higher education advance to the next stage of internationalization without relying on additional *Dejima*.

Note

1 In this chapter, 'EMI course' is used to refer to an individual unit of study, whilst 'EMI program'refers to a degree or other qualification made up of multiple courses.

References

Brown, H. (2014). Contextual factors driving the growth of undergraduate English-medium instruction programmes at universities in Japan. *Asian Journal of Applied Linguistics*, 1(1), 50–63.

Brown, H., & Iyobe, B. (2014). The growth of English medium instruction in Japan. *JALT 2013 Conference Proceedings*. 9–19.

Clark, B. (1983). *The Higher Education System: Academic Organization in Cross-national Perspective*. Oakland: University of California Press.

Dearden, J. (2015). *Report: English as a Medium of Instruction – A Growing Global Phenomenon*. UK: British Council.

Funabashi, Y. (2000). *Aete Eigo kouyougo ron [Opinion to Make English as the Second Public Language in Japan]*. Tokyo: Bungeishunju.Maruyama, M. & Kato, S. (1998). *Honyaku to Nihon no kindai [Translation and Modern Japan]*. Tokyo: Iwanami Shoten.

Matsuo, Y. (2015). *Nihongo no kagaku ga sekai wo kaeru [Sciences in Japanese Will Change the World]*. Tokyo: Chikuma Shobo.

MEXT. (2008). *Outline of the Student Exchange System*. Retrieved December 15, 2015, from www.mext.go.jp/a_menu/koutou/ryugaku/081210/001.pdf

MEXT. (2009). *Gurobaru 30 Kobo-yoryo [Global 30 Application Guideline]*. Retrieved from www.mext.go.jp/component/a_menu/education/detail/__icsFiles/afieldfile/2009/05/13/1260324_01_1.pdf

MEXT. (2016). *Daigaku ni okeru kyoiku naiyo-tou no kaikaku jyokyo nitsuite [Survey on the Educational Reform in Higher Education]*. Retrieved from www.mext.go.jp/a_menu/koutou/daigaku/04052801/__icsFiles/afieldfile/2017/12/06/1380019_1.pdf

MEXT. (2017). *Gakko kihon chousa [School Basic Survey]*. Retrieved from www.mext.go.jp/component/b_menu/other/__icsFiles/afieldfile/2017/12/22/1388639_3.pdf

Mitchell, D. (2010). *The Thousand Autumns of Jacob de Zoet*. New York: Random House.

OECD. (2015). *Education at a Glance 2015*. OECD Publishing. Retrieved from www.oecd.org/edu/education-at-a-glance-19991487.htm

Ota, H. (2014). Japanese universities' strategic approach to internationalization: accomplishments and challenges. In A. Yonezawa, Y. Kitamura, A. Meerman, & K. Kuroda (Eds.), *Emerging International Dimensions in East Asian Higher Education* (pp. 227–252). Netherlands: Springer.

Phillipson, R. (1992). *Linguistic Imperialism*. Oxford, UK: Oxford University Press.

Poole, G. S. (2016). Administrative practices as institutional identity: bureaucratic impediments to HE "internationalisation" policy in Japan. *Comparative Education*, 52(1), 62–77.

Sakakibara, E. (2010). *Nihonjin ha naze kokusaijin ni narenainoka [Why Japanese people cannot be internationally-minded]*. Tokyo: Toyo Keizai Inc.

Sanno Institute of Management. (2015). Shinnyushain no gurobaru ishiki chousa [Survey on new employees' attitude toward globalization]. Retrieved from www.sanno.ac.jp/research/vbnear0000000q91-att/global2015

Se, T. (2015). *Eigo-ka ha gumin-ka [Englishization Makes Japan Down]*. Tokyo: Shuueisha.

Shimauchi, S. (2016). *Higashi ajia ni okeru ryugakusei-idou no paradaimu tenkan [The Paradigm Shift on International Student Mobility in East Asia]*. Tokyo: Toshindou.

Tsuneyoshi, R. (2005). Internationalization strategies in Japan: the dilemmas and possibilities of study abroad programs using English. *Journal of Research in International Education*, 4, 65–86.

Wächter, B., & Maiworm, F. (2014). *English-Taught Programmes in European Higher Education: The State of Play in 2014*. Bonn: Lemmens.

Wilkinson, R. (2013). English-medium instruction at a Dutch university: challenges and pitfalls. In A. Doiz, D. Lasagabaster, & J. M. Sierra (Eds.), *English-Medium Instruction at Universities: Global Challenges* (pp. 3–24). Clevedon, UK: Multilingual Matters.

Chapter 3

Internationalization and indigenization

Transforming Canadian higher education

Sonja Knutson

Internationalization researchers, advocates, and practitioners agree that there is no basic theoretical framework to give coherence to the field with respect to overarching vision, values, processes, and desired outcomes (Brandenburg & de Wit, 2011; Maringe & Foskett, 2010; Mestenhauser, 2011). In the absence of a common approach or worldview, or indeed any aligned discourse, internationalization is by and large an institutionally located process, and thus practice is fragmented and often marginalized unless there is strong executive support (Heyl, 2007; Hudzik, 2011; Merkx & Nolan, 2015). In Canada, institutional disparity is exacerbated by the ambiguity of federal versus provincial oversight of international education. The launch of a national internationalization strategy (Foreign Affairs and International Trade Canada, 2012) was met with some optimism that Canada would articulate an inspiring internationalized vision, but the higher education community has since critiqued its focus on soft power and economic benefits (Trilokekar, 2016). Nevertheless, the economically focused discourse of Canadian national policy persists, and is now evident in institutional strategic plans and agendas (Trilokekar, 2016).

As internationalization wrestles with its existential purpose, the relationship of Canada to Indigenous peoples has become a national priority. Indigenization has become a prominent preoccupation for higher education in Canada, largely motivated by the Truth and Reconciliation Commission's Calls to Action for the "eliminat[ion] of educational and employment gaps between Aboriginal and non-Aboriginal Canadians" (Truth and Reconciliation Commission, 2015b, pp. 1–2). Indigenization challenges universities in Canada to undertake seismic transformation to decolonize and deconstruct dominant cultural paradigms (Alfred, 2004; Battiste, Bell, & Findlay, 2002; Kuokannen, 2007; Ottman, 2013). Indigenization of the academy does not have a singular definition or approach in Canada, but it does have widespread high-level rhetorical commitment. Yet Canadian institutions remain challenged to move beyond token initiatives such as the superficial addition of Indigenous worldviews to existing curriculum or policy (Kovach, 2009).

While efforts to indigenize the academy gain momentum, ironically, the Canadian international education discourse is largely silent when it comes to analysis of marginalized peoples and knowledges. Many of the activities associated with internationalization are grounded in monocultural paradigms and the favorable positioning of "valued Western knowledge" (Dixon, 2006, p. 326). For example, approaches to partnership agreements, research collaborations, and supports for students who are not part of the dominant culture tend to privilege curriculum, perspectives, and academic norms of the West. A handful of global scholars are calling for a critical examination of internationalization's role in perpetuating global inequity (Altbach & Knight, 2007; Marginson, 2004). In this quest to address global issues, "Indigenous peoples are perhaps best positioned to inspire and lead others" (Battiste et al., 2002, p. 91). Those involved in international education in Canada have the opportunity now – through respectful learning from the decolonizing, emancipatory, and activist perspectives of indigenization – to develop the foundations for a critical approach to internationalization, unique to the Canadian context but perhaps with broader relevance.

Canadian context of internationalization and indigenization

Indigenization and internationalization of higher education are challenging Canadian institutions to transform core purposes and structures. According to Buller (2015), change drivers in higher education emerge contextually, from demographic, political, economic, technological, or other external factors, deeply impacting the university core business of teaching and learning, research, and engagement. Transformation of higher education policies and practices in Canada presents a set of unique navigational challenges, particularly given the governing jurisdictional complexities.

The federal/provincial dichotomy of education in Canada

Canadian higher education's responsiveness to change is affected by the nature of Canada's decentralized educational jurisdictions. Education is the sole responsibility of each province and territory, and each sets up its own structure "that, despite the many similarities, reflect[s] the distinctive character of regions separated by considerable distances and the diversity of the country's historical and cultural heritage" (Council of Ministers of Education, Canada, 2001, p. 11). To complicate matters, both Indigenous and international affairs are federal responsibilities, adding layers of complexity to the implementation of federal initiatives focused on indigenization or internationalization of the academy.

At the institutional level the jurisdictional ambiguities, increasing commercial importance of internationalization, and the growing political and academic prominence of indigenization make for a deeply nuanced and complex higher education landscape. Institutional arrangements across Canada tend towards separate and distinct organizational structures and affiliations for the offices that oversee indigenization and internationalization. Yet both offices struggle at the frontlines of the dominant worldview of academia, advocating for students and scholars, and against cultural assimilation. The potential for transformative solidarity in the Canadian context is leading to an incipient, yet admittedly fledgling, dialogue on the international/Indigenous axis.

Definitions, rationales, and motivations for indigenization and internationalization

Despite jurisdictional challenges and operational differences, there are apparent purposive parallels between internationalization and indigenization. International education purports to initiate transformational change by "alter[ing] the culture of the institution by changing underlying assumptions and overt institutional behaviors, processes and structures" (Eckel, Green, & Hill, 2001, p. 5). Indigenizing the academy, according to Alfred (2004, p. 88) should

> change universities so that they become places where the values, principles, and modes of organization and behavior of our people are respected in, and hopefully even integrated into, the larger system of structures and processes that make up the university itself.

Yet the potential for synergistic activity is increasingly corrupted by growing fundamental and oppositional differences between internationalization and indigenization, as the former is swept into increasingly commercial activities, while indigenization focuses on institutional capacity for reconciliation, ecosystem stewardship, and activism.

Internationalization of higher education

Internationalization is still broadly understood as a *process*: how to embed international, intercultural, and global mindsets into core university business (Knight, 2003). To many in the field, though, there is a lack of a clear purpose for internationalization. There is a call for internationalization to "dig deeper, place the options within a new set of values and rationales, and ensure that we really achieve what is meaningful" (Brandenburg & de Wit, 2011, p. 16). The process-driven preoccupation with *how* to internationalize does not address the *why*, and a theoretical foundation, which could provide an anchor in meaningful values, remains elusive (Mestenhauser, 2011).

The multiplicity of rationales for internationalization, as a change process for pedagogy; a description of mobility across borders with associated revenue potential; a path to global peace and understanding; and a way for nations to compete globally, have given rise to internationalization being used "as an umbrella term for the range of institutional strategic responses to globalization in universities" (Maringe & Foskett, 2010, p. 8). Universities are developing internationalization strategies and agendas with "little reference to or supporting theoretical and strategic frameworks, and without a sound and substantial evidence base for either policy-making or operational activities" (Maringe & Foskett, 2010, p. 7). While the field of international education arguably developed from goals of improving equitable access for all (Deardorff, de Wit, & Heyl, 2012), new and intensifying global pressures have left the field adrift in new territory as the work itself becomes more revenue-driven and focused on student recruitment, research dollars, and offshore programs.

Indigenizing the academy

The concept of indigenizing the academy encompasses many distinct and diverse views, which cannot all be addressed adequately here. Generally there is consensus that indigenization requires fundamental transformational change, since Canadian higher education "accomplish[es] the acceptance and normalization of Western ideas, the glorification of Western societies as the highest form of human organization" (Alfred, 2004, p. 96). Alfred (2004) also contends that, in attempting transformation, "Indigenous people immediately come into confrontation with the fact that universities are intolerant of and resistant to any meaningful 'Indigenizing'" (p. 88). The academy is a place where Indigenous peoples are continually forced into a position of resistance to identity threats and assimilation; thus indigenization requires an entire mindset change, not simply the improvement of student supports or the development of a new vision or mission statement (Kuokannen, 2007).

Indigenization of higher education is a policy priority across Canada as a recognition of, and response to, the historic oppression of Indigenous peoples, knowledges, and worldviews. Colonization has resulted in multiple devastating impacts, documented in the final report of The Truth and Reconciliation Commission (2015a). Educational establishments are not benign, safe places for Indigenous peoples, and instead have been used as tools for assimilation, resulting in fragmented familial and community relations and disrupted traditional patterns of Indigenous knowledge transmission (Grande, 2004). Low university program completion rates by Indigenous youth in all educational endeavors are one glaring issue (Ottman, 2013), but there are multiple examples of how academic gatekeeping continues "to monitor, dispel and discourage Indigenous scholars and . . . allies" (Mihesuah, 2004, p. 32). There is strong critique, for example, of the design of student 'supports' as being "primarily about the insiders and how much or how little they will have to adjust their practices and share their privileges in order to 'respond' to (by once again determining) outsiders' 'needs'" (Battiste et al., 2002, p. 83). Thus, the deconstruction of colonial systems that persist in Canadian higher education is necessary because the "consequence of academic affirmation of colonialism – currently undertaken in the name of global competiveness – has been to diminish the value and potential relevance of Indigenous knowledge in education" (Battiste et al., 2002, p. 83).

Transformation: meanings and motives in context

In Canada, then, is it possible for indigenization and internationalization, despite fundamental differences, to find intersectional and supportive solidarity by motivating transformational and decolonizing change? While universities acknowledge their role in developing a new generation prepared to work globally in diverse contexts, to program these diverse perspectives into all aspects of the academy requires transformative, disruptive change. No matter what the driver, attempts to effect fundamental shifts "are sure to meet strong resistance [. . . because that] approach violates the unique quality of the academic institutions in which collaboration and consensus are central to the social and institutional fabric" (Williams, 2013, p. 178). Kuokannen (2007) proposes instead that, to transform, universities must commit to "engaging in the slow and demanding process of ethical singularity" (p. 156), meaning the creation of a space for authentic collaboration and relationship-making between the diverse voices in a university community.

Transforming through Indigenous frameworks

Indigenous frameworks of transformation in higher education are grounded in activist approaches that are "disrupting social injustice and transforming inequitable and oppressive power relations" (Garcia & Shirley, 2012, p. 80). The Indigenous approach to transformation engages all voices, and is not imposed through hierarchical structure disconnected from community relationships (Wilson, 2008). The goals are powerful and clear, requiring courageous, "intentional and strategic confrontation" (Ottman, 2013, p. 8). Classroom practice must be introspective on both the personal and professional levels, since "organizational change begins with individuals [. . .who] will either further the cause of decolonization and Indigenization of the academy or impede it" (Ottman, 2013, p. 15). Indigenization of the academy allows emergence of Indigenous ways of knowing, establishes academic policies which allow Indigenous expertise to be recognized, and transforms the academy to a place where Indigenous worldviews are valued and respected (Ottman, 2013).

Transforming through internationalization frameworks

Unlike indigenization, internationalization is vague about transformation, describing it as "deep, pervasive, intentional [and] long-term" (Heyl, 2007, p. 8) but with no explicit vision of why it is driving institutional change. There is a pervasive belief that internationalization, if comprehensively organized within an institution, inherently provides benefits to universities and their national contexts (Hudzik, 2011). Internationalization makes great strides on outcomes related to revenue, reach, and 'footprint,' but when it comes to its capacity to transform perspectives, and develop humanistic values, the balance sheet is woeful. The university community continues to 'other' international scholars, and their knowledge and experience are disconnected from the core values of the academy, not integrated into policy or curriculum (Hayes, 2017). University policies, processes, and structures force assimilation, as they are firmly grounded in dominant cultural values, leaving no space for the culturally different. Transformation "requires multilateral processes of understanding and unpacking the central assumptions of domination, patriarchy, racism, and ethnocentrisms that continue to glue the academy's privileges in place" (Battiste et al., 2002, p. 84). Transformation of this order is not evident in internationalization perhaps because there is little guidance to clarify the main issue, which is: transformation to what end (Slimbach, 2015).

Differences in purposes for transformation

While both internationalization and indigenization are considered to be agents of change in higher education, the underpinnings of internationalization related to commercialization and assimilation of difference conflict with Indigenous ideologies. International education is increasingly tied to national goals related to political and economic outcomes, and to institutional goals related to finances and rankings. Internationalization is "driven by globalization, privileges Western models" (Radford, 2013, p. 55), whereas Indigenous scholars warn the academic community "about globalization and neo-liberal economic policies and practice" (Smith, 2012, p. 220) that maintain unequal global relations.

Scholars of internationalization of higher education are struggling to reconcile expectations for internationalization to contribute to national economic and political goals with long-held assumptions of being the "white knight of higher education, the moral ground that needs to be defended, and the epitome of justice and equity" (Brandenburg & de Wit, 2011, p. 16). Growing inequity is evident in how international student and labor market flows are driving talent asymmetrically into wealthier nations (Marginson, 2004). It is seen in the increasing, yet contentious, use of English for transmitting knowledge, which homogenizes what is acceptable and accessible knowledge (Altbach & Knight, 2007). At issue is the driving force of globalization, which "tends to concentrate wealth, knowledge and power in those already possessing these elements" (Altbach & Knight, 2007, p. 291). Global inequity is a factor of concern for all higher education caught in "the move of the university from a service profile to a market profile" (Dixon, 2006, p. 320). Higher education's attempts to respond to global pressures and opportunities through international education activities, far from contributing to the public good, are instead furthering the concentration of prestige and wealth in the already privileged nations.

Meanwhile, indigenization of the academy seeks to expose the underlying epistemological basis of racism and intolerance of Western higher education to Indigenous knowledge (Kuokkanen, 2007; Mihesuah, 2004; Smith, 2012). Indigenization tackles higher education as being a tool of colonization, which perpetuates global inequity, because it is "a way of thinking about oneself and others always in terms of domination and submission" (Alfred, 2004, p. 89).

Far from advocating for other ways of knowing, internationalization instead has been positioned as providing the highly valuable 'gift' of knowledge through access to Western curriculum (Dixon, 2006). This knowledge is shared through the 'benevolence' of Western higher education as 'knowledge holder' to improve global education overall (Dixon, 2006). Indigenization opposes this approach to knowledge as inequitable, forcing those from other worldviews to engage their energies to combat constant threats to their own values and identities within the higher education realm.

How to engage in transformation that benefits all?

Indigenization continues to challenge the academy to be transformed by Indigenous perspectives. Explicit outcomes related to transformational change are clear and firmly framed as both a means and an end for institutional transformation. Internationalization, on the other hand, is facing an identity crisis exacerbated by the lack of a humanistic epistemological foundation to support transformation (Brandenburg & de Wit, 2011; Radford, 2013). Internationalization in Canada can learn from two important aspects of Indigenization: the importance of active leadership, and meaningful theoretical foundations to engage in institutional transformation.

Active leadership for transformation

Internationalization literature on managing change focuses on identifying the different stakeholder rationales for engagement with international education and the necessity to modify communication to engage the values of each particular stakeholder audience (Haigh, 2014). Not only must campus leaders manage messaging to internal audiences; they must also manage the external environment within the context of constant global shifts and crises. As Heyl states, leading change in international education is fraught with challenges and "persistence emerges as a key trait" (2007, p. 10). In contrast, Mihesuah and Wilson's (2004) work on indigenizing the academy identifies "activism and persistence" (p. 5) as key traits to leading transformational change. The identification of activism is a missing component in the literature on transformative leadership in internationalization. Indigenous calls for activism are manifested in resistance to the colonizing aspects of the system and institution of academia, while internationalization calls for its leaders to persist in convincing each stakeholder of the value that internationalization could provide them.

Transformational theoretical basis for internationalization

International education has been critiqued for being ill prepared for the current context of globalization and consequential global inequity (Maringe & Foskett, 2010). While rhetoric continues to frame internationalization as "a transformative phenomenon, moving institutions – and even national and supranational actors – to adjust everything from administrative policies to entire frames of reference" (Rumbley, Altbach, & Reisberg., 2012, p. 13), the lack of transformative purpose remains of grave concern. Lacking its own meaningful grounding, the theoretical basis for internationalization today is increasingly tied to globalization with its push to increase the influence of Western academic norms and the dominance of the English language (Brandenberg & de Wit, 2011; Brewer & Leask, 2012; Maringe & Foskett, 2010). Dixon's (2006) research found that individuals involved in international education activities "were loath to speak . . . in terms of globalization" (p. 328). If internationalization resists self-scrutiny, it cannot engage in a deep examination of institutionalized and epistemological racism, or "what is considered legitimate epistemology in the academy" (Kuokannen, 2007, p 67). The challenge for the field is to examine its philosophical grounding: to acknowledge and to transform.

Conclusions

Despite increasing concerns over its role in the unequal distribution of global wealth and opportunity (Egron-Polak & Hudson, 2014), internationalization of higher education in Canada remains focused on enhancing Canadian prosperity. Canada, similar to other countries, engages with internationalization of higher education as a way to drive economic and political strategies that impact how institutions pursue new opportunities (Maringe & Foskett, 2010). Yet, for internationalization in Canada "to respond to global challenges in service of the public good . . . a foundational epistemology is required" (Radford, 2013, p. 70). Problematizing internationalization activities through Indigenous worldviews could lead to a reimagining of internationalization's stance, in particular an understanding of the historic role played by Canadian education in relation to colonization and the perpetuation of a monocultural, hegemonic worldview. Canada's international education leaders can learn from Indigenous approaches, and begin to develop a new framework for transformative outcomes of "human solidarity across cultures, inequities, and manufactured differences" (Radford, 2013, p. 70), thus far elusive in the internationalization of higher education.

References

Alfred, T. (2004). Warrior scholarship: Seeing the university as a ground of contention. In A. W. D. A. Mihesuah (Ed.), *Indigenizing the Academy: Transforming Scholarship and Empowering Communities* (pp. 88–99). Lincoln, NE: University of Nebraska Press.

Altbach, P. G., & Knight, J. (2007). The internationalization of higher education: motivations and realities. *Journal of Studies in International Education, 11*(3–4), 290–305.

Battiste, M., Bell, L., & Findlay, L. M. (2002). Decolonizing education in Canadian universities: an interdisciplinary, international, indigenous research project. *Canadian Journal of Native Education, 26*(2), 82–95.

Brandenburg, U., & de Wit, H. (2011). The end of internationalization. *International Higher Education, 62,* 15–17.

Brewer, E., & Leask, B. (2012). Internationalization of the curriculum. In D. Deardorff, H. de Wit, J. Heyl, & T. Adams (Eds.), *The SAGE Handbook of International Higher Education* (pp. 245–265). Thousand Oaks, CA: SAGE Publications.

Buller, J. L. (2015). *Change Leadership in Higher Education: A Practical Guide to Academic Transformation.* San Francisco: John Wiley & Sons, Inc.

Council of Ministers of Education, Canada. (2001). *The Development of Education in Canada, September.* Council of Ministers of Education, Canada. Retrieved from www.cmec.ca/Publications/Lists/Publications/Attachments/34/ice46dev-ca.en.pdf

Deardorff, D. K., de Wit, H., & Heyl, J. (2012). Bridges to the future: the global landscape of international higher education. In D. Deardorff, H. de Wit, J. Heyl, & T. Adams (Eds.), *The SAGE Handbook of International Education* (pp. 457–485). Thousand Oaks, CA: SAGE Publications.

Dixon, M. (2006). Globalization and international higher education: contested positionings. *Journal of Studies in International Education, 10,* 319–333.

Eckel, P., Green, M., & Hill, B. (2001). *On Change V: Riding the Waves of Change: Insights from Transforming Institutions.* Washington, DC: American Council on Education.

Egron-Polak, E., & Hudson, R. (2014). *Internationalization of Higher Education: Growing Expectations, Fundamental Values.* Paris: International Association of Universities.

Foreign Affairs and International Trade Canada. (2012). *International Education: A Key Driver of Canada's Future Prosperity.* Retrieved from www.international.gc.ca/education/assets/pdfs/ies_report_rapport_sei-eng.pdf

Garcia, J., & Shirley, V. (2012). Performing decolonization: lessons learned from indigenous youth, teachers and leaders' engagement with critical indigenous pedagogy. *Journal of Curriculum Theorizing, 28*(2), 76–91.

Haigh, M. (2014). From internationalization to education for global citizenship: a multi-layered history, *Higher Education Quarterly, 68*(1), 6–27.

Hayes, A. (2017). Why international students have been "TEF-ed out." *Educational Review, 69*(2), 218.

Heyl, J. (2007). *The Senior International Officer (SIO) as Change Agent.* Durham, NC: AIEA.

Hudzik, J. (2011). *Comprehensive Internationalization: From Concept to Action.* Washington, DC: NAFSA Association of International Educators.

Knight, J. (2003). Updating the definition of internationalization. *International Higher Education 33,* 2–3.

Kovach, M. (2009). *Indigenous Methodologies: Characteristics, Conversations, and Contexts.* Toronto, ON: University of Toronto Press.

Kuokannen, R. (2007). *Reshaping the University: Responsibility, Indigenous Epistemes, and the Logic of the Gift.* Vancouver: UBC Press.

Marginson, S. (2004). National and global competition in higher education. *Australian Educational Researcher, 31*(2), 1–28.

Maringe, N., & Foskett, N. (2010). *Globalization and Internationalization in Higher Education: Theoretical, Strategic and Management Perspectives.* New York: Continuum.

Merkx, G. W., & Nolan, R. (2015). The challenge of internationalization. In G. W. Merkx & R. Nolan (Eds.), *Internationalizing the Academy: Lessons of Leadership in Higher Education* (pp. 213–223). Cambridge, MA: Harvard Education Press.

Mestenhuaser, J. A. (2011). *Reflections on the Past, Present and Future of Internationalizing Higher Education: Discovering Opportunities to Meet the Challenges.* Minneapolis, MN: University of Minnesota.

Mihesuah, D. A. (2004). Academic gatekeeping. In D. A. Mihesuah & A. C. Wilson (Eds.), *Indigenizing the Academy: Transforming Scholarship and Empowering Communities* (pp. 31–47). Lincoln, NE: University of Nebraska Press.

Mihesuah, D. A., & Wilson, A. C. (Eds.). (2004). *Indigenizing the Academy: Transforming Scholarship and Empowering Communities.* Lincoln, NE: University of Nebraska Press.

Ottman, J. (2013). Indigenizing the academy: confronting "contentious ground." *Morning Watch: Education and Social Analysis, 40*(3–4), 8–24.

Radford, W. (2013). Post secondary internationalization and hyper-diverse city contexts. Unpublished doctoral dissertation, Simon Fraser University, Vancouver, BC.

Rumbley, L., Altbach, P., & Reisberg, L. (2012). Internationalization within the higher education context. In D. Deardorff, H. de Wit, J. Heyl, & T. Adams (Eds.), *The SAGE Handbook of International Higher Education* (pp. 3–26). Thousand Oaks, CA: SAGE Publications.

Slimbach, R. (2015). Reinventing international education: purpose, product, place and pedagogy. *International Educator, 23*(5), 58–63.

Smith, L. T. (2012). *Decolonizing Methodologies. Research and indigenous peoples.* London: Zed Books.

Trilokekar, R. D. (2016). Strategic internationalization: At what cost? *Trends and Insights, February,* 1–5. Retrieved from www.nafsa.org/_/File/_/ti_february2016.pdf

Truth and Reconciliation Commission. (2015a). *Honouring the Truth, Reconciling for the Future: The Final Summary of the Report From the Truth and Reconciliation Commission of Canada.* Retrieved from http://nctr.ca/assets/reports/Final%20 Reports/Executive_Summary_English_Web.pdf

Truth and Reconciliation Commission. (2015b). *Truth and Reconciliation: Calls to Action.* Retrieved from http://nctr.ca/assets/reports/Calls_to_Action_English2.pdf

Williams, D. A. (2013). *Strategic Diversity Leadership: Activating Change and Transformation in Higher Education.* Sterling, VA: Stylus Publishing, LLC.

Wilson, S. (2008). *Research is Ceremony.* Winnipeg, MB: Fernwood Publishing.

Chapter 4

Innovation and internationalization in university-based schools and faculties of education

Mark S. Johnson, Chelsea Blackburn Cohen, and Andrea Ferrer

This chapter seeks to describe and analyze recent transformations in university-based schools and faculties of education, with a special focus on policy debates about the allegedly urgent need for 'disruptive innovation' and new approaches to internationalization. Schools and faculties of education take on diverse forms around the world, with a fundamental distinction being that not all institutions emphasize both teacher education and educational research. In fact, that is the single most important fault line that runs through the middle of this sector. On the one side, there are those university-based schools and faculties that are primarily (or exclusively) focused on the traditional mission of pre-service teacher education (often at the undergraduate level) and in-service professional development for teachers and educational leaders, designed to meet primarily local or national needs. On the other side, there are university-based schools and faculties that combine the core mission of teacher education (sometimes only at the graduate or postgraduate level) with an expanding emphasis on peer-reviewed interdisciplinary research and policy development, often together with diverse external and global partners.

In the United States, long the pace-setter in the development of schools and faculties focused on both teacher education and research, there have been both positive and negative trends in recent years. Positively, the research profile and available grant funding for highly ranked schools and colleges of education have been rising, and many institutions have benefited from greater international student mobility into their degree programs, especially at the professional master's and doctoral levels. Negatively, many public U.S. schools and colleges of education have been subjected to repeated state-level budget cuts, while private institutions have seen drops in enrollment in the face of rising tuition costs and emerging competition from online and for-profit teacher training programs that charge lower tuition fees and have lower barriers-to-entry. Some institutions have suffered from overly political attacks on public-sector teachers' unions and ideologically motivated attempts to establish looser or 'alternative' teacher licensure programs. Many schools and colleges of education in the United States have also been criticized for having low academic standards, allowing grade inflation, and for being resistant to 'reform' movements such as vouchers and charter schools (for an incisive historical analysis of these conflicts and institutional marginalization, see Labaree, 2004). In other developed countries, in contrast to the United States, the profiles of university-based programs in education have been rising, and many have seen significant infusions of government funding in pursuit of policy-relevant research and a more highly skilled teaching corps (most notably in Singapore, Korea, China, Taiwan, some provinces in Canada, and many nations in Europe). Unfortunately, in many developing and disadvantaged countries, it seems that teacher education programs are also struggling, especially if they are isolated in narrowly profiled or specialized pedagogical institutions.

This chapter represents a first look at findings from a larger research project on these global policy trends, which will ultimately encompass comparative and qualitative analyses of about twenty university-based schools and faculties focused on education. An overview of broad historical trends is provided, as well as insights from five brief institutional examples. The larger project will also analyze some of the universities that are currently grouped together in the International Network of Education Institutions (INEI), an informal grouping of nine leading schools and faculties of education. The chapter will also draw on insights generated by an international 'summit' of more than twenty deans of schools of education that was convened by the deans of the Graduate School of Education of Peking University and the National Research University Higher School of Economics (Moscow), which was held in St. Petersburg, Russian Federation, in June of 2016.

The politics of 'disruptive innovation' in global higher education: U.S. perspectives

The early 2000s witnessed a remarkable period of upheaval in U.S. and global higher education, which accelerated during the great recession of 2008–2009 and, at least in the United States, was only partially ameliorated by President Obama's American Recovery and Reinvestment Act (ARRA, the 'stimulus' bill) of 2009–2011. Other nations, especially in Europe and Latin America, faced similar higher education budget crises and only in parts of East Asia were state-led stimulus efforts seemingly equal to the severity of the recession. Faced with this budget crisis, university leaders, media commentators, and venture capitalists highlighted the inevitability of 'disruptive innovation' in higher education, which they argued would rapidly destabilize 'old' service providers, much as analogous changes had done in other cultural sectors (Christensen & Eyring, 2011). The driving forces behind these allegedly inexorable transformations were said to be the globalization of the higher education market; new platforms for information technology and digital media; the rapid global growth in the online availability of course content; and emerging models for governance, academic labor, and revenue generation compared to the allegedly 'obsolete' traditional universities. In light of the emergence of aggressive for-profit and online providers, and in the context of ongoing disinvestment by many governments, almost all of the large comprehensive public universities began embracing ambitious programs for 'innovation' and the commercialization of university products and services with a greater sense of urgency.

There was significant attention around the world to the disruptive and 'revolutionary' potential of these new digital tools and emerging instructional practices. The *New York Times* declared that 2012 was the 'Year of the MOOC,' with widespread interest in how massive open online courses could transform both global access and content provision (Haber, 2014). Other enthusiastic accounts described how students anywhere in the world could pursue a 'do-it-yourself' (DIY) education online and assemble their own majors and degree programs outside of traditional institutions, or seek new content and experiences 'unbundled' from residential requirements (Selingo, 2013). Common themes throughout this burgeoning 'movement' were that technology was rapidly ending the traditional need for the 'co-presence' of instructors and students; that competency-based education (CBE) and prior learning assessments (PLA) would finally end the 'archaic' credit-hour standards of residential degree programs and traditional accreditation; and that new digital tools and staffing models could constrain both academic labor and facilities costs. Looking ahead, enthusiastic journalists and advocates argued that emerging interactive functionality and the potential of predictive analytics in learning management systems (LMSs), along with adaptive learning software and new assessment tools, would revolutionize teaching and learning worldwide and create vast opportunities for 'visionary' venture capital to transform the higher education sector (Carey, 2015). It must be noted that these utopian prescriptions often failed to account for the types of degree programs that are purposefully place-specific or nationally bounded, for our purposes most notably teacher education and locally relevant educational research and policy analysis.

Predictably, there were also critics and skeptics who questioned the inevitability of disruptive innovation, perhaps especially those who lamented the potential eclipse of faculty leadership and traditional models of shared governance. Higher education analysts drew attention to the inevitably complex realities of implementation, especially the vital role of experienced faculty members in implementing such new approaches and establishing new organizational cultures (Law, Yuen, & Fox, 2015). Some educators came to see the inevitability of change and the transformational potential of the new digital technologies, but stressed the need for serious and sustained research on the impact of new approaches to teaching and learning, and on how to best adapt new digital tools to the needs of distinctive academic disciplines and institutional missions. Thus, the challenge facing university-based schools and faculties of education in the last decade has been how to blend the pressure to pursue such 'innovation' in principled ways, while at the same time dealing with budget pressures to achieve autonomy and greater financial self-sufficiency, and simultaneously wrestling with policy imperatives to embrace internationalization.

The first generation: cross-cultural travelers, pedagogy, and boundary crossings

In broad outline, the dynamics of internationalization in university-based faculties and schools of education have gone through at least three stages or generations, with only a relatively small number of institutions worldwide seeming to break through to a new 'third generation' of interdisciplinarity, sustained innovation, and strategic internationalization. In such a schema, in the first generation (from the late 18th century until the middle of the 20th century), cross-cultural influences were spread informally through travelers and personal accounts of visits to innovative schools and with individual scholars, such as visits to see Johann Pestalozzi's schools in Switzerland or the tours of Horace Mann in Europe. While there were some early efforts to foster more scholarly approaches to 'comparative education,' these did not lead to university-based degree programs until well into the 20th century (Manzon, 2011). Similarly, efforts to professionalize teacher education were, necessarily, local or at best nationally focused, in which normal schools and institutes or academies of education trained local teachers for service in local schools, or in which schools of education contributed to the role of nation building in newly independent countries through support for native-language instruction, curriculum development, and citizenship education. In almost all cases, these efforts were institutionally separate from leading public and private universities.

Internationalization in this context was often accidental or incidental: the recruitment of teachers from expatriate or missionary families (and thus with foreign language skills), and the influential role played by privately funded missionary schools in colonial settings. While such colonial schools undeniably constituted a form of 'cultural imperialism' and often did grievous damage to local languages and cultures (Altbach & Kelly, 1978), in some settings they also fostered opportunities for cross-cultural communication, mutual recognition, and anti-colonial resistance. For example, what began as the informal recruitment of American teachers into early colonial ventures in the Philippines, Hawaii, and Puerto Rico evolved into systematic efforts to recruit teachers and deploy them around the world in the Peace Corps and other U.S.-government-funded international aid programs. As Zimmerman (2006) has detailed, these programs sometimes caused participants to question the individualism and materialism of American society, or to cultivate a deep appreciation of non-Western cultures. These efforts were paralleled by ambitious teacher education and mobility programs from the Soviet Union and the socialist bloc (Muller, 1967), with Soviet-style specialized 'pedagogical institutes' established in many newly independent countries, with their strong emphasis on traditional school curricula and formal 'didactics' for teaching. To summarize, throughout this period, institutional missions around the world remained almost entirely focused on the core mission of pre-service teacher education and in-service professional development, as well as in some cases policy-relevant research and educational evaluation.

The second generation: an ethos of global cooperation yet with constricted resources

In a 'second generation' of institutional development that began in the 1960s, the core mission of teacher education remained, but was supplemented in many leading institutions by a growing array of interdisciplinary and international initiatives. Organizational experiments include the International Bureau of Education (IBE), which began in the 1920s, survived the World War II, and later merged with UNESCO (founded in 1945), with its emphasis on global cooperation in adult literacy and teacher education (ILO/UNESCO, 1966). The agenda of teacher professionalization was also advanced by the International Institute of Educational Planning (IIEP, established in 1962) and 'official development assistance' programs undertaken by a variety of countries on both sides of the Cold War.

In this expansive context, many university-based schools and faculties of education sought to raise their research profile and scholarly status, which often entailed drawing in expertise and methodological rigor from the quantitative social and behavioral sciences, especially in educational psychology and measurement. The post-World War II era provided new opportunities for research in comparative education, cooperation in international educational development, and ambitious cross-cultural studies, which arguably began in earnest with the founding of the International Association for the Evaluation of Educational Achievement (IEA) in 1958. Some institutions began to require or encourage study abroad or teaching practicums abroad as part of their certification programs, although in the United States this remains limited as a result of state-level licensing and residency requirements (Mahon, 2010). Other institutions undertook the active recruitment of international students into their postgraduate degree programs, in pursuit of both global connections and new revenue. Of course, the tensions of the Cold War and violent struggles over decolonization also resulted in attacks on schools and teachers in proxy wars and liberation struggles, pressure against teachers' labor organizations, and ideological suspicions about those who had studied in either the United States and the West or the Soviet Union and the socialist bloc.

These years also saw ambitious efforts to articulate new approaches to global studies and global citizenship education (Stearns, 2008), although many of these efforts were later undercut by declining resources in the 1980s and 1990s. Ironically, the economic decline of the socialist bloc and the winding down of the Cold War also led to sharply curtailed mobility opportunities and constricted resources for international teacher education. Furthermore, after the end of the Cold War in 1991, the United States shifted away from strategic educational aid programs to more laissez-faire and market-based approaches to global mobility. This occurred as higher education became increasingly conceived of as a private good and a consumer product, in which private, corporate, and for-profit educational providers would be encouraged to compete with more established public colleges and universities.

More positively, during these same decades, numerous other countries – especially in parts of the (soon-to-be-former) socialist bloc and East and Southeast Asia – came to require comparative education courses for all future teachers, and emphasized global policy trends and lessons for improved practice to be gleaned from such comparative study. In the West, there was also a renaissance of comparative studies of pedagogy and teaching practice (Alexander, 2001; Baker & LeTendre, 2005), as well as a renewed emphasis on an ethos of 'global education' and cross-cultural curricula (Acedo, 2012). However, arguably, many of these innovations remained somewhat peripheral, especially as both international aid from the superpowers and domestic budgets began to constrict in the 1980s and after. While the Education for All (EFA) movement spurred increased attention to rigor and quality in teacher education, austerity budgets also constrained the public sector, and emphasized market-driven solutions in professional and teacher education.

The third generation: towards interdisciplinary research and sustained innovation

In a new or 'third generation' of innovation and internationalization, some leading schools and faculties of education have recently been pushing into genuinely new terrain. Exemplars of this new approach include the University of Toronto, the University of British Columbia, Seoul National University, the National Institute of Education in Singapore, Peking University and Beijing Normal University, the National Research University Higher School of Economics in Russia, the University of Melbourne, the University of Sydney, University College London, and numerous U.S. and other institutions. These institutions are (in most cases) working to sustain their core mission in teacher education (Sieber & Mantel, 2012), while at the same time aggressively developing revenue-generating 'innovations' such as professional master"s degree programs and 'mixed modality' executive PhD and EdD programs. Many of these institutions are also systematically incorporating global mobility into their graduate and postgraduate programs, and are encouraging university-wide and deeply interdisciplinary grant development and research projects. Many are also aggressively recruiting international faculty, and developing the administrative and staff capacity to sustain ambitious cross-border collaborations.

Another critical factor that seems to tie together these institutions is a close alignment with sub-national and national school reform strategies, and a more integrated and coherent approach to the professional development of teachers and educational leaders (even if not all of these goals are achieved consistently in practice). All of these leading institutions work to support national-level initiatives to raise the quality of students coming into university-level education programs; to require a bachelor's degree in an academic field along with a certificate or additional degree in education; and, in many cases, to require a master's or

Master of Arts in Teaching (MAT) degree along with extensive practice teaching or school-based practicums before beginning to teach. Most of these programs are also predicated upon an expectation of academic rigor within their courses; the prospect of relatively high salaries in the public sector upon graduation; and the provision of high-quality professional development support while teaching. In other words, the rigor and quality of university-based schools and faculties of education seems to depend in almost every case on a sustained national commitment to educational achievement and equity, even if those goals are often legitimated through the policy language of global competitiveness.

For example, University College London (established in 1862) merged in 2014 with the Institute of Education (IOE) to become UCL IOE, and has been ranked first in the QS subject rankings in Education for several years (UCL IOE has more than 6,000 students and 800 staff). UCL has embraced a university-wide strategy for strategic internationalization, through its Global Engagement Strategy (GES) and Global Engagement Office (GEO), with perhaps the most striking institutional innovation being the appointment of seven pro-vice-provosts intended to coordinate university-wide activities across seven world regions. UCL has also laid out a vision for 2034 (UCL, 2014), with a focus on four grand challenges (global health, sustainable cities, intercultural understanding, and human well-being). UCL IOE offers interdisciplinary research grants to faculty and students who reach across the disciplines, and has recently launched a well-resourced Centre for Global Higher Education to cultivate global partnerships and policy-relevant cooperation with major international organizations and partner universities.

Similarly, the University of Melbourne (established in 1853) combined its Graduate School of Education (2006) with the Melbourne Centre for the Study of Higher Education (CSHE) and the L. H. Martin Institute, which focuses on innovation in tertiary education and revenue-generating professional programs and executive education. The Melbourne Graduate School of Education offers a Master of Education and a Master of Teaching, and coordinates a number of large-scale research projects in science, technology, engineering, and mathematics (STEM) teaching and learning; workplace literacy; and school-to-university transitions; as well as a network of partnership schools. Melbourne also offers a residential Master of Arts (MA) degree in international education policy, and an MA in global studies in education as an online revenue-generating program with a focus on East and Southeast Asia. Research is coordinated through an array of centers, including the Melbourne Education Research Institute (MERI), the International Centre for Classroom Research (ICCR), and the CSHE. In other words, Melbourne seeks to balance graduate-level teacher education with revenue-generating programs and professional training. Additional interdisciplinary efforts include the Melbourne Social Equity Institute (MSEI) – focused on university-wide research in health, law, education, housing, work, and transportation – as well as the Science of Learning Research Centre, designed to foster interdisciplinary and university-wide research in neurobiology and the learning sciences.

In 1996, the University of Toronto (UT) was consolidated together with the Ontario Institute for Studies in Education (OISE, established in 1847), and now functions as a combined faculty of education, state-funded research center, and province-wide hub for advanced professional development and executive education. UT OISE offers Bachelor of Arts (BA), MA, PhD, and EdD degrees. Prominent research hubs include the Centre for the Study of Comparative and International Higher Education (CIHE) and Comparative, International and Development Education Centre (CIDEC), as well as a growing presence in indigenous education. Prominent themes for these programs include ethnicity, globalization, global governance, social equity, conflict resolution, and community development. Significantly, many UT OISE faculty are affiliated with other faculties, such as the Munk School of Global Affairs or the professional schools in health, law, and business. The UT branch campus in Mississauga is also focused on 'internationalization at home' through its Global Education Centre, including support for students to add global content and experiences to their degrees and assistance for foreign students who are studying in Canada. Both campuses also seek to increase Canadian students' participation in study abroad. It should be noted that UT OISE combines funding from revenue-generating programs with a substantial base of provincial government support, as well as the aggressive pursuit of competitive external grant funding.

In an interesting variation on this pattern, what is generally recognized as the leading education program in the Russian Federation is in a relatively new university, the National Research University Higher School of Economics (HSE) in Moscow (Froumin, 2011), which was in part designed precisely to break with the Soviet legacy of specialized 'pedagogical' training. HSE has led the process of raising research standards in the social sciences as well as in conducting policy-relevant research for various ministries, especially related to the Bologna Process, new finance models in higher education, and a new national testing system for university admissions. HSE's Graduate School of Education and Institute of Education (as consolidated in 2012) offer hybrid professional MA degrees, as well as residential MA and PhD degrees in areas such as teacher education (with a special focus on history, political science, and language education); evidence-based policy research; institutional leadership; and educational measurement and testing. Research and postgraduate training at HSE is intended to be both relevant to policy and practice within Russia, as well as informed by international methodologies and comparative analysis. HSE doctoral students are funded for a period of research at an international partner university; and HSE has also led efforts at professional capacity building in Russian education, most notably through its peer-reviewed journals and the creation of the Russian Association of Higher Education Researchers (RAHER). As with the other institutional examples cited in this chapter, HSE combines revenue-generating 'innovative' programs with a core of government funding and in-house capacity to aggressively pursue external and national research funding.

Finally, the College of Education at Seoul National University (SNU-COE) offers a similar dynamic of institutional consolidation and high-profile professional education aligned with national policy goals. COE emerged from the Hansung Normal School (1895), and became one of the founding units of SNU (established in 1946). SNU-COE offers BA, MA, and PhD degrees in teacher education, educational leadership, sports science, counseling, arts education, and how to teach Korean language and literature. SNU-COE is also affiliated with a network of laboratory schools, and is actively developing study abroad programs for pre-service teachers through its international networks.

The strategy that ties all of these leading institutions together is bringing teacher education and educational research into the heart of major research universities, as well as leveraging comprehensive and coherent approaches to internationalization – along with institutional resources – to pursue these strategies.

Conclusions: combining principled innovation and strategic internationalization

The selection of these examples is not intended to suggest that other institutions are not comparably innovative: one could also look to the University of Bristol, the University of Sydney, the University of Hong Kong, the University of British Columbia, Michigan State University, Arizona State University, University of Wisconsin-Madison, Boston College, and numerous others for similar efforts to combine their core mission with new approaches to innovation and internationalization (Hudzik, 2015; Quezada, 2015). While there are risks in a short-term focus on 'disruptive innovation' and narrowly commercial approaches to revenue generation, many of these leading institutions have been successful in continuing to generate significant state funding and competitive grant funding, and many of their professors are involved in multidisciplinary and multinational research collaborations.

Perhaps the most obvious lessons for institutions in the United States are the necessity of maintaining a stable core of government funding for such programs as well as embracing research-based policymaking instead of ideological or partisan dogmas. In fact, it is entirely possible that many U.S. programs, perhaps especially in public universities, may fall behind in this increasingly competitive global policy environment. In the most highly regarded of these new 'third generation' schools and faculties of education, there are ongoing efforts underway to develop robust networks of international partnerships; to craft more strategic approaches to global student and faculty mobility (through sustained and often subsidized 'pipelines' with partner institutions); and to closely cultivate their global alumni networks. Of course, many schools and faculties of education will remain local or regional institutions, or will remain committed to the traditional core mission of teacher education. The key policy issue then becomes our ability to draw out lessons that might be learned from these exemplars, and the ways in which their approaches to principled innovation and strategic internationalization can be used to support and enrich more traditional or locally focused programs, perhaps through professional associations or new university consortia.

References

Acedo, C. (2012). Internationalization of teacher education. *Prospects 42*, 1–3.

Alexander, R. (2001). *Culture and Pedagogy: International Comparisons in Primary Education*. Malden, MA: Blackwell.

Altbach, P. G., & Kelly, G. P. (Eds.). (1978). *Education and Colonialism*. New York: Longman.

Baker, D. P., & LeTendre, G. K. (2005). *National Differences, Global Similarities: World Culture and the Future of Schooling*. Stanford, CA: Stanford University Press.

Carey, K. (2015). *The End of College: Creating the Future of Learning and the University of Everywhere*. New York: Riverhead Books.

Christensen, C., & Eyring, H. J. (2011). *The Innovative University: Changing the DNA of Higher Education From the Inside Out*. San Francisco, CA: Jossey-Bass.

Froumin, I. (2011). Establishing a new research university: the Higher School of Economics, the Russian Federation. In P. G. Altbach & J. Salmi (Eds.), *The Road to Academic Excellence: The Making of World-Class Research Universities* (pp. 293–321). Washington, DC: World Bank.

Haber, J. (2014). *MOOCs*. Cambridge, MA: MIT Press.

Hudzik, J. K. (2015). *Comprehensive Internationalization: Institutional Pathways to Success*. New York: Routledge.

ILO/UNESCO. (1966). *Recommendations Concerning the Status of Teachers*. Geneva/Paris: ILO/UNESCO.

Labaree, D. F. (2004). *The Trouble with Ed Schools*. New Haven, CN: Yale University Press.

Law, N., Yuen, A., & Fox, R. (2015). *Educational Innovations Beyond Technology: Nurturing Leadership and Establishing Learning Organisations*. Dordrecht: Springer.

Mahon, J. (2010). Fact or fiction? Analyzing institutional barriers and individual responsibility to advance the internationalization of teacher education. *Teaching Education 21*(1), 7–18.

Manzon, M. (2011). *Comparative Education: The Construction of a Field*. Hong Kong: Springer/CERC.

Muller, K. (1967). *The Foreign Aid Programs of the Soviet Bloc and Communist China*. New York: Walker.

Quezada, R. (2015). *Internationalization of Teacher Education*. New York: Routledge.

Selingo, J. (2013). *College (Un)Bound: The Future of Higher Education and What it Means for Students*. Boston: Harcourt.

Sieber, P. & Mantel, C. (2012). The internationalization of teacher education: an introduction. *Prospects, 42*, 5–17.

Stearns, P. (2008). *Educating Global Citizens in Colleges and Universities: Challenges and Opportunities*. New York: Routledge.

UCL. (2014). *UCL 2034: A New 20-Year Strategy for UCL*. London: University College London.

Zimmerman, J. (2006). *Innocents Abroad: American Teachers in the American Century*. Cambridge, MA: Harvard University Press.

Chapter 5

Constructing transnational partnerships

New forms and spaces for internationalization in East African universities

Jackline Nyerere and Milton Obamba

Partnerships spanning diverse organizational and geographical boundaries have emerged in recent decades as the dominant paradigm for organizing innovative research activities, strengthening institutional research and teaching capacities, as well as organizing international development policy and practice (Koehn & Obamba, 2014). The growing focus on the partnership framework is driven partly by an increasing realization that communities worldwide are interdependent and many of the world's most challenging problems are complex and invariably transcend territorial boundaries (Koehn & Rosenau, 2010; Zeleza, 2005). Partly as a result of this emerging perspective, there has been a remarkable increase in the scope and significance of agencies, human power, policy systems, and financial resources directed at creating and promoting transnational knowledge-based partnerships among higher education institutions as well as between universities and other non-university organizations (Zeleza, 2007). At the global scale, transnational academic collaborations and networks have become increasingly ubiquitous, embedded in diverse organizational cultures, and are increasingly organized in a wide variety of structural forms and for diverse purposes among individual researchers, academic institutions, research institutes, donor agencies, governments, and intergovernmental agencies (Bradley, 2007; Obamba & Mwema, 2009). The importance of diasporic networks for revitalizing research in developing countries has also been widely documented (Obamba, 2013).

Transnational research partnerships and diasporic networks can contribute to capacity building, knowledge production and sharing, as well as mobilization of financial and human resources across boundaries (Katz & Martin, 1997; Kinser & Green, 2008). This has the benefit of creating synergies and complementarities for mutual benefits and promotion of economic growth. The need has become increasingly urgent in developing regions and around the world for more effective collaborative knowledge-based initiatives and what are commonly described by some researchers as 'transnational competencies,' which transcend geographical borders (Koehn & Rosenau, 2010).

Recent literature and policy documents from diverse contexts show that knowledge-based partnerships involving universities are also increasingly considered as key tools for realizing the goals of international and sustainable development (Koehn & Obamba, 2014). In Europe, for example, the European Research Area (ERA) emphasizes that transnational cooperation and mobility are at the core of the broader ERA strategy for building a more competitive and sustainable knowledge economy. Meanwhile, in recent years, a growing body of major policy publications has suggested that African universities must lead the way in creating and consolidating collaborative partnerships and networks at the national, regional, and international levels if Africa is to benefit meaningfully from the global circuits of knowledge and build its own internal capacity for innovation, economic growth, and development (African Union Commission, 2014; International Science and Technology Institute, 2004). Some of these policy documents include the Africa Action Plan (African Union, 2008), Abuja Declaration on Sustainable Development in Africa (Association of African Universities, 2009), and Africa-Europe Higher Education for Development Cooperation White Paper (EUA-AAU, 2010).

How are transnational research collaborations in African universities constructed?

Increased attention has been paid in the recent literature to the effective governance and management of research activities (Morris, 2002; Schuetzenmeister, 2010). Certain studies have focused on research management in African universities, highlighting existing practices and structural weaknesses (Association of Commonwealth Universities, 2012; Kirkland & Ajayi-Ajagbe, 2013). This heightened interest in more efficient research governance is driven by the increasing scarcity and competitiveness of critical research funding, a greater focus on the economic and social impacts of scientific research, as well as the growing complexity and interdependence of institutional environments in which research organizations are embedded (Morris, 2002).

Although research governance is a relatively recent phenomenon that is still evolving at different speeds across the world, there has been a shift towards what can be described as the professionalization of research management. Research governance or management can be understood as "the day-to-day activity in which the complex and permanently changing institutional environment of scientific work has to be taken into account in order to make research possible" (Schuetzenmeister, 2010, p. 2).

Transnational academic partnerships and networking are at the core of Africa's agenda for revitalizing higher education and stimulating a knowledge-based approach to sustained economic growth and development across the continent. The New Partnership for Africa's Development (NEPAD) has emphasized that revitalizing Africa's universities to play their critical role in development "will require partnerships not only with local and regional actors and stakeholders, but also with the universities, businesses, and governments of the developed world" (NEPAD, 2005, p. 21). Universities across Africa are increasingly embedded within diverse networks, partnerships, and consortia that transcend the nation-state and operate at multiple levels, based on disciplinary, geographical, historical, and institutional complementarities and similarities (Koehn & Obamba, 2014; Zeleza, 2005).

North-South, South-South, and diasporic networks represent some of the innovative existing forms of transnational organizational and structural arrangements that are becoming increasingly common among African universities. These partnerships and networks are tremendously useful for mutual capacity building and enhancing socioeconomic innovations and growth (Obamba & Mwema, 2009). In the emerging context of increasing transnational academic cooperation and closer interconnectedness between research and socioeconomic development priorities, the governance of higher education research systems and their boundary-spanning configurations becomes a complex and challenging affair (King, 2009). This increased complexity, significance, and fluidity of research arrangements draws our attention to the urgent need for a radical shift from traditional locally bounded governance structures to a new focus on transnational governance of research systems (King, 2009), which embraces multi-level and multi-actor modes of governance processes and structures (Jongbloed, Jurgen, & Carlo, 2008).

Transnational research partnerships in Kenya and Uganda

This chapter presents early findings from a study still in progress that aims to critically examine the organization and governance of transnational research partnerships in six universities in Kenya and Uganda, including how existing research networks interface with national innovation systems. The study seeks to identify and analyze the management processes and structures as well as the actors embedded at the interface between transnational research partnerships, institutional research management structures, and national innovation systems.

The research utilizes a rigorous multi-method and multi-level approach, addressing the macro- and micro-level dimensions and contexts of transnational partnerships. The macro-level dimension involves critical reviews of key policy documents and literature that have shaped the trajectory of transnational academic partnerships at the regional and national levels. National policy blueprints on economic development, higher education, research management, and innovation systems in Kenya and Uganda are critically examined and compared. The research also involves conducting key informant interviews focused on respondents in governmental and sub-governmental agencies.

Although the study will ultimately include data from universities in both Kenya and Uganda, the findings presented in this chapter are drawn exclusively from the data collected from three universities in Kenya: Kenyatta University, Masinde Muliro University of Science and Technology, and United States International University – Africa. Rather than collecting data concurrently in the two countries, the research activity was organized in a two-phase arrangement, starting with Kenya before moving into Uganda, due to considerable differences in time and requirements for gaining access to the sample institutions in these two East African countries.

Institutional context for partnership governance

We suggest that governance of transnational partnerships refers to how decisions are made within the partnership, and provides the overarching framework for matters of authority, accountability, and the lines of communication that support transnational research projects and engagements. At both the institutional and project levels, research management requires suitable structures and processes in order to operate efficiently and achieve desired results. Preliminary findings suggest that research and higher education partnerships have been anchored in various policy frameworks at institutional, national, regional, continental, and global levels. At the institutional level, the findings indicate that policymaking to streamline higher education partnership formation and management is becoming increasingly common across higher education institutions in Kenya. Each of the three universities in this case study demonstrated the existence of at least some specific policy framework document and organizational structure put in place for the purpose of regulating the planning, establishment, and management of higher education partnerships and cooperation.

Research partnerships at Kenyatta University (KU) are handled by the Centre for International Programs and Collaboration as well as the Directorate of University-Industry Partnerships. Of the three case study universities, KU displays the most articulate and comprehensive policy framework and organizational structure for the development and effective management of higher education partnerships. The *Kenyatta University Partnerships Policy, 2015* (Kenyatta University, 2015) demonstrates that partnership and cooperation are core to the university's triple mission of teaching, research, and community service. It states that "KU has prioritized partnerships as a mechanism for achieving its strategic objectives that include infrastructure development, innovation, training, research, and community service" (p. 7). This policy instrument articulates a whole range of matters pertaining to partnership development, including key principles and aims, university structures for partnership management, procedures, the legal framework for partnerships (which must be grounded in Memoranda of Understanding or Memoranda of Agreement), and the various categories of partnerships the university is mandated to engage in. Some of the core principles articulated in the partnership policy require that partnerships are guided by the broader KU statutes and vision; are based on written and legally binding agreements; clearly define activities and benefits to the university; are valid for five years and renewable on satisfactory review; protect and enhance KU's core interests; and are of the highest standard of quality in terms of contributing to the university's triple mission of teaching, research, and community service (Kenyatta University, 2015). The KU policy framework further demands that partnerships adhere to the university's own established statutes and promote its own academic and economic goals, while also aspiring to meet higher standards of quality. This suggests that KU has its own clear standards and goals and is therefore more likely to engage in higher-quality partnerships, and in a more structured and strategic fashion, rather than in an informal or haphazard manner.

Masinde Muliro University of Science and Technology (MMUST) manages its partnerships through the Directorate of International Relations and Academic Linkages (DIAL) established in 2010. Like Kenyatta University, the university also had in place a partnership policy guiding its functions pertaining to partnership development and management (MMUST, 2015). Like KU, MMUST also considers partnership-building as critical to the achievement of its goals and the university is therefore seeking to create a uniform and well-defined regulatory framework for partnership development across the institution. The document, for instance, outlines the aims of the DIAL, including attainment of the university's vision and mission; facilitating exchange programs; and connecting the university to other universities, organizations, and communities at various levels (MMUST, 2015, p. 2). The document does not articulate any principles guiding the university's partnership strategy or the processes and criteria to be followed in partnership identification and development. In relative terms, the MMUST policy document is generally less articulate, less radical, and less comprehensive compared to the KU partnership policy document. The document at least showed the university's general interest to develop partnerships but the framework for construction and governance of these partnerships is not clearly articulated.

The United States International University – Africa (USIU-A), on the other hand, manages partnerships through the Institutional Planning and Advancement (IPA) unit under the Academic Research Office (ARO). Unlike KU and MMUST, USIU-A's research and partnerships activities are coordinated by a senior office, the Academic Research Office, headed by the Associate Deputy Vice Chancellor for Academic Affairs. The office handles institution-wide research efforts, whereas the schools and department-based partnerships are managed by respective schools and departmental committees, but in consultation with the ARO. ARO is responsible for, among other activities, the collaborations and management of university research affairs.

The main document guiding research partnership activities at USIU-A was the university strategic plan (United States International University – Africa, 2015). Under its LAGICS (linking academics, government, industry civil society, and sponsors) framework, the plan envisions an interdisciplinary approach to partnerships that links the university to the community as well as with local and international organizations. This fits in with one of the five goals of the strategic plan, which is to provide globally competitive and innovative academic programs that focus on research and collaborations (USIU-A, 2015). In the fashion already observed at Kenyatta University, the USIU-A also portrays a deliberate and strategic approach to partnership building and management that embraces various actors, elements, and activities both within and outside the boundaries of the university. However, as mentioned earlier, the KU policy framework is still more comprehensive and radical compared to the USIU-A partnership document.

Overall, there is evidence of various forms of organizational structures for governance of research and partnerships in each of the three case study universities. Survey data from the study indicate that the three universities in Kenya have established various structures and initiatives for running research partnerships. Respondents surveyed at departmental levels across the three universities identified a range of structures pertaining to partnership management, including international offices, research and outreach units, university policy frameworks, program directors/coordinators, university committees, school/faculty committees, and administrative department units – in various combinations to facilitate partnership activities at both university and project levels. It would seem reasonable to suggest that the growing importance of transnational partnerships and cooperation has precipitated the proliferation and institutionalization of organizational structures at various levels across higher education institutions for the purpose of planning, initiating, and governing international collaborative operations.

National and regional agendas on research and partnerships

The three Kenyan institutions in the current study have attempted to various extents to align their research activities with a range of system-wide government policies, particularly the country's overarching economic blueprint, *Kenya Vision 2030* (Republic of Kenya, 2007), and the National Commission for Science Technology and Innovation (NACOSTI) policy objectives. *Kenya Vision 2030* and the establishment of NACOSTI are part of a wider pattern of increasing institutional elaboration and policy thickening around the need and rhetoric to embed research and knowledge into the government's national development agenda. There is a substantial set of other policy frameworks that are presumably established to shape research and the overall functioning of Kenya's higher education system, including a new discourse around knowledge creation and applications to national development. Important examples of these instruments include the *Ministry of Education, Science and Technology Strategic Plan 2013–2017* (Republic of Kenya, 2013), the *National Science, Technology and Innovation Policy and Strategy* (Republic of Kenya, 2008), and the *Universities Act* (Republic of Kenya, 2012). These documents represent a new body of policy instruments and guidelines that articulate the Kenyan government's new emphasis on a knowledge-based economic order, and demonstrate the growing importance of science, technology, and innovation capacity for national development. The question of whether this new knowledge-based policy discourse remains largely in the rhetorical sphere or whether it translates into actual implementation and practice remains the subject of considerable debate and uncertainty in Kenya (Jowi & Obamba, 2013).

Under *Kenya Vision 2030*, the country aims to "provide a globally competitive quality education, training and research for sustainable development" (p. 126). Specifically, the country seeks to encourage and strengthen partnerships and linkages with key stakeholders, including the private sector, to enhance relevant training, and to mobilize funding for research capacity development (Republic of Kenya, 2007). *Kenya Vision 2030* clearly emphasizes multiple linkages and dimensions of cooperation:

> In order for Kenya to realize the maximum benefits of research [and training] there is need to adopt a systems approach to address innovation dynamism in all sectors of the economy by examining interdependencies, interconnections, and interrelations. The current system does not encourage access, use, generation, and diffusion of knowledge within business systems.
>
> (Republic of Kenya, 2007, p. 24)

Drawing from *Kenya Vision 2030*, NACOSTI also aims to coordinate science, technology, and research activities so as to achieve harmonization of efforts and resources among science, technology, and innovation (ST&I) players across the country.

At the regional and continental levels, higher education institutions in Kenya are guided by the Inter-University Council for East Africa (IUCEA) and the *Africa Agenda 2063* framework, both of which emphasize the need to develop a common higher education area in East Africa, a phenomenon resembling the European Research Area initiative (African Union Commission, 2015).

Regionally, IUCEA is a participant in East Africa's integration process in which the East African Community (EAC) is establishing systems to implement four regional integration pillars: Customs Union, Common Market, Monetary Union, and Political Federation. IUCEA's vision is to become a strategic institution of the EAC responsible for promoting, developing, and coordinating human resources development and research. Among other activities, IUCEA plans to develop systems for the harmonization of higher education to make East Africa a common higher education area; to promote research linked to education, postgraduate training, innovation, and community engagement; as well as to link academia with private enterprise through engagement with the public sector.

At the continental level *Agenda 2063: The Africa We Want* (African Union Commission, 2015) is considered a strategic framework for the growth and sustainable development of Africa. The Agenda is pushing for quality in the delivery of education through cutting-edge research, innovation, and the promotion of information sharing and mutual learning, as well as the establishment of communities of practice in the education space. It envisions the establishment of an increased number of world-class regional/continental research centers, which are expected to provide critical research outputs in priority areas for Africa. To date this has been realized partly through the establishment of more than 40 research centers of excellence across Africa. These centers have been established to strengthen specialization and collaboration among African higher education institutions. They are expected "to deliver relevant and quality education and applied research to address key development challenges facing the region" (Makoni, 2015). The centers encourage the mobility of academics, researchers, staff, and students to foster collaborative knowledge creation and dissemination.

Initiating partnerships

The formation and development of transnational partnerships involve a range of complex processes and considerations, including initiation, planning, management, and structural integration, all of which entail the need to build mutual trust and establish common grounds (Koehn & Obamba, 2014). The early stages of a higher education partnership are also critical, since "success and sustainability of the collaboration have their roots in the initial context of formation of the partnership" (Koehn & Obamba, 2014, p. 83). Partnerships in higher education are assembled to solve complex problems requiring multiple and cross-cutting scientific viewpoints and backgrounds and thus work best when they are situated in environments that can easily adapt and evolve as studies take new turns and directions (Koehn & Obamba, 2014; Koehn & Rosenau, 2010). There is a need, therefore, to focus on developing environments that are dynamic, flexible, and adaptive.

Transnational higher education partnerships can take a range of different forms. Adholla and Warner (2005), for instance, have identified a variety of models including cases where one partner acts as a subcontractor of the other (mostly a Northern partner), or where the partners get external research funding mainly managed by one partner. There are also cases where partnerships operate as franchises, which draw on financial resources from the main partner. In other cases, partnerships involve networks of institutions with a shared interest and complementary competences in similar or related thematic research. In this study, we identified a mix of different models in different partnership projects implemented by the three institutions in Kenya. The dominant model involves institutions participating in a competitive research fund managed by one of the partners, which often served as the lead partner and tended to be predominantly based in the global North but also increasingly in the global South (see Obamba, 2013). Another common form of partnership was where one or more Southern and Northern partners draws funding from a third party. In addition, some partnerships are situated within a network of institutions with shared interests in research. In practical terms, the preliminary findings suggest that many of these partnership models tend to be overlapping rather than distinctive, and the nature of a partnership changes and evolves over time for various reasons.

This study also identified a variety of ways in which partnerships were initiated across the three universities. In line with other studies, in-depth interviews with university officials and academics indicated that personal and informal connections were important triggers of partnership creation. Academics and individual researchers described how chance or serendipitous encounters or interactions during conferences, academic visits, social gatherings, exchange programs, or other kinds of external engagement were the source of major and long-term partnership initiatives. These initial personal or informal contacts then became the seed through which a partnership was nurtured and formalized through the university's own formal procedures and structures. We found little evidence of transnational partnerships being formally and independently initiated and implemented at the university's senior management level. Overall, partnership initiation seemed to proceed in diverse patterns from a relatively informal, amorphous, unplanned, and personalized form before evolving and transitioning into a more formalized and structured phenomenon involving the university's formal governance structures.

The second pathway through which transnational partnerships were formed entailed instances where researchers from different institutions were attracted to a call for joint research grant bids or other forms of funded collaborative activity. In these cases, the institutions or academic units involved either reached out to potential external collaborators or were approached by their counterparts to form a partnership for the purpose of developing a collaborative research grant application. Initiation or participation in such partnership activity was observed at various levels and in different ways, ranging from the institution, to specific research units, departments, or faculties, through to participation as individual researchers. There were also a few cases where international offices and research offices in the respective universities initiated research projects and contacted the relevant institutions to form the partnerships directly between the universities. In some cases, individual schools, departments, or individuals started partnership initiatives and thereafter the university provided them with support and resources through central research management and legal services. Our preliminary findings suggest that even where an application for an international collaborative research grant was the main trigger for a partnership, the role of informal networks and previous personal contacts still remained critical and important at the initial stages of the partnership initiative. As other studies have noted, viable research partnerships and joint initiatives tend to grow out of previous or ongoing formal and informal encounters. Initiation or participation in such partnership activity was seen at various levels, ranging from the institution as a whole, to specific research units, departments or faculties, to individual researchers (Koehn & Obamba, 2014).

Conclusions

A wide range of factors can trigger the initiation of a transnational partnership among higher education institutions. Calls for collaborative research or development initiatives seem to be a major catalyst for partnership formation. However, our preliminary findings are clear that previous or existing personal connections and informal encounters play a fundamental and indispensable role in enabling a partnership to be initiated, developed, and sustained. These informal encounters are still crucial at the initial phases regardless of whether the partnership is also driven by other factors, such as joint research and other interests.

The three universities participating in this study in Kenya had traditionally embraced various forms of transnational partnerships and collaborations as a source of third-stream revenue, academic capacity development, as well as reputational enhancement. The universities were increasingly adopting the practice of developing relatively more formal organizational structures as well policy and regulatory frameworks to guide their partnership development and management practices. This might signal a new shift towards the formalization and institutionalization of partnership initiatives. It is clear from the preliminary findings that there is no 'one size fit all' prescription for the governance or structure of transnational higher education partnerships. A variety of models or combinations of approaches can be explored based on mutual agreement, and the form, core objectives, or management structure of such partnerships can also change over time, reflecting changing interests, needs, and circumstances.

References

Adholla, S. M., & Warner, M. (2005). *North-South Research Partnerships: A Guidance Note on the Partnering Process.* London: Overseas Development Institute.

African Union. (2008). *The AU/NEPAD African Action Plan.* Addis Ababa: AUC.

African Union Commission. (2014). *Science, Technology and Innovation Strategy 2024.* Addis Ababa: AUC.

African Union Commission. (2015). *Agenda 2063: The Africa We Want.* Retrieved from www.un.org/en/africa/osaa/pdf/au/agenda2063.pdf

Association of African Universities. (2009). *Abuja Declaration on Sustainable Development in Africa: The Role of Higher Education.* Accra: AAU.

Association of Commonwealth Universities. (2012). *Survey of Current Research Management Practices within the African and Caribbean Regions 2011/2012.* London: ACU.

Bradley, M. (2007) *North-South Research Partnerships: Responses and Trends* (Canadian Partnerships Working Paper No. 1). Ottawa: IDRC.

European University Association-African Association of Universities. (2010). *Africa-Europe Higher Education Cooperation for Development: Meeting Regional and Global Challenges.* Brussels: EUA-AAU.

International Science and Technology Institute. (2004). *Assessment of Higher Education Partnerships for Global Development Program*, Vol. 1. Arlington, VA: IST Inc.

Jongbloed, B., Jurgen E., & Carlo, S. (2008). Higher education and its communities: interconnections, interdependencies and a research agenda. *Higher Education, 56,* 303–324.

Jowi, J. O., & Obamba, M. O. (2013). *Research and Innovation Management: Comparative Analysis of Ghana, Kenya and Uganda.* Report commissioned for OECD Programme on Innovation, Higher Education and Research for Development (IHERD). Paris: OECD.

Katz, J. S., & Martin, B. R. (1997). What is research collaboration? *Research Policy, 26,* 1–18.

Kenyatta University. (2015). *Kenyatta University Partnerships Policy, 2015.* Nairobi: Kenyatta University.

King, K. (2009). The promise and peril of partnership. *NORRAG News, 41* (December), 7–11.

Kinser, K., & Green, M. (2008). *The Power of Partnerships: A Transatlantic Dialogue.* Washington, DC: American Council on Education.

Kirkland, J., & Ajayi-Ajagbe, P. (2013). *Research Management in African Universities: From Awareness Raising to Developing Structures.* London: British Academy of Sciences.

Koehn, H. P., & Obamba, M. O. (2014). *The Transnationally Partnered University: Insights from Research and Sustainable Development Collaborations in Africa.* Basingstoke, UK/ Gordonsville USA: Palgrave Macmillan.

Koehn, H. P., & Rosenau, J. N. (2010). *Transnational Competence: Empowering Professional Curricula for Horizon-Rising Challenges.* Boulder, CO: Paradigm Publishers.

Makoni, M. (2015, August 14). New centres of excellence for East and Southern Africa. *University World News, 377.*

Masinde Muliro University of Science and Technology (MMUST). (2015). *Masinde Muliro University of Science and Technology Partnerships Policy, 2015.* Nairobi: MMUST.

Morris, N. (2002). The developing role of departments. *Research Policy, 31,* 817–833.

New Partnership for Africa's Development, (2005). *Renewal of Higher Education in Africa: Report of AU/NEPAD Workshop.* October 27–28, Johannesburg.

Obamba, M. O. (2013). Transnational knowledge partnerships: new calculus and politics in Africa's development. *COMPARE: Journal of International and Comparative Education, 43*(1), 124–145.

Obamba, M. O., & Mwema, J. K. (2009). Symmetry and asymmetry: new contours, paradigms, and politics in African academic partnerships. *Higher Education Policy, 22*(3), 349–372.

Republic of Kenya. (2007). *Kenya Vision 2030.* Nairobi, Kenya Government Printers.

Republic of Kenya. (2008). *National Science, Technology and Innovation Policy and Strategy.* Nairobi: Kenya Government Printers.

Republic of Kenya. (2012). *Universities Act.* Nairobi: Kenya Government Printers.

Republic of Kenya. (2013). *Ministry of Education, Science and Technology Strategic Plan 2013–2017.* Nairobi: Kenya Government Printers.

Schuetzenmeister, F. (2010). *University Research Management: An Exploratory Literature Review.* Berkeley, CA: Institute of European Studies.

United States International University – Africa. (2015). *2015–2020 USIU Strategic Plan.* Nairobi: USIU-A.

Zeleza, P. T. (2005). Transnational education and African universities. *Journal of Higher Education in Africa, 3*(1), 1–28.

Zeleza, P. T. (2007). The internationalization of African knowledges. In Paul T. Zeleza (Ed.), *The Study of Africa,* Vol. 2, *Global and Transnational Engagements* (pp. 1–24). Dakar: CODESRIA.

Chapter 6

From periphery to the center

International aspirations of regional universities in Siberia

Dina Uzhegova

Internationalization has become one of the top priorities for higher education institutions (HEIs) and national governments. While most countries today have a common aspiration to have internationally competitive higher education (HE) systems, the process of internationalization plays out differently for HEIs in various contexts and depends on various external and internal factors. The literature on internationalization reflects the inequality within the international knowledge system. Most of the research on the internationalization of HE comes from and focuses on the experience of "wealthy, White, and Western countries, especially the major, developed Anglophone nations" (Welch & Yang, 2011, p. 63). In countries with emerging economies, attention is only given to a small group of top universities with ambitions to become 'world-class.' In the case of Russia, 'best practice' is usually presented by HEIs located in major cities, Moscow in particular (e.g., Froumin & Leshukov, 2016).

Furthermore, internationalization is generally discussed within local, national, or global contexts. Where regional aspects of internationalization are considered, these are usually analyzed through the prism of macro-regions, such as the European Higher Education Area (EHEA) or the Association of Southeast Asian Nations (ASEAN). Little research has been conducted on internationalization in micro-regions – territorial entities that exist "between the 'national' and the 'local' (municipal) level, and are either sub-national or cross-border" (Söderbaum, 2005, p. 87). This chapter aims to provide insight into the unique challenges faced by Russian regional HEIs in their internationalization efforts, by focusing on Siberia[1] as a new context where internationalization has recently moved to the forefront of institutional agendas. Based on an advanced Ph.D. study, the discussion in this chapter draws on interviews with administrative leaders responsible for international activities in a group of leading Siberian HEIs, as well as on analysis of institutional development strategies, offering a perspective on internationalization from HEIs located in the Russian periphery.

The Russian context

Situated in an emerging economy, Russian HEIs are mainly peripheral in a global academic context (Altbach, 2016). In the last decade, the Russian government has acknowledged the importance of having an HE system compatible with international standards and HEIs competitive in the global education arena for the wellbeing of the whole country. It has also emphasized the need to regain Russia's international competitiveness in research, technology, and HE (Medveded, 2013). While ambitious, the aspiration to regain the status that Soviet HE lost during a period of post-Soviet "uncertainty and chaotic adaptation" (Froumin & Leshukov, 2016, p. 174) to the new market economy is not impossible. There are examples of parts of HE systems or HEIs that moved from the periphery to the center of global academe or have the potential to do so (Altbach, 2016). In relation to Russia, China provides the most vivid example. While HE systems in both countries were influenced by the Soviet model for many years, strong political commitment supported by reforms and large investment in HE and research have allowed China to achieve much greater success in the modernization of its HE system over the past two decades than Russia (Marginson, 2016).

The agenda of the Russian government "to maximize the competitive position of a group of leading Russian universities in the global research and education market" (Russian Academic Excellence Project, n.d.) is funded through the Russian Academic Excellence Project 5–100. The 21 HEIs selected to participate in this project have begun to actively integrate into the global HE landscape. Such initiatives to invest in a group of leading HEIs and priority research areas, although criticized by some international HE scholars (e.g., Altbach & Hazelkorn, 2017) for their overall negative effect on HE systems, are popular around the world. For large HE systems like Russia, it is difficult to equally support the entire HE system, therefore focusing on leading HEIs and merging smaller ones to create centers of research and excellence is often a viable alternative. Such state support is especially necessary for regional HEIs, where inter-regional migration and demographic shortfalls have caused a decline in the number of university applicants and made university admission less competitive.

Prior to the launch of Project 5–100, the Russian government had already identified a group of leading HEIs that were granted status of 'federal' or 'national research' university. However, almost half of these HEIs are located in Moscow and St. Petersburg. While this can be justified by the historical role of these cities in the development of Russian HE, as well as their current high population density, this concentration of government investment in the universities in these two cities creates social inequality in HE among the regions (Latova & Latov, 2013). In addition to the high concentration of leading Russian HEIs around Moscow and St. Petersburg, the proximity of these cites to Europe and the historical relationships with that region have influenced the government's interest in adopting a European model of HE development and integrating Russian HE into the EHEA. With Russia stretched across two continents, following certain HE trends creates different attitudes across the country. According to the European University Association report on trends shaping the European Higher Education Area (EUA, 2007), HEIs in the western regions of Russia express a strong interest in adapting to the European approach to HE, while those located in the central and eastern regions of the country give preference to cooperation with Asia and the United States.

Russia is an extremely capital-centric country, and as such has developed strong center-periphery dynamics between Moscow and the other regions, including Siberia and the Russian Far East, regions that are often referred to as "Russian Asia." While there is a clear state agenda to modernize and internationalize Russian HE, these reforms do not affect the different regions of the country in the same way. Given the size of Russia, its regional inequality, and relatively complex HE system, the rationales, strategies, and challenges faced by HEIs in their attempt to internationalize vary in different regions. Therefore, it is necessary to consider specific regional conditions when analyzing internationalization in Russian HEIs.

The place of Siberia in Russia

For the Russian government, Siberia is a valuable region, given its abundance of natural resources including coal, hydrocarbon, and drinking water (Ministry of Economic Development of the Russian Federation, 2010). Due to the nature of its economic development, the region is often used as Russia's economic colony (Zhdanov, 1995). While Siberia is also "the quintessence of Russia's Eurasian status and a natural bridge between Europe and Asia" (Vodichev & Lamin, 2008, p. 127), the advantage of this geographic location has never been developed to its full capacity.

Despite its various natural resources, the standard of living in Siberia is quite low and the region is dependent on central government subsidies. The center-periphery imbalance creates an internal inter-regional migration flow from the eastern territories to the Moscow region, a phenomenon called 'Western drift.'[2] The big city environment, with better work and educational opportunities, makes Moscow very attractive and, for many Russians and residents of former Soviet countries, "migration to the capital presents an alternative to moving abroad, because Moscow serves the role of 'domestic abroad'" (Zaionchkovskaya, Mkrtchian, & Tyuryukanova, 2014, p. 234). Siberia, located in the geographic center of the country, can to some extent compensate for the inter-regional migration to the capital by way of arrivals from the Far East and the Commonwealth of Independent States, but its population is still declining.

Siberia is often depicted in literature (e.g., Frazier, 2010; Wirick, 2006) and media (Terskikh & Malenova, 2015) as the 'middle of nowhere' and a place with a severe climate and history of political exile. Few people know that the third largest city in Russia, Novosibirsk, is located in Siberia, and that the first HEI in Siberia opened more than a hundred years ago. There are currently five leading universities in the region. These are the Siberian Federal University and four national research universities: Novosibirsk State University, Irkutsk State Technical University, Tomsk State University, and Tomsk Polytechnic University. Four of these universities are currently participating in the 5–100 Project.

- Established during the period of imperial rule, Tomsk State University (1878) and Tomsk Polytechnic University (1896) were the first universities located to the east of the Ural Mountains. Both universities have been designated as historical and cultural monuments by Presidential Decree.
- Irkutsk State Technical University was founded in 1930 when Irkutsk became a center of the Siberian gold industry.
- Novosibirsk State University, established in the period 1957–1959 as a part of the Siberian Branch of the Russian Academy of Sciences, is located in the heart of Akademgorodok, 'city of science.' At the time of its establishment, Siberian Akademgorodok was a symbol not only of progress and the development of rich Siberian resources but also of the decentralization of science from Moscow and St. Petersburg (Josephson, 1997).
- Siberian Federal University, the youngest university in this group, emerged through the amalgamation of four HEIs in 2006 and one additional institution in 2012. Russian federal universities are intended to develop a system of professional education "on the basis of optimizing regional educational structures and strengthening links of educational institutions of higher education with economics and social sphere of the federal districts" (National Training Foundation, n.d., n.p.).

While these HEIs are prestigious in the region and have long histories and academic traditions, as well as a special role in the development of Siberia, they are not well-known internationally. Peripheral location of Siberia makes their pursuit of internationalization even more challenging.

Regional aspirations for HE internationalization in Siberia

The insights in this section of the chapter are based on in-person semi-structured interviews with administrative leaders responsible for international activities in leading Siberian HEIs conducted during campus visits during the period August–September 2014. The interviews showed a common perception of the importance of the internationalization process for HEIs in Siberia. They confirmed the view that internationalization drivers in regional HEIs in Russia include *inter alia* a necessity to increase prestige, attractiveness, and competitiveness at a national and international level (Garusova & Piginesheva, 2013). One interviewee said that their institutions "faced the necessity that every university faces, of increasing the visibility on national, as well as on international market, including education services, research, and scientific developments. And therefore, the word 'internationalization' came into usage." An interviewee from another university commented that "Internationalization will first of all contribute to the popularization of our university in the world. It's very important in this way." The internationalization rationale to raise a university's international profile is also stated in the strategic development plans of some Siberian HEIs (e.g., Siberian Federal University).

There is also the potential impact of the internationalization of HEIs on municipal and regional development. As one interviewee suggested, "Internationalization significantly contributes to the position of the university on the academic and also political map. Significance of the region in many aspects depends on the extent to which university has collaborations with international partners." Tomsk Polytechnic University considers the positioning of the city of Tomsk as a unique global research and academic center to be one of its strategic goals in increasing international competitiveness.

In addition to the visibility and recognition on national and international levels, the importance of internationalization was also linked to the geographic marginality of Siberia. Internationalization was thus regarded as a means of diminishing the remoteness of the region by providing HE with international perspectives, as captured in this view:

> Internationalization is very important. It is probably important for any HEI, but for [an] HEI that is located not in the center of the universe it is, I think, even more important. So that, firstly, people do not feel disconnected and, secondly, so that people keep up with the rest of the world.

Internationalization was also understood from a competency perspective, where interviewees saw its role in relation to student outcomes:

> [A] specialist, even if this specialist is being prepared for local needs, cannot be efficient if s/he doesn't know global trends in the[ir] field of specialization . . . Preparation of high class and high quality specialists, which is a mission of our university, is not possible without the broad-mindedness and global comprehension of professional market.

Regional tensions and challenges

In addition to a number of factors influencing internationalization in HEIs across Russia –such as language, bureaucracy, and the recognition of Russian qualifications abroad – there are specific factors affecting this process in regional HEIs. The historical, socio-economic, and geographic characteristics of Siberia add more complexity to the internationalization process of its HEIs. During the interviews, university administrators commented on the great efforts and resources they have put into foreign student recruitment and how little effect that has had on student numbers. One of the interviewees stated that the return on investment in student recruitment was only around 15 percent. The remoteness of Siberia was not considered to be the main challenge in recruiting foreign students and professors. Indeed, distance matters less as infrastructure develops and transportation becomes cheaper. However, the negative image of Siberia, often based on stereotypes, is what seems to hinder academic mobility. This was highlighted in the following comments: "All because we are located in Siberia – the word

'Siberia' is scary" and "Siberia, the name 'Siberia' itself has a very, very negative image that is hard to fight. We are located in Siberia and for them [foreign students] it is scary." It is argued that international profiling is very important for HEIs on the periphery, as the places where they are situated are often not very well-known (Klemenčič, 2017). Yet, in the case of Siberia, this is different. The concept 'Siberia' is recognized internationally due to its figurative meanings, such as 'a place with an extremely cold weather' or 'a place that is far away.'

Of those students who do come to study in Siberia, the majority are from the former Soviet republics and Asia. Students from developed countries come to Siberia very rarely, usually just for short exchange programs, as an 'exotic' experience. Moscow, St. Petersburg, and the European part of Russia, in general, are more attractive for foreign academics and students. Furthermore, the socio-economic challenges and the burden of regionality and provinciality of Siberia force many talented local high school graduates to leave the region.

Meanwhile, although far from the capital, Siberia does not escape close central government control, and the broader political situation in the country affects the region. During the Cold War, some Siberian cities required government permission for entry, due to their proximity to so-called 'closed administrative-territorial formations' or 'closed cities,' where nuclear or other secretive research was being conducted. At that time, this hindered the ability of HEIs to engage in international activities with countries outside of the Communist Bloc. As such, many Siberian HEIs only began to internationalize in earnest after 1991, when the iron curtain was lifted and HEIs acquired the autonomy to engage in various international activities.

Yet, this lack of international exposure has influenced the attitudes of some professional and academic staff towards internationalization. For example, one interviewee believed that "narrow-mindedness of people is one of the obstacles to internationalization." The need to change the current mindset of academic and professional staff, to internationalize perspectives, and make ways of thinking more flexible was identified as a challenge and a desired outcome of internationalization in many responses. One interviewee stated that "internationalization has to happen in the mind. People need to start looking a little bit differently at the world and cooperation in general. People need to be more flexible towards the world and other things."

Despite the recent modernization of HE, "many rudiments and systematic restrictions of the Soviet past" are still evident in Russian HEIs (Yudkevich, 2014, p. 1465). The strong organizational culture of Soviet HE – underpinned by principles of uniformity, top-down administration, and one-man management (Kuraev, 2016) that developed over decades – cannot disappear in a short period of time. On the one hand, the aging generation of academics is challenged to adjust to the rapid transformation in the HE environment and change their old practices. On the other hand, it may take time for young academics to gain the necessary experience to move Russian HEIs beyond these traditional modes, as explained by one of the interviewees:

The majority of people [at the university] were brought up in a completely different paradigm. Aging people, they will never learn a foreign language anymore and the young people who began coming and staying to work at the university, they may have language skills, but they do not have the background.

For the internationalization process to be successful, it is argued that it must intertwine all spheres of university life. In reality, this process is still marginalized in two main areas: institutional governance (where the strategy and vision for internationalization are developed) and international offices (where the operational side of this strategy is implemented). Despite the fact that more academic staff are now engaged in international activities, not everyone is ready to embrace internationalization practices:

> Individual teachers or heads of some departments are not always with great interest meeting the idea that a bunch of foreign students will come [to their faculty or class], because of whom they will have to teach a bit differently, because of whom they will have to teach in English. This creates additional difficulties. And to say that they all are jumping with joy is impossible. Yes, you have to [internationalize], but at the same time they [longtime faculty] have been living perfectly before this. So we do meet some resistance on the ground.

Different factors, including lack of institutional support, various individual barriers, as well as the multiple understandings of internationalization, affect the level of faculty's international engagement in HEIs worldwide (Proctor, 2015). Internationalization of Siberian HEIs is unlikely to be effective unless all university staff support this process and unless they possess the skills and knowledge needed to introduce international activities.

Creating action and finding a way forward

Leading Siberian HEIs are facing tremendous pressure not just to engage in international activities but also to fully integrate into the international HE space as competitive HEIs. Located in the periphery of the country, HEIs in Siberia are at disadvantage in comparison with other Russian HEIs. Their status nationally is diminished by their geographic location and their position in the international HE space is yet to be established.

State support is important for internationalization of HEIs in peripheral locations. However, funding provided by the Russian government through the excellence initiative has come with a set of key performance indicators and reporting procedures related to the allocation of funds and the achievement of targets. Regional differentiation was not taken into consideration when the government's policy on the internationalization of HE was adopted. Pressure to make Russian HEIs more globally competitive has to be balanced against local realities and the current needs of HEIs. The opportunity to innovate and find context-sensitive and context-specific approaches to internationalization is the key to the effective internationalization of Siberian HEIs moving forward.

Given that such inherited factors – like geographic location, history, economy, culture, and language – are beyond institutional control, HEIs positioned in the periphery are especially in need of a carefully designed internationalization strategy (Klemenčič, 2017) that can address the challenge of finding the right balance between their local, national, regional and global roles (de Wit, 2017). Klemenčič (2017) suggests that peripheral HEIs need to work closely with their cities and micro-regions to enhance the internationalization of the whole community and to create an attractive learning environment. While the quality of life in Siberia's cities is important for attracting talent, hosting a sizable student population is vital for the stable development of Siberian cities. Therefore, collaboration between HEIs and city governments could be mutually beneficial.

Internationalized Siberian HEIs have the potential to become attractive centers for young people and to slow down the inter-regional migration to the west of Russia. Leading HEIs in Tomsk and Novosibirsk already attract students from smaller Siberian cities. In 2013, the largest proportion of the non-resident students from other regions and countries were enrolled in HEIs in Tomsk, St. Petersburg, Novosibirsk, and Moscow, respectively (Hadaev, 2013). The "formation of [a] center of attraction for young scientists and talented youth in the Baikal and Far Eastern regions, which will significantly reduce the outflow to the European part of the country and abroad" is a part of the development strategy of Irkutsk State Technical University (Irkutsk National Research Technical University, 2010).

Furthermore, if the fierce competition between Siberian HEIs does not overpower their cooperative strategies, the distinctive regional geography of HEIs could be used to develop a unique Siberian HE hub. Regional cooperation is seen as a 'promising ideal' for HEIs in the periphery, as this process can allow them to combine their resources to build an academic and intellectual infrastructure (Altbach, 2016) and strengthen their collective international status and visibility (Klemenčič, 2017). For some Siberian HEIs, especially for Novosibirsk and Tomsk State Universities, which are in the top 10 Russian universities, this will require a shift in focus from their national to the micro-regional status. Given that the concept 'Siberia' is already well-known internationally due to its metaphorical use, transforming the negative image of the region into a positive one through the network of leading Siberian HEIs can be the key to internationalization, not only in Siberia's HEIs but also the region as a whole.

Notes

1 While in geographic terms Siberia is the Russian territory to the East of Ural Mountains, in this chapter Siberia is referred to as the Siberian Federal District.
2 "'Western drift' – population movement from the east of the country to the center, Volga region and the south, which reflects Far East residents' desire to resettle in the European part of the country – is the main vector of interregional migration during the post-Soviet period" (Zaionchkovskaya, Mkrtchian, & Tyuryukanova, 2014, p. 32).

References

Altbach, P. G. (2016). The university as center and periphery. In P. G. Altbach (Ed.), *Global Perspectives on Higher Education* (pp. 149–170). Baltimore: Johns Hopkins University Press.

Altbach, P., & Hazelkorn, E. (2017, January 8). Why most universities should quit the rankings game. *University World News*. Retrieved from www.universityworldnews.com/article.php?story=20170105122700949&query=altbach

de Wit, H. (2017, February 24). Internationalisation of HE may be accelerating. *University World News*. Retrieved from www.universityworldnews.com/article.php?story=20170220232342276

European University Association (EUA). (2007). *Trends V: Universities Shaping the European Higher Education Area*. Brussels: EUA.

Frazier, I. (2010). *Travels in Siberia*. New York: Farrar, Straus and Giroux.

Froumin, I., & Leshukov, O. (2016). The Soviet flagship university model and its contemporary transition. In J. A. Douglass (Ed.), *The New Flagship University: Changing the Paradigm from Global Ranking to National Relevancy* (pp. 173–179). Basingstoke, UK: Palgrave Macmillan.

Garusova L. N., & Piginesheva A. P. (2013). Strategiya mezhdunarodnogo sotrudnichestva universitetov otechestvennyy i zarubezhnyy opyt [Strategies for internationalization of higher education: Russian and international experience]. *Territoriya Novykh Vozmozhnostey. Vestnik Vladivostokskogo Gosudarstvennogo Universiteta Ekonomiki i Servisa*, *4*(22), 134–152. Retrieved from http://science.vvsu.ru/scientific-journals/journal-eng/current/article/id/2145393558/Strategies%20for%20Internationalization%20of%20Higher%20Education:%20Russian%20and%20International

Hadaev, A. (2013, August 26). Tomsk i Novosibirsk stali liderami po chislu inogordnih studentov [Tomsk and Novosibirsk became leaders in the number of interstate students]. *Rossiyskaya Gazeta*. Retrieved from https://rg.ru/2013/08/26/reg-sibfo/studehty-anons.html

Irkutsk National Research Technical University. (n.d.) *Program of the Development of the State Educational Institution of Higher Education "Irkutsk State Technical University" in 2010–2019*. (Approved by Ministry of Education and Science of the Russian Federation from June 11, 2010, No. 604). Retrieved from www.istu.edu/eng/deyatelnost/niu/programma_razvitiya

Josephson, P. R. (1997). *New Atlantis Revisited: Akademgorodok, the Siberian City of Science*. Colby College. Retrieved from http://digitalcommons.colby.edu/cgi/viewcontent.cgi?article=1000&context=facultybooks

Klemenčič, M. (2017). Internationalisation of higher education in the peripheries: the "gear effect" of integrated international engagements. In J. Gacel-Avila, E. Jones, N. Jooste, & H. de Wit (Eds.), *The Globalization of Internationalization: Emerging Voices and Perspectives* (pp. 99–109) (Internationalization in Higher Education series). London: Routledge.

Kuraev, A. (2016). Soviet higher education: an alternative construct to the western university paradigm. *Higher Education, 71*, 181–193.

Latova, N. V., & Latov, I. V. (2013). "Capital cities centrism" as the cause of social inequality in the Russian system of higher education. *Russian Education & Society*, *55*, 53–83.

Marginson, S. (2016). *The Role of the State in University Science: Russia and China Compared* (Centre for Global Higher Education Working Paper No. 9). London: Centre for Global Higher Education, UCL Institute of Education. Retrieved from www.researchcghe.org/perch/resources/publications/wp9.pdf

Medvedev, D. (2013, July 5). *Dmitry Medvedev Attends a Meeting of the Council for Promoting the Competitiveness of Russia's Leading Universities Among the World's Leading Research and Education Centres.* Retrieved from http://government.ru/en/news/2798/

Ministry of Economic Development of the Russian Federation (2010). *Strategy of Socio-economic Development of Siberia Through 2020.* (2010). Retrieved from http://economy.gov.ru/minec/activity/sections/strategterplanning/komplstplanning/strategstplanning/index

National Training Foundation (n.d.). *Creation of new universities in federal districts.* Retrieved from http://eng.ntf.ru/p96aa1.html

Proctor, D. (2015). Faculty and international engagement: has internationalization changed academic work? *International Higher Education, 83*(special issue), 15–17. Retrieved from https://ejournals.bc.edu/ojs/index.php/ihe/article/view/9082

Russian Academic Excellence Project. (n.d.). *The Goal of Project 5–100.* Retrieved from http://5top100.com/

Söderbaum, F. (2005). Exploring the links between micro-regionalism and macro-regionalism. In M. Farrell, B. Hettne, & L. Van Langenhove (Eds.), *Global Politics of Regionalism: Theory and Practice* (pp. 87–103). Ann Arbor, MI: Pluto Books. Retrieved from www.jstor.org/stable/j.ctt18fs9dj.10

Terskikh, M., & Malenova, E. (2015). Metaphorical conceptualization of the concept of Siberia in modern American mass media discourse. *Procedia – Social and Behavioral Sciences, 214*, 1125–1133. Retrieved from www.sciencedirect.com/science/article/pii/S1877042815060814

Vodichev, E. G., & Lamin, V. A. (2008). Russian identity and Siberia's self-identification. Historical traditions in the global world. In D. W. Blum (Ed.), *Russia and Globalization. Identity, Security and Society in the Era of Change* (pp. 111–139). Washington, DC/Baltimore, MD: Woodrow Wilson Center Press/Johns Hopkins University Press.

Welch, A., & Yang, R. (2011). A pearl on the Silk Road? Internationalizing a regional Chinese university. In J. Palmer, A. Roberts, Y. Ha Cho, & G. Ching (Eds.), *The Internationalization of East Asian Higher Education: Globalization's Impacts* (pp. 63–89). New York: Palgrave Macmillan.

Wirick, R. (2006). *100 Siberian Postcards.* London: Telegram Books.

Yudkevich, M. (2014). The Russian University: recovery and rehabilitation. *Studies in Higher Education, 39*(8), 1463–1474.

Zaionchkovskaya, Z., Mkrtchian, N. V., & Tyuryukanova, E. V. (2014). Russia's immigration challenges. In T. Akaha & A. Vassilieva (Eds.), *Russia and East Asia: Informal and Gradual Integration* (pp. 200–243) (Routledge Contemporary Russia and Eastern Europe Series). Retrieved from www.hse.ru/mirror/pubs/lib/data/access/ram/ticket/47/14943727739674be537f20a60996bdb04fa9455201/%D0%A1%D1%82%D0%B0%D1%82%D1%8C%D1%8F-%D0%97%D0%9C%D0%A2.pdf

Zhdanov, V. A. (1995). Contemporary Siberian regionalism. In S. Kotkin & D. Wolff (Eds.), *Rediscovering Russia in Asia – Siberia and the Russian Far East* (pp. 120–132). Armonk, NY: M. E. Sharpe.

Chapter 7

Internationalizing higher education in an era of austerity

The case of Ireland

Linda Hui Yang

Introduction

Using a 'glonacal' perspective, Marginson and Rhoades (2002) contend that higher education is now influenced far beyond the nation-state, by regional trading blocs and associations, such as the European Union (EU) or the North American Free Trade Agreement (NAFTA), and by nongovernmental organizations, such as the Organisation for Economic Co-operation and Development (OECD) or the World Bank. As Case (2013) suggests, social and political expectations of the role that higher education institutions should play have continued to expand.

Given the impact of austerity on higher education systems, an intellectual concern with the significance of austerity's impact on engagement with internationalization seems appropriate. The Republic of Ireland is an interesting case study in this regard, as the global recession had a significant impact on that country's economy, as it did in many countries. However, national factors, such as the impact of the Irish sovereign debt and the ensuing financial crisis, had even more serious repercussions for the country. During this period, successive Irish governments sought new approaches to maximize efficiencies in the public sector, which in the Irish context includes higher education institutions. The combined forces of austerity and new policy approaches to higher education provide a unique opportunity to explore the impact of global, national, and local factors, as well as agents, on the development of internationalization across the Irish higher education sector.

This chapter will examine the approaches to internationalization adopted by national agencies in Ireland in response to the collapse of Ireland's national finances in the wake of the global economic crisis of 2008. The study is based on the examination of public documents, and on an analysis of the impact of global, national, and local agencies on the development of these approaches.

Glonacal agency heuristic

Marginson and Rhoades (2002) introduced what they termed a 'glonacal agency heuristic' to provide an approach to understanding and comparing globalization of higher education. This heuristic emphasizes the simultaneous significance of global, national, and local dimensions and forces. It also combines two meanings of the word 'agency.' The first meaning is that of an established organization. Established organizations impacting on the internationalization of higher education exist at the global level (e.g., the United Nations Educational, Scientific and Cultural Organization [UNESCO], the EU, and the International Association of Universities), the national level (e.g., governments, departments of education or higher education, semi-state organizations, and groups representing all or some of the higher education institutions), and the local level (e.g., higher education institutions themselves).

The second meaning of 'agency' captured in the heuristic is that of an individual or collective action. These actions can occur on any of the three levels, but the impact of the actions may flow through to either or both of the other levels. For example, the action by one country's immigration agency to restrict the number of international students coming into a country may impact at the local level on the financial viability of that country's higher education institutions, but may also impact at the global level if the flow of students to that country is diverted to other countries.

In this study, the glonacal agency perspective is used to explore the internationalization of Irish higher education over the period of austerity following the 2008 global financial crisis. The key agents and actions at each level which contributed to this internationalization are identified and analyzed for their global, national, and local interactions.

The Irish higher education landscape

The Republic of Ireland is a relatively small European country with a population of 4.76 million (Central Statistics Office, 2016). It has been independent since 1922 and is a unitary parliamentary republic (Prakke, Kortmann, & van den Brandhof, 2004, p. 429). The government department with responsibility for higher education is the Department of Education and Skills (DES), which is responsible for all state-supported education and for ensuring the quality of all education, from pre-primary through primary, secondary, and tertiary levels (DES, n.d.). Under the Secretary General of DES, a Deputy Secretary General has specific responsibility for higher education, and is assisted by the Higher Education Authority (HEA), a statutory authority which has responsibility for governance and regulation of higher education institutions and the higher education system (HEA, n.d.).

Ireland has seven universities, thirteen institutes of technology, and a small number of private colleges (Education in Ireland, n.d.). The universities and institutes of technology are all public institutions, with the universities governed independently by governing authorities established under the Universities Act, 1997 (Irish Statute Book, 1997).

Before the financial crisis – the Celtic Tiger years

From the mid-1990s to 2008, Ireland experienced a period of rapid economic growth coinciding with significant foreign direct investment. At the start of the 1990s, Ireland was a relatively poor country by West European standards, with high unemployment, high inflation and low growth (Girvin, 2010). However, the Irish economy expanded at a higher rate than any other OECD country between 1995 and 2000, and continued to grow until 2008, transforming the country into one of the wealthiest countries in Europe (Garcimartin, Rivas, & De Sarralde, 2008).

During this time, relatively little attention was paid to the internationalization of higher education. The *Department of Education and Science Statement of Strategy 2005–2007*, written in 2004, mentions "promoting Ireland as a centre for international excellence in education" and "linking with Asia through education" (DES, 2005, p. 38), but by the time the *Statement of Strategy 2008–2010* was written in 2007, the international aspect of higher education was not mentioned, and instead the Government committed to "develop a national strategy for higher education to guide the future development of the sector" (DES, 2008, p. 40).

The financial crisis and the period of austerity

In the later part of the Celtic Tiger period, mortgage loans in Ireland increased from €16 billion in the first quarter of 2003 to €106 billion by the third quarter of 2008, and property-related loans to construction businesses went from €45 billion in 2003 to a peak of €125 billion in the first quarter of 2008. This coincided with very significant increases in the price of Irish property assets over the period and a boom in property development (Whelan, 2014).

In late 2007 and in 2008, the world experienced a global financial crisis, triggered by a high default rate in the subprime home mortgage sector in the United States following the bursting of a housing bubble in that country (Financial Crisis Inquiry Commission, 2011). Once this global financial crisis struck, the fragile cashflows of Irish property developers were exposed. With the value of most of the assets securing the loans declining in line with the property market, the liabilities of the six Irish domestic banks became much greater than their assets (Whelan, 2014).

After a series of moves to prevent the Irish banks from collapse, including nationalization of the Allied Irish Banks (AIB) and Bank of Ireland, and the transfer of toxic loans to a newly created National Asset Management Agency, in 2010 the Irish Government was forced to accept a financial bailout package from the EU and the International Monetary Fund (IMF) (Whelan, 2014). This package was accompanied by severe restrictions on public expenditure and public employment.

The effect of the financial crisis on the higher education sector was severe. Between 2008 and 2015, funding to Irish universities was cut by 28 percent and reductions were made in staff head count, while student numbers increased by 18 percent. This led to an increase in the student–staff ratio from 16:1 to 21:1, well above the OECD average of 14:1 (Irish Universities Association, 2016).

Emergence of a national International Education Strategy

In December 2008, in an attempt to resurrect the economy, the Government published a strategy entitled *Building Ireland's Smart Economy: A Framework for Sustainable Economic Renewal* (Taoiseach's Office, 2008). This strategy contained many actions, most of which proved unaffordable as the crisis deepened. However, one is of particular relevance here: "We will seek to position Ireland as a destination of choice in the international education market through new regulatory and marketing co-ordination arrangements that will enhance the promotion of Irish education overseas" (p. 72).

The next step taken by the Government to accomplish this action was the creation of a High-Level Group on International Education. This is recorded in the introductory text to the International Education Strategy published later:

> In that context, and arising from the national strategy for economic renewal . . . the Government established the High-Level Group on International Education to co-ordinate a national approach to internationalization and to develop a strategy for Ireland's enhanced performance in this area. The High-Level Group brings together the relevant Government departments and State agencies with representatives of the higher education and English-language sectors.
>
> (DES, 2010, p. 21)

This High-Level Group consisted of leaders from the Department of Education and Skills; the Department of Jobs and Skills; the Department of Justice and Immigration; the Department of Transport, Tourism, and Sport; the Department of Foreign Affairs; the Higher Education Authority; Enterprise Ireland (the Irish state agency responsible for supporting the development of manufacturing and internationally traded services companies); Science Foundation Ireland; and Fáilte Ireland (the Irish state agency responsible for promoting Ireland as a tourist destination). Of the twenty-four members of the group, there were only two representatives from the university sector. However, the group also included two representatives from the institutes of technology, one from the private colleges and one from the English language teaching sector.

From a glonacal point of view, the High-Level Group can be seen as a national agency incorporating other national agencies, but with individual representatives from local agency groups. This conclusion is clear from the balance of representatives on the committee – Ireland has seven universities, fourteen institutes of technology, eight private colleges, and approximately a hundred English language colleges, yet only 25 percent of the committee comprised of representatives from these local institutions, while each and every government and semi-government unit with any interest at all in the higher education sector was represented.

Critique of the national International Education Strategy

The primary rationale for the Irish international education strategy is embedded in the name of the strategy: *Investing in Global Relationships.* Accordingly, this strategy promotes

> investment in future global relationships, with students we have educated in Ireland becoming our advocates overseas, with education institutions that will be research and teaching partners of the future, and with the countries that will be Ireland's next trading and business partners.
>
> (DES, 2010, p. 27)

Two secondary rationales were also given: that internationalization enhances the quality of learning, teaching, and research, enriching the classroom experience for all students by providing intercultural experiences and perspectives; and that educational services could make a significant contribution to economic recovery (DES, 2010, p. 27).

The strategy sets out thirteen goals (calling them objectives or targets), of which the first 11 relate to increasing international student numbers in higher education and in the English language education sector. Examples include "Increase total international student numbers . . . in higher education institutions to 38,000, an increase of over 12,000 or 50% on current numbers" (the first goal) and "Enhance the total economic impact of international education by some €300 million to approximately €1.2 billion in total." Only the final two goals, which proposed increases in the number of Irish staff and students spending time overseas, and the strengthening of institutional relationships with priority countries, are related to broader aspects of internationalization (DES, 2010, p. 31).

The strategy then sets out ten 'strategic actions' to achieve these targets, covering policies (e.g., making visa and labour market access policies competitive), organization (e.g., creating a new framework for the promotion of international education), and activities (e.g., redeveloping and strengthening the Education Ireland brand). The majority of the actions are focused on increasing the recruitment of international students, and 'actions' directed at broader aspects of internationalization are vague and are left to the institutions (DES, 2010, pp. 35–64).

Taken as a whole, the alignment of the majority of the document is with the third rationale, the opportunity for international education to make a contribution to Ireland's economic recovery. Consequently Ireland's International Education Strategy 2010–2015 could reasonably be seen as a coherent Government-level strategy for selling international education as a service. This interpretation is supported by repeated references in the document to 'markets.'

National strategy for higher education to 2030

As referenced above, the Department of Education and Skills' *Statement of Strategy 2008–2010* (DES, 2008), written before the crash, committed to the development of a national strategy for higher education. This task was undertaken by the Higher Education Authority, which established a 'Strategy Group' with significant higher education expertise, including three university/institute of technology presidents, supported by an 'International Panel of Experts' sourced from around the world.

The Strategy Group eventually published its report (DES, 2011) four months after *Investing in Global Relationships* was published. This report made 26 recommendations across the broad areas of teaching and learning, research, engagement with wider society, system governance, developing a coherent framework for the higher education system, funding, and internationalizing higher education. The two specific recommendations concerning internationalizing higher education were that "Higher education institutions should set out their international vision in an institutional strategy that: is related to their institutional mission and to wider national policy goals; and considers internationalization and global engagement in the widest perspective" and "Higher education institutions should put in place appropriate supports to promote the integration, safety, security and well-being of international students" (DES, 2011, p. 85).

The report refers to the International Education Strategy and to the opportunity which internationalization represents for Ireland, but cautions that "The internationalisation of Irish higher education needs to happen as part of a long-term and sustainable process, based on high-quality, holistic and balanced engagement with international partners" (p. 82), and refers to reputational damage that can occur when internationalization is not supported adequately. These quotes suggest that the Strategy Group took a more holistic view of internationalization than the High-Level Group on International Education, and may even have been concerned with the emphasis of the International Education Strategy on international student recruitment. This is not surprising, as the majority of the Strategy Group were higher education professionals, while the majority of the High-Level Group were career civil servants.

However, others have seen this report as an "attempt by the Irish state to re-construct higher education in accordance with economic utilitarian objectives" (Walsh & Loxley, 2015, p. 1128), and Hazelkorn (2014, p. 1350) noted that only one member of the Strategy Group "worked in the area of educational research and policy."

From a glonacal perspective, the Strategy Group could be seen as having a national focus, but being influenced by global trends and global thinking through the support of the international panel of experts. Bearing this in mind, the criticisms by the commentators quoted appear rather harsh.

Higher Education System Performance Framework

The National Strategy for Higher Education report also suggested that the HEA engage in strategic dialogue with higher education institutions to align the strategies of individual institutions with national priorities, and to agree on key performance indicators (KPIs) against which institutional performance could be measured (DES, 2011, p. 91).

This recommendation was embraced by the Department for Education and Skills and by the HEA, and in May 2013 the Minister for Education and Skills approved a 'whole-of-system' approach to the governance of the Irish higher education system, including a performance framework. The document, *Higher Education System Performance Framework 2014–2016* (DES, 2014), indicates that "The HEA will use this framework as the context for conducting a process of strategic dialogue with individual institutions where institutions will agree performance compacts with the HEA with institutional KPIs reflecting their contribution to overall system objectives" (p. 1).

The performance framework set out seven key system objectives for 2014–2016 in support of the Government's national objectives. The objective relevant to international education was "To ensure that Ireland's higher education institutions will be globally competitive and internationally oriented, and Ireland will be a world-class centre of international education" (DES, 2014, p. 2). Supporting this objective were a number of high level indicators, including "Proportion of overall student body of international students – progress towards 15% national target" (p. 8). Institutions set targets against these indicators within their performance compacts, which were drafted in the latter part of 2013. Following individual strategic dialogue meetings between the HEA and the institutions in early 2014, these compacts were signed off by both the HEA and the institutions. The introduction of this process was widely seen as an attempt by the Irish Government to reduce the autonomy of the higher education institutions (e.g., Hazelkorn & Harkin, 2014).

However, from a glonacal perspective, the new process could also be seen as an innovative attempt to bring together national and local imperatives in order to obtain the best overall result from the Irish state.

The post-crash Irish government glonacal approach to international education

The approach that the Irish Government took towards international education during the post-crash period can be interpreted as a glonacal approach, as it uses agents at the national and local level, and recognizes the need for actions to be taken at the global, national, and local levels. The international education market is global, in the sense that students travel from many countries around the world to study internationally, and the competition for students in that market is global. Competition for students exists on a national and local level, as countries try to market their educational environment as a whole, and institutions try to market their own quality and the quality of the educational experiences they offer.

The setting up of the High-Level Group on International Education was an attempt to create a national agency through which the engagement of Ireland in the international education market could be coordinated. As the Government only had control over its own (national) departments through this group (including its national agencies that were already engaging globally), engagement with the higher education institutions had to happen through a different route. From a glonacal perspective, this meant using national policy and national agents to influence the actions of local agents.

Since the HEA is the agency through which the Irish higher education institutions are funded, it is also the agency through which the Irish Government can exercise some control over those institutions. The higher education system performance framework allowed specification of key system objectives to support identified national objectives. The system of performance compacts with each institution created a mechanism through which the local agency of the institutions could be aligned to national level objectives.

The system performance framework allowed the efforts of the institutions to complement the efforts of other national agencies in order to achieve the Government's global objective of attracting more international students to Ireland. Consequently, the approach taken by the Irish Government could be classified as a glonacal approach.

Renewal of the International Education Strategy

On October 7, 2016, the Irish Minister for Education and Skills launched Irish Educated, Globally Connected: An International Education Strategy for Ireland 2016–2020 (DES, 2016). This document included an analysis of trends in international student numbers in Ireland and the economic contribution of those students, which showed that the targets of the previous strategy had been significantly exceeded. Notably:

> In 2010/2011, 20,995 students attended publically and privately-funded Irish HEIs [higher education institutions]. This increased by 58% to 33,118 in 2014/2015. The increase over the period was primarily driven by increases in the non-EU student cohort, which increased by 85% from 11,604 to 21,440 (compared to a 25% increase in the EU student cohort).
>
> (DES, 2016, p. 18)

These results suggest that the approach taken by the Irish Government may have been effective. However, as mentioned above, funding to the Irish higher education institutions has been cut significantly over the period of austerity. Despite the emergence of Ireland from recession and significant improvements in the national finances, there has yet to be any significant return to investing in higher education, where funding remains at levels much lower than prior to the economic crisis. Consequently, the only way institutions have been able to improve their financial circumstances has been by recruiting more international students. Due to EU laws, which mandate that fees charged to EU students must be at an equivalent level to those for Irish students, non-EU students are more attractive recruits than EU students (Europa, n.d.).

Ireland's first national international education strategy did not express a preference to target non-EU students, yet the numbers quoted above from the second national strategy show that, since 2010, non-EU student numbers have increased by 85 percent, while non-Irish EU student number have increased by just 25 percent. This differential suggests that the HEIs, as autonomous local agents, are preferentially targeting non-EU students due to the higher return these students provide to the institution. Since the HEIs have a financial incentive to recruit more non-EU students, much of their activity in this area may have occurred without the Irish Government's attempt to manage the process.

However, it is more likely that the Irish success in increasing the number of international students studying at the country's higher education institutions has been influenced by factors at the global, national, and local levels. The alignment of activities of the various government departments and agencies through the High-Level Group is likely to have contributed positively to efforts to attract international students, while the individual efforts of the institutions are also likely to have contributed, as are global and national factors which may have made other English-speaking destinations less attractive.

The new strategy contains more overt references to the economic benefit of the broader aspects of internationalization, but, as with the first strategy, most of the actions presented for execution by the government departments and agencies are directed at increasing international student recruitment, while the broader aspects of internationalization are confined to the single action "Internationalisation plans will be included in the overall plans of Higher Education Institutions and continue to be monitored through the strategic dialogue process" (DES, 2016, p. 43).

As a result, this second strategy should also be seen primarily as a strategy for international student recruitment, with the target numbers updated from the first strategy. The structures and policies for achieving this have not changed from the first strategy. Consequently, the approach continues to fit within a glonacal framework.

Conclusions

Through an investigation of public documents, this chapter has demonstrated that, in response to the economic crisis of 2008, one of the strategies the Irish Government pursued was an attempt to increase the number of international students coming to study in Ireland, expressed by way of a broader international education strategy. The execution of this strategy involved national and local agencies interacting at local, national, and global levels, and the process by which this interaction occurred has been considered effectively through the lens of Marginson and Rhoades' (2002) glonacal agency heuristic. Notably the national interests of the Irish Government were expressed most clearly in the two international education strategies (DES, 2010, 2016), which were developed by a group dominated by national agencies. In contrast, the national higher education strategy, developed by a group with a greater number of representatives from local agencies and informed by an international panel with a global perspective, proposed a process of strategic dialogue between the main national agency operating between the Irish Government and the higher education institutions (the HEA) and the local institutions on an individual basis to attempt to align national and local priorities. Although it is difficult to prove that this process was causal, the HEA system performance report (HEA, 2016) indicates that the system met, and in fact exceeded, the targets set for the national priorities in the period 2014–2016.

Although the Irish situation is unusual in terms of the relatively small number of higher education institutions involved, the approach is likely to also be useful in analyzing interactions between government, government agencies, and higher education institutions in relation to the internationalization of higher education.

References

Case, J. M. (2013). *Researching Student Learning in Higher Education: A Social Realist Approach*. London: Routledge.

Central Statistics Office. (2016). *Census of Population 2016 – Preliminary Results*. Retrieved from www.cso.ie/en/census/census2016reports/census2016preliminaryreport/

DES. (n.d.). *Management and Organisation*. Retrieved from www.education.ie/en/The-Department/Management-Organisation/

DES. (2005). *Department of Education and Science Strategy Statement 2005–2007*. Retrieved from www.education.ie/en/Publications/Corporate-Reports/Strategy-Statement/strategy_statement_05_07.pdf

DES. (2008). *Department of Education and Science Statement of Strategy 2008–2010*. Retrieved from www.education.ie/en/Publications/Corporate-Reports/Strategy-Statement/des_strategy_statement_2008_2010.pdf

DES. (2010). *Investing in Global Relationships: Ireland's International Education Strategy 2010–2015*. Retrieved from www.education.ie/en/Publications/Policy-Reports/Ireland-s-International-Education-Strategy-2010-2015-Investing-in-Global-Relationships.pdf

DES. (2011). *National Strategy for Higher Education to 2030 – Report of the Strategy Group*. Retrieved from www.hea.ie/sites/default/files/national_strategy_for_higher_education_2030.pdf

DES. (2014). *Higher Education System Performance Framework 2014–2016*. Retrieved from www.education.ie/en/The-Education-System/Higher-Education/HEA-Higher-Education-System-performance-Framework-2014-2016.pdf

DES. (2016). *Irish Educated, Globally Connected: An International Education Strategy for Ireland 2016–2020.* Retrieved from www.education.ie/en/Publications/Policy-Reports/International-Education-Strategy-For-Ireland-2016-2020.pdf

Education in Ireland. (n.d.). *Where Can I Study in Ireland?* Retrieved from www.educa tioninireland.com/en/Where-can-I-study-/.

Europa (n.d.). *University Fees and Financial Help.* Retrieved from http://europa.eu/youreurope/citizens/education/university/fees-and-financial-help/index_en.htm

Financial Crisis Inquiry Commission. (2011). *The Financial Crisis Inquiry Report.* Washington, DC: US Government Printing Office. Retrieved from www.gpo.gov/fdsys/pkg/GPO-FCIC/pdf/GPO-FCIC.pdf

Garcimartin, C. R., Rivas, L. A., & De Sarralde, S. D. (2008). Accounting for Irish growth: a balance-of-payments-constraint approach. *Journal of Post Keynesian Economics, 30*(3), 409–433.

Girvin, B. (2010). Before the Celtic tiger: change without modernisation in Ireland 1959–1989. *Economic and Social Review, 41*(3), 349–365.

Hazelkorn, E. (2014). Rebooting Irish higher education: policy challenges for challenging times. *Studies in Higher Education, 39*(8), 1343–1354.

Hazelkorn, E., & Harkin, S. (2014). Restructuring Irish higher education through collaboration and merger. In A. Curaj, L. Georghiou, J. Casingena Harper, R. Pricopie, & E. Egron-Polak (Eds.), *Mergers and Alliances in Higher Education: International Practice and Emerging Opportunities* (pp. 105–121). Dordrecht: Springer.

HEA. (n.d.). *About the HEA.* Retrieved from www.hea.ie/en/about-hea

HEA. (2016). *Higher Education System Performance: First report 2014–2016.* Retrieved from www.education.ie/en/Publications/Education-Reports/Higher-Education-System-Performance-First-report-2014-2016.pdf

Irish Statute Book. (1997). *Universities Act, 1997.* www.irishstatutebook.ie/eli/1997/act/24/enacted/en/html

Irish Universities Association. (2016). *Press Statement – Report of the Expert Group on Future Funding of Higher Education (Cassells Group) – 11th July 2016.* Retrieved from www.iua.ie/iua-press-statement-report-of-the-expert-group-on-future-funding-of-higher-education-cassells-group-11th-july-2016/

Marginson, S., & Rhoades, G. (2002). Beyond national states, markets, and systems of higher education: a glonacal agency heuristic. *Higher Education, 43,* 281–309.

Prakke, L., Kortmann, C. A. J. M., & van den Brandhof, J. C. E. (2004). *Constitutional Law of 15 EU Member States.* Deventer: Kluwer.

Taoiseach's Office. (2008). *Building Ireland's Smart Economy: A Framework for Sustainable Economic Renewal.* Retrieved from www.taoiseach.gov.ie/BuildingIrelands SmartEconomy_1_.pdf

Walsh, J., & Loxley, A. (2015). The hunt report and higher education policy in the Republic of Ireland: an international solution to an Irish problem? *Studies in Higher Education, 40*(6), 1128–1145.

Whelan, K. (2014). Ireland's economic crisis: the good, the bad and the ugly. *Journal of Macroeconomics, 39,* 424–440.

Chapter 8

Boundaries, bridges, and barriers
Collaboration in the borderland context

Jermain Griffin and Robin Matross Helms

One key approach to advance internationalization in higher education is to foster institutional partnerships. Recent literature shows that partnerships offer institutions innovative ways to engage students, faculty, and staff with peers abroad (Helms, 2015; Knight, 2005). Specific rationales for such arrangements vary by institution, but generally, objectives include building institutional reputation and prestige, enhancing teaching and learning, and pursuing shared goals (Eddy, 2010). Partnership outcomes can range from inactivity, to 'parasitic' engagement – where one partner dominates at the expense of the other – to reciprocal engagement, where both partners experience equitable benefits of the collaboration (Gatewood & Sutton, 2017).

This chapter explores higher education partnerships in the unique space of borderland regions, where the progress of such alliances can be subject to a variety of issues, including the complexities of economics, politics, language, and quality of life. It offers an overview of existing research and information about borderland collaborations, as well as a detailed case study derived from an American Council on Education (ACE) report on U.S.-Mexico higher education partnerships (Helms & Griffin, 2017). While each border context is unique, the examples and analysis included illustrate the particular types of opportunities and challenges that arise in cross-border academic collaborations, and provide insights on borderland partnership dynamics that may be helpful in guiding the development and success of such relationships in other parts of the world.

Understanding borderlands

Regionalisms, structures or processes for guiding policy coordination, have been an instrument for key regional alliances such as the European Union (EU) or the North American Free Trade Agreement (NAFTA), which can serve as strategic partnerships for nation-states (Chao, 2014; Dent, 2008). However, these regional alliances do not always imply cohesiveness, as intra-regional issues such as border engagement can represent underlying complexities that challenge geopolitical, economic, environmental, or sociocultural coordination (Dent, 2008; Haselsberger, 2014). The *borderland* or border region typically represents a geographic area that links two or more communities and/or nation-states in a centralized space that can be separated by a variety of barriers including politics, law, and religion (Haselsberger, 2014; Popescu, 2008). Haselsberger (2014) distinguishes between 'thick' borders – those that are linear, have clear demarcations established by states, and are restrictive for passage – and 'thin' borders or border regions that also have official demarcations, but are more apt to permeability.

Several relatively recent examples illustrate the complexity of borderland relationships, and the potential for collaboration or contention. For instance, the dissolution of the Soviet Union in 1991 yielded new, political border relationships between former Soviet-controlled states such as the Romania-Ukraine-Moldova borderlands (Popescu, 2008). Soviet-era ethnic and borderland tensions were gradually replaced by new alliances stemming from Romania's joining the EU in 2007 and increased economic and political cooperation in the Eastern Europe border region (Popescu, 2008).

In Africa, nearly 50 years of civil war in Sudan eventually led to the independence of South Sudan in 2011 and ongoing negotiations over disputed border areas with the Republic of Sudan. These contested areas, which have vast natural resources and tactical entry points from neighboring Ethiopia, are claimed by both sides with no clear resolution on the horizon (Deng Kuol, 2014). In Asia, a current dispute between emerging global powers China and India over the Doklam region, which also crosses Bhutan, represents a struggle for road access with the promise of greater regional economic prowess (Kalwani, 2017; Saran, 2017).

In the Americas, the U.S.-Mexico borderland region – the setting for the case example highlighted later in this chapter – spans more than 2,000 miles, covering four U.S. states (Arizona, California, New Mexico, and Texas) and six Mexican states (Baja California, Chihuahua, Coahuila, Nuevo León, Sonora, and Tamaulipas). With a large Mexican immigrant population living in U.S. border states, cultural, historic, and economic ties between communities on either side of the border are robust. However, the border region also struggles with a variety of complex issues, including the trafficking of drugs and humans, border security, and poverty. Intensifying political and cultural animosities resulting from President Trump's 2016 presidential campaign promise to build a border wall at the expense of Mexico are also impacting the borderland climate and the extent to which it fosters collaboration – including in the higher education realm (Davis, 2017).

Higher education engagement in borderland regions

Though complex and sometimes contentious, borderlands present potentially myriad opportunities for bi-national or multinational partnership in a broad range of areas including governance, industry, environmental protection, and higher education cooperation. The latter is an under-researched area that offers a new context for the discussion of the internationalization of higher education, and its potential to contribute meaningfully to the development of institutions and the communities in which they are situated. While existing literature is scarce, there are some examples – mainly from Europe – that highlight both opportunities and challenges inherent in borderland academic collaboration, and set the stage for an in-depth analysis of the U.S.-Mexico case.

Higher education coordination in European borderlands

Referred to as 'Euro-regions,' a series of multilateral alliances has been established or reconfigured throughout Europe between the latter half of the 20th century and the early part of the 21st century. There are now more than 100 of these inter-governmental regions throughout Europe where coordination contributes to the sustainability or expansion of regional networks (Haselsberger, 2014; Popescu, 2008). A number of these regions involve countries that share borders, and have given rise to higher education collaborations of various stripes centered in border-land regions.

The European Confederation of Universities on the Upper Rhine (EUCOR), for example, is a consortium of five universities in the French-Swiss-German border region. In 1989, the Universities of Basel, Freiburg, Haute-Alsace, and Strasbourg, and the Karlsruhe Institute of Technology established an official part-nership referred to as 'The European Campus' (EUCOR, 2017). Still in opera-tion today, the partnership connects students and faculty from affiliate institutions through research, student mobility, and curriculum and instruction opportunities (EUCOR, 2017).

National-level initiatives involving Northern Ireland and the Republic of Ireland can also be considered borderland collaboration. Universities Ireland, a consor-tium of institutions in Northern Ireland and the Republic of Ireland (Universities Ireland, 2017), offers an example of successful higher education partnership in a post-conflict border region (Osborne, 2006; Universities Ireland, 2017). The network supports student mobility between the two Irelands through scholar-ships for postgraduate study and other initiatives (Universities Ireland, 2017).

An example from the Nordic states is in the Øresund region, which spans the borders of Denmark and Sweden, and is recognized for its joint ventures, involv-ing actors from both the public sector and private sector, that foster collaboration on several issues including environment, food policy, housing, and technology (Maguire, Marsan, & Nauwelaers, 2013). In 1998, a cross-border education net-work of 14 Danish and Swedish institutions formed Øresund University as a voluntary association to contribute to the region's economic growth and innova-tion through joint-research and student mobility programs (Maguire et al., 2013; Osborne, 2006). Due to differences in national regulations for higher education, Øresund University shut down in 2010, but institutions in the region continue to collaborate on a smaller scale (Maguire et al., 2013).

An examination of borderlands where the potential for academic collabora-tions seems to exist but has not been fulfilled also sheds lights on complexi-ties and challenges. Though not specific to higher education, Kovach's (2015) analysis of border relationships in the Carpathian Euro-region, which links the five Central and Eastern European nations of Hungary, Poland, Romania, Slovakia, and Ukraine, highlights how geopolitical and administrative barriers can impede borderland partnership, including between academic institutions. Kovach (2015) identifies the Slovakia-Ukraine border as a weak area within this Euro-region due to several inefficiencies including unemployment, lack of access to financial resources, and poor road access. Another challenge for partnership is that Ukraine is not a member of the European Union and only the western region of the country is linked with the Carpathian Euro-region initiative (Kovach, 2015). Eastern Ukraine has experienced armed conflict in recent years, which provides an added layer of uncertainty for engagement that extends well beyond higher education collaboration (Smith, 2014). Furthermore, a recent change of legislation in Hungary has restricted the ability of Hungarian higher education institutions to award degrees from non-Hungarian institutions, potentially harming the ability of its larger institutions to remain solvent (Custer, 2017).

Research from other regions

Outside of Europe, research and information about higher education partnership activity in borderland regions is sparse. Scholarly organizations devoted to borderlands studies such as the Association for Borderland Studies (2017), the African Borderlands Research Network (2017), and the Asian Borderlands Research Network (2017) address a range of issues, including migration, trade, stability, conflict, and governance, but have given little attention to the role or impact of higher education collaboration in borderlands. Regional academic networks and associations, such as the ASEAN University Network, promote student mobility and other collaboration among institutions in member countries, but do not specifically target borderland areas (Chao, 2014).

   The next section begins to fill this gap with a case from the Americas, where a critical area of focus is the U.S.-Mexico border region. In this region, scholarship about borderland realities has covered a wide array of issues including public health, drug-related violence, and migration. Higher education partnership in this context is an area of exploration that can offer perspectives on diverse border regions across the globe that are confronted with some of the same experiences and challenges highlighted by the U.S.-Mexico case.

Higher education engagement in U.S.–Mexico borderlands

In March 2017, the American Council on Education (ACE) released a report, supported by Universia/Banco Santander, that examined the depth of partnership activity between US and Mexican higher education institutions. While the geographic scope of the study included the two countries in their entirety, a key finding was that higher education collaboration is largely concentrated in the border region. Of 150 bilateral exchange programs documented, for example, the majority originated from institutions located in the four U.S. border states; the most active Mexican higher education institution in terms of collaboration with U.S. counterparts (the Monterrey Institute of Technology or 'Tecnologico de Monterrey') is located in the Mexican border state of Nuevo León (Helms & Griffin, 2017). An examination of an array of partnerships, programs, and projects across a number of institutions in borderland areas, combined with interviews with select senior international officers at those institutions, allowed for the identification of particular opportunities and challenges inherent to academic collaborations in the borderland context.

Opportunities

Innovative models for student mobility

One key opportunity for higher education collaboration in border regions is the use of innovative models for mobility that capitalize on shared geography. For example, San Diego State University in California coordinates trans-border courses on sustainable development and sociology in Tijuana, Mexico (located one hour away by car) with regional partners Colegio de la Frontera Norte and Universidad Autónoma de Baja California. These courses, which can last for a few weeks or for an entire semester, involve class time on campus in both San Diego and Tijuana, and students are expected to conduct field research on a topic that specifically addresses a trans-border issue (San Diego State University, 2017).

Another example of student mobility from the San Diego–Tijuana border region is an undergraduate field internship program sponsored by the University of California at San Diego's Cross-Border Initiative, which links with local organizations in San Diego and Tijuana to address shared concerns in the region, such as economic development, poverty, and public health, through student internships. The internship placements are with organization or institution partners on either side of the San Diego–Tijuana border (Helms & Griffin, 2017).

These examples of student mobility illustrate unique ways that students can have international experiences that are both local and culturally unique. The institutions involved were able to link course content to broad issues of relevance to both countries.

Community development

Faculty or student mobility programs that are coordinated with regional or local actors to primarily serve community interests are also good examples of higher education collaboration in border contexts. Such programs can involve coordination among institutions, or between institutions and community partners. One model is the use of service-learning courses that allow students to visit border communities and collaborate on discipline-related projects that benefit the region. The University of Arizona's Border Health Service Learning Institute, for example, links public health scholars and students with community organizations in the Naco, Arizona–Naco, Sonora border region to carry out migration, health, and economic development projects (University of Arizona, 2017).

Short-term service trips are another vehicle for community development-focused border engagement. In 2016, the Health International mission program at Loma Linda University offered students the opportunity to participate in one-week to three-month mission trips to the Baja California region to volunteer at the Mount of Olives Children's Village, a shelter for orphans and street youth (Haas, 2016; Helms & Griffin, 2017). Such projects illustrate the potential to tie student mobility to specific development needs in the region. Ideally, they are driven by active participation of partners in the university and the communities across borders, creating bilateral engagements with local impact.

Research on shared issues

The prevalence of joint research projects was also a key finding of the ACE study. Several examples highlight the role of borders in helping institutions in the region to shape research priorities. For example, the University of Arizona's Mel and Enid Zuckerman College of Public Health has partnered with El Colegio de Sonora, located in the Mexican state of Sonora, to develop several public health research projects, including research on dengue prevention and diabetes prevention, which have benefited communities in the Arizona-Sonora border region. Another research partnership captured by the ACE inventory (between researchers with the Center for U.S.-Mexican Studies at the University of California-San Diego, the Colegio de la Frontera Norte and the CaliBaja Region Initiative) assesses cross-border employment and business opportunities in the Southern California–Baja California, Mexico region. The project aims to address several bilateral issues, including cross-border governance, trade, and quality of life (Helms & Griffin, 2017; University of California-San Diego, 2017).

Multifaceted 'transformational' partnerships

The U.S.-Mexico borderland offers partnership opportunities that cut across several communities and states. Colegio de la Frontera Norte, located in the San Diego–Tijuana region, has research partnerships with public health scholars at the University of Arizona. One recent study between the two institutions focused on reproductive health needs in the Sonora region (University of Arizona, 2017). This study was funded by the Research Program on Migration and Health (PIMSA), a border health research consortium launched in 2003 by the University of California system in partnership with Mexico's National Council for Science and Technology (CONACYT) and Mexico's Secretary of Health. The consortium has grown to include institutions from all four U.S. border states and additional U.S. institutional partners outside of the border region. The network of institutional partners from within and outside of the borderland commits resources to research aimed at critical border health issues such as mental health, women's health, and infectious diseases (University of California-Berkeley, 2017).

While exciting, such an example is atypical and requires a significant commitment of resources from multiple partners in order to sustain. ACE's U.S.-Mexico report (Helms & Griffin, 2017) noted that such large-scale research projects involving multiple entities in each country are relatively rare; however, they illustrate the potential for long-term, multilateral collaboration with deep impact.

Challenges

Government policy

In recent years, the U.S.-Mexico relationship has been driven by the North American Free Trade Agreement (NAFTA), ratified in the early 1990s to boost trade relations. More recently, the Bilateral Forum on Higher Education, Innovation and Research (FOBESII), a cross-border higher education collaboration, was established in 2013 by Mexican President Enrique Peña Nieto and former U.S. President Barack Obama (Federal Government of Mexico, Secretary of External Relations, 2017; Ramirez, 1999). Since the 2016 U.S. presidential election, however, the Trump administration has signaled major changes in American policy toward Mexico in a number of areas, including, as noted previously, the proposal to build a wall between the two countries – as well as stricter immigration policies aimed at deporting undocumented Mexicans and other Central American nationals from the United States, and raising tariffs on imports from Mexico. As a result, tensions between the two countries are at their highest point in decades. Higher education collaboration is likely to be impacted both by the policies themselves – particularly immigration policies that may restrict student and scholar mobility – as well as a discouraging climate that may dampen enthusiasm for creating bilateral relationships.

In even the most stable of contexts, international higher education partnerships can be susceptible to changes in government policy (Maguire et al., 2013; Osborne, 2006). Public policy that fosters bilateral tensions can potentially harm partnership networks that may rely on government funding for research and subsidy for student travel. The fragility of partnerships can be amplified in border regions, particularly where barriers exist such as language and economic challenges (Helms & Griffin, 2017).

Crossing the border vs. cross-border experience

While border proximity can provide unique opportunities for student mobility programming and services, it can represent an unusual challenge for partnership activity in border regions. There are cases where, for example, proximity makes cross-border exchange less attractive for students. Three international officers interviewed for ACE's U.S.-Mexico partnerships project discussed the challenge of attracting students to spend more than a few weeks at sites in Mexico (Helms & Griffin, 2017). The proximity to the Mexican border seemed to diminish the importance of crossing it as an education abroad experience, compared with boarding a plane to the United Kingdom or to Costa Rica. Another interviewee observed an issue specific to students of Mexican descent on U.S. campuses, citing a lack of interest in reconnecting with Mexican culture on the part of these students or their parents. Border proximity and cultural connections, it seems, do not necessarily enhance the appeal of long-term student mobility, and in fact may have the opposite effect.

Unexpected differences, magnified impact

A senior international officer quoted in a recent ACE report on U.S.-U.K. higher education partnerships noted that the impact of differences is magnified when they are unexpected (Helms, Griffin, & Brajkovic, 2017). Because borderlands are uniquely shared spaces, often with distinct cultures of their own, it can be easy to forget that they are part of broader national economic and higher education systems that influence institutional culture and operations, and can impact cross-border relationships.

In the U.S.-Mexico case, while many parts of the borderland are areas of considerable economic vitality, there are substantial economic disparities between the two countries as a whole. The US has one of the largest economies in the world, while Mexico is considered to be an emerging economy (Calderon, Lee, & Wilson, 2015; Jahan, 2015). When it comes to academic collaborations, whereas U.S. institutions, particularly state flagship research universities such as those in Texas and California, often have access to a diverse set of funding sources (government funds, tuition fees, endowments, alumni donations, etc.) to support their cross-border activity, their Mexican counterparts typically rely on (quite limited) government funding. Even with other factors, such as those noted in the previous section, working in favor of borderland partnerships, imbalanced resource levels can hinder reciprocity, and lead to the "parasitic" relationships, described by Gatewood and Sutton (2017), that lack equitable distribution of benefits, and often are not sustainable over time. A considerably greater flow of students from the US to Mexico than from Mexico to the US raises concerns along these lines (Helms & Griffin, 2017).

Beyond economic disparities, even when countries and institutions share many cultural and historical elements, there are likely to be subtle variations that can impact academic collaboration. While cultural commonalities and familiarity may create an initial sense of comfort for students, faculty, and staff involved in borderland partnership activities, seemingly small differences – often unnoticed at the start – may add up. Differences in interpersonal communication styles, classroom conduct, expectations for student-faculty interactions, academic writing conventions, and social and professional norms stemming from the broader national context of each country may cause confusion and frustration over time. And, because they are often subtle and perhaps unanticipated, they may be difficult to for institutions – and individuals themselves – to identify and manage effectively (Helms et al., 2017).

Conclusion

The benefits of institutional partnerships in border regions can include unique student mobility initiatives and shared research projects that add value to regional communities. Border higher education networks, however, are vulnerable to changes in politics, economic conditions, and security among other conditions that can adversely affect border communities. The U.S.-Mexico border is a unique example that is not fully comparable to other border regions across the globe; however, real complexities of the border can be found everywhere – even in the European context, where cross-border integration has been a hallmark of political and social policy for several decades (Haselsberger, 2014).

Despite political uncertainties, senior international officers working in the U.S.-Mexico borderland remain optimistic about their capacity and that of bilateral counterparts to remain engaged because of established relationships and shared interests (Helms & Griffin, 2017). The U.S.-Mexico case illustrates that higher education partnerships can contribute to the building of bilateral relations in borderland regions by tapping into shared interests with potential to benefit the wider region such as workforce development, improved infrastructure, and access to public health. Ultimately, college and university networks in border regions need to cultivate strong ties that can weather the volatility of markets, politics, and region-specific issues that create potential barriers to achieving the full potential of these unique international partnerships.

References

African Borderland Research Network. (2017). *Where ABORNE Members Work*. Retrieved from www.aborne.org/map-of-research-areas.html
Asian Borderlands Research Network. (2017). *About the Asian Borderlands Research Network*. Retrieved from www.asianborderlands.net/
Association for Borderland Studies. (2017). *Journal of Borderland Studies*. Retrieved from http://absborderlands.org/journal/.
Calderon, A. A. B., Lee, E., & Wilson, C. (2015). *Competitive Border Communities: Mapping and Developing U.S.-Mexico Transborder Industries*. Washington, DC: Wilson Center.
Chao, R. Y. (2014). Pathways to an east Asian higher education area: a comparative analysis of East Asian and European regionalization processes. *Higher Education, 68*, 559–575.
Custer, S. (2017, April 5). Hungary's CEU defiant after restrictive HE law passes in parliament. *The PIE News*. Retrieved from https://thepienews.com/news/hungarys-ceu-defiant-restrictive-he-law-passes/

Davis, J. H. (2017, January 25). Trump orders Mexican border wall to be built and plans to block Syrian refugees. *New York Times*. Retrieved from www.nytimes.com

Deng Kuol, L. B. (2014). Confronting civil war: the level of resilience in Abyei area during Sudan's civil war in the 1990s. *Civil Wars, 16*, 468–487.

Dent, C. M. (2008). *East Asian Regionalism*. New York: Routledge.

Eddy, P. L. (2010). Organizational partnerships. *ASHE Higher Education Report, 36*, 17–53.

EUCOR (2017). *About EUCOR – The European Campus*. Retrieved from www.eucor-uni.org/en/eucor-european-campus

Federal Government of Mexico, Secretary of External Relations (2017). *What Is FOBESII? And Why Is it so Important for the Youths of Mexico and the US?* Retrieved from www.gob.mx/sre/articulos/what-is-fobesii-and-why-is-it-so-important-for-young-people-in-mexico-and-the-u-s

Gatewood, J., & Sutton, S.B. (2017). *Internationalization in Action: International Partnerships, Part One: Definitions and Dimensions*. Washington, DC: American Council on Education.

Haas, C. (2016, April). SIMS program returns to Mexico for first time since 2010. *Loma Linda University Health*. Retrieved from https://news.llu.edu/sites/news.llu.edu/files/docs/today/TODAY%20Apr%202016w.pdf

Haselsberger, B. (2014). Decoding borders. Appreciating border impacts on space and people. *Planning Theory and Practice, 15*, 505–526.

Helms, R. M. (2015). *International Higher Education Partnerships: A Global Review of Standards and Practices*. Washington, DC: American Council on Education.

Helms, R. M. & Griffin, J. (2017). *U.S.-Mexico Higher Education Engagement: Current Activities, Future Directions*. Washington, DC: American Council on Education.

Helms, R. M., Griffin, J., & Brajkovic, L. (2017). *U.K.–U.S. Higher Education Partnerships: Firm Foundations and Promising Pathways*. Washington, DC: American Council on Education.

Jahan, S. (2015). *Human Development Report 2015: Work for Human Development*. New York: United Nations Development Programme. Available at http://hdr.undp.org/en/2015-report/download

Kalwani, G. (2017, July 20). The Doklam standoff is the beginning of a troubling new era in India-China Ties: The Doklam standoff is just the beginning of challenging times for India. *The Diplomat*. Retrieved from http://thediplomat.com/2017/07/the-doklam-standoff-is-the-beginning-of-a-troubling-new-era-in-india-china-ties/

Knight, J. (2005). Cross-border education: an analytical framework for program and provider mobility. In J. Smart & W. Tierney (Eds.), *Higher Education: Handbook of Theory and Practice* (vol. 1, pp. 345–396). Dordrecht: Springer.

Kovach, V. I. (2015). Carpathian euroregion as an example of euroregional cross-boundary cooperation. *Economy of AIC, 11*, 96–111.

Maguire, K., Marsan, G. A., & Nauwelaers, C. (2013). *The Case of Oresund (Denmark-Sweden) – Regions and Innovation: Collaborating Across Borders* (OECD Regional Development Working Papers No. 21). Paris: OECD Publishing.

Osborne, R. D. (2006). Cross-border higher education collaboration in Europe: lessons for the "two Irelands"? *European Journal of Education, 41*(1), 115–129.

Popescu, G. (2008). The conflicting logics of cross-border reterritorialization: geopolitics of euroregions in Eastern Europe. *Political Geography, 27*, 418–438.

Ramirez, D. P. (1999). Higher education along the northern border of Mexico: a historical approximation, *Journal of Borderlands Studies*, *14*(2), 93–112.

San Diego State University. (2017). Trans-border opportunities certificate: the border beyond the headlines. *Joan B. Kroc School of Peace Studies*. Retrieved from www.sand iego.edu/peace/programs/border-certificate/

Saran, S. (2017, July 25). Is a China-centric world inevitable? Nations must determine when to confront Chinese aggression; for India, Bhutan is a priority. *YaleGlobal Online*. Retrieved from http://yaleglobal.yale.edu/content/china-centric-world-inevitable

Smith, B. (2014). India evacuates students from eastern Ukraine. *The Pie News*. Retrieved from https://thepienews.com/news/india-evacuates-students-eastern-ukraine/

Universities Ireland (2017). *Universities Ireland – About Us*. Retrieved from http://uni versitiesireland.ie/about-us/

University of Arizona. (2017). Border and immigration: current projects. *Southwest Institute for Research on Women*. Retrieved from https://sirow.arizona.edu/border-immigration

University of California-Berkeley. (2017). *What Is PIMSA?* Retrieved from https://hia. berkeley.edu/what-is-pimsa/

University of California-San Diego (2017). *Research: Cross-Border*. Retrieved from https://usmex.ucsd.edu research/cross-border.html

Part II

New modes

Chapter 9

New modes of research

Understanding and improving the international student experience using data

Richard Garrett and Rachael Merola

main question ⟶

How are universities using data to improve higher education? How can we use new modes of research to better understand the motivations and intentions of students around the world?

The number of international higher education students has increased from 2 million in 2000 to more than 5 million in 2015, according to the latest Organisation for Economic Co-operation and Development (OECD) estimates (OECD, 2015). For many colleges and universities, international students represent not just much-needed revenue but are a key ingredient to internationalizing the curriculum and the domestic student experience.

It is in the interests of institutions, government sponsors, and of course students themselves, to ensure a rich and detailed understanding of what constitutes a strong international student experience. However, despite its importance, much research on the topic is based on small-scale, qualitative studies, with a notable lack of quantitative, large-scale, and longitudinal datasets (Garrett, 2014).

An additional difficulty is that data are often not shared among institutions or researchers. Under these circumstances, measuring more than international student headcount can be a challenge, let alone gaining a deeper understanding of their experiences. This lack of cross-institutional and cross-country data on the international student experience represents a significant gap that inhibits efforts to enhance fit, quality, and value (Garrett, 2014).

The International Student Barometer (ISB), an independent survey developed since 2005 by a company called i-graduate in the United Kingdom and implemented by colleges and universities around the world, seeks to address this gap. The ISB has gathered responses from over 2.5 million students from institutions ranging from English language training (ELT) institutes to comprehensive research universities, and covering the full cycle of the student experience – from application to graduation. In total, it constitutes the most comprehensive set of insights to date.

The ISB serves universities that seek to better understand their students' experiences and how they compare to other universities. With this knowledge, universities can more effectively formulate recruitment strategies, support students, and engage alumni. Universities commonly employ ISB data to answer questions related to learning, living, and support services, as these data offer both quantitative (through a rated response) and qualitative (through written-in comments) measures of these areas.

The ISB has uncovered patterns at a scale not possible through other means. For example, survey data suggest that among students studying in the United Kingdom, university ranking does not impact student satisfaction at undergraduate level – only at graduate level (Archer, 2015). In turn, one factor that *has* been found to have a strong influence on satisfaction among undergraduates studying in the United Kingdom, United States, or Australia is whether a student will be the first in his or her family (i.e., a "first generation student") to enter and complete tertiary education (Garrett, 2014).

Knowing where differences exist – and where they do not – is the first step to understanding the nuanced picture of what leads to a satisfying university experience. An understanding of these relationships is important because there is a proven connection between a student's reported satisfaction at their institution and his or her likelihood of recommending the institution to other prospective students, with all the benefits such endorsements imply in terms of referrals and strong alumni relations (Garrett, 2014).

Despite the clear benefits of such data, over the twelve years since the ISB was developed there has been little usage of the resulting data in international higher education research. Largely, this is due to a lack of well-defined pathways for sharing or collaboration. To remedy this, in 2015 i-graduate created a system to facilitate connecting researchers to ISB data through specialized data requests, which is now being used for a number of ongoing research projects.

This chapter explores the ISB's origins and methodology, examples of ISB data and analysis, and how universities have used the survey to make changes to policy and practice. Finally, it looks at the limitations of ISB data, innovations and changes, and how higher education institutions and researchers may gather and use data differently in the future.

ISB uses and methodology

The ISB has been implemented by more than 1,400 institutions since its foundation, with 196 institutions having used the ISB in 2016 alone. The survey tracks and compares the decision-making, expectations, perceptions, and intentions of international students from pre-enrollment to plans post-graduation. In addition to their own results, universities are able to benchmark against a selected group of peer universities, viewing their anonymized results to gain deeper insights.

Gathering data is only the first step; equally important is how the data are used. Universities that have implemented the ISB have used the results to identify areas in which they are doing well, as well as those that need improvement.

benmarking —

Results of the ISB can be benchmarked against competitor or peer groups, as well as national and international indices, allowing universities to better understand the global picture of student experience. Competitor groups consist of the aggregated results of a selected group of other participating universities, ensuring that no institution would ever be identifiable or have their anonymized data displayed alone.

Benchmarking allows a new layer of insight – for example, a university that has a low score on elements of their student accommodations might find it useful to know that other universities have a higher, or lower, average score in that area. In an increasingly competitive market, and with students having more choice than ever before, the benchmarking element is a critical part of the ISB.

Range of satisfaction scores in the sample

The i-graduate International Student Barometer measures satisfaction, both overall and with respect to specific components, on a four-point scale:

- 4 = very satisfied
- 3 = satisfied
- 2 = dissatisfied
- 1 = very dissatisfied.

Notably, there is no "neutral" option on the scale, which forces students to make a choice about their satisfaction levels. Offering a "neutral" category might result in some students deferring to that option in the case that they do not already have an opinion on the topic, to expedite the survey process, or due to a desire to avoid extremes. A "central tendency" in ratings could decrease the reliability of the data and so is avoided by presenting a forced-choice scale.[1]

The use of a four-point scale is deliberate, though some institutions express a desire for a wider scale that could allow for greater nuance. Research indicates that the optimum number of choices on a scale is between four and seven. Fewer than four choices may decrease the reliability and validity of the results (Shaftel et al, 2012), while offering more than four to five scale points does not increase the reliability of the data (Lozano et al., 2008). If the scale were to be changed, it would impact the ability to conduct longitudinal analysis on data using the former scale.

ISB example analyses

The ISB can lend insight into the decision-making, perceptions, and expectations of students, allowing nuanced understanding of key differences among students using variables included in the survey. Nationality and year of study, for example, are revealed to be predictors of student satisfaction, as shown below.

Impact of nationality on international student satisfaction

Previous analyses of ISB data have revealed key differences across a number of variables related to nationality, international student populations, and satisfaction levels (Garrett, 2014), including:

- negative correlation between a higher international student ratio and satisfaction with lecture quality and time with faculty outside class
- negative correlation between the ratio of international undergraduates from China and integration among international students
- higher satisfaction among students from Europe than students from most parts of Asia and the Middle East.

Using data from the 2015 ISB, we have explored possible differences in satisfaction according to the nationality of the student as well as their year of study. For the purposes of this analysis, we looked only at ISB data from students hailing from the top three countries of origin among international students – China, India, and South Korea – studying at the top three destination countries for international students – the United Kingdom, the United States, and Australia.

Looking at the average satisfaction levels reported by students from China, South Korea, and India reveals significant differences. Indian students report the highest level of satisfaction (3.21), followed by Chinese students (3.02) and South Korean students (2.98). An analysis of variance (ANOVA) was conducted to compare the differences in satisfaction between international students from these three countries. Results indicate that there are statistically significant differences between the satisfaction levels of students from China and India, and South Korea and India. However, such differences do not exist between students from China and South Korea.

Seeing that these differences exist is a first step; explaining why they exist requires additional research into the social, academic, and cultural dimensions of the student experience. To this end, the ISB provides measures of satisfaction with comprehensive aspects of the student experience, including their arrival on campus, living environment, learning experience, and support services. Digging deeper into these areas can reveal where differences lie. This lends itself to further quantitative or qualitative investigations of differences.

Impact of year of study on international student satisfaction

To examine differences in satisfaction levels by year of study, three categories were used: "first year/single year," "other year," and "last year." The average satisfaction rating of students decreases by year: first year students report an average satisfaction score of 3.07, other year students report an average satisfaction score of 3.04, and final year students report an average satisfaction of 3.02.

Digging deeper, an ANOVA test reveals that variations between the mean satisfaction levels of first year and last year students differ significantly. There were not, however, statistically significant differences between the satisfaction levels of students in other years and those in first or last years.

What contributes to the difference in satisfaction levels between first year and final year students? There could be a "honeymoon" effect at play, in which the students upon arrival tend to perceive their experience as positive. It takes time for issues that could impact student satisfaction – such as integration difficulties, learning support, or living arrangements – to build and intensify.

Likewise, students in their last year are likely more cognizant of any dissatisfaction they might be experiencing, having had had plenty of time to identify and ruminate over problems. There may also be a tendency in the final year of study to evaluate the student experience with a more critical lens, as the student prepares for their next step, whether further study, joining the labor market, or other plans. Institutions that achieve higher satisfaction ratings are able to count on students and alumni to be active ambassadors for their institution. In a world where word of mouth, often via social media, is of paramount importance, ensuring that students are satisfied is of paramount importance. More satisfied students are also more likely to be engaged and generous alumni.

Overall, the average level of satisfaction among the students at the institutions participating in the ISB is high and, on average, satisfaction scores have risen slightly over time as institutions work hard to make improvements: the 2014 UK Competitive Advantage report shows a 3 percent increase over 2008–2014 in the percentage of undergraduate international students who were satisfied or very satisfied with their arrival experience. While this increase is not large, the percentage of satisfied students was already high in 2008 – 87 percent – so a marginal gain of 3 percentage points may be more difficult to attain than if there were fewer satisfied students.

Beyond the hard work that these institutions do to ensure the satisfaction of their international students, there may be a few other factors influencing satisfaction. First, participants in the ISB are a self-selecting group of institutions that are, in some instances, already paying special attention to international students, and therefore may be doing a better-than-average job at keeping them satisfied.

There may also be an element of cognitive dissonance at play, in which students are disposed to find their experience satisfying, since ultimately they were usually the ones deciding whether or not to attend. If a student chose to attend a certain university, they would like to believe it was for good reason and based on their sound judgment: in some way, reporting lower levels of satisfaction might cause the student to question their own judgment in having chosen the university in the first place.

Innovative uses of ISB data in admissions and student support

Universities have used their results from the ISB in a number of innovative ways related to admissions and student support services. The following examples come from universities that have leveraged their data to make institution-wide changes.

University of Cincinnati

The University of Cincinnati, in the United States, learned from benchmarking their ISB results that they took three weeks longer on average than their competitors to make admissions decisions for international undergraduates.

This galvanized the university to create a dedicated International Admissions Office and shorten the decision timeframe. In the years following this change, ISB survey results have shown that the university has become one of the top universities in this category. Another change due to ISB feedback included opening a study room in the main library that is open 24 hours a day, seven days a week.

University of Aberdeen

The University of Aberdeen, in Scotland, used ISB data to transform its organizational structure as well as to improve its student support services. All support areas now report directly to the Director of Student Life, including student support, chaplains, sport, catering services, careers services, residential services, recruitment, and admissions. This provides a more collaborative approach to working toward objectives and a clear-cut structure.

Additionally, Aberdeen opened an "Infohub", designed to increase communication and collaboration between students and the university. The Infohub answers all student queries, including those related to information technology, registrar matters, finance, admissions, and accommodation. All of these changes were inspired and supported by data from the ISB.

University of Adelaide

As a final example, at the University of Adelaide in Australia, ISB results identified a lack of integration between international and domestic students at the university. To address this, the university created a space where students meet, study, make social connections, and exchange ideas. This space, called "Hub Central," occupies 10,500 square meters over three floors on the university's main campus.

Using ISB data to identify and address this weakness led to significant improvements in the university's scores in the integration and student support services categories.

Institutional changes to how data is shared

Universities are inclined to use ISB data in ways that will be of greatest benefit and maximum impact to their specific context. One common challenge is how to share and act on data across sometimes large and disparate networks, when the wider benefits may be less obvious. The following universities have found ways to maximize the impact of their data by formulating novel ways to organize and share it.

Australian National University

Since 2012, the Australian National University (ANU) has implemented the ISB and its counterpart, the Student Barometer (SB), which measures the student experience of domestic students, and gathered responses from over 22,000 students. The data they receive include a report and presentation provided by i-graduate – a wealth of data, but difficult to share across the ANU network in a way that would prompt swift and coordinated actions. To maximize dissemination and utility of the findings, the university decided to undertake a more condensed and focused reporting process, with each service division and academic area receiving a tailored report.

To this end, ANU created individual topic papers for the different service divisions and academic areas based on ISB results as well as results from their own internal data collection. The topic papers were informed by the areas of improvement identified by the ISB and issues of importance on the ANU campus, such as learning resources, safety, student support, graduate employability, and pastoral care in residences. Each service division at ANU received the papers with top line information backed up by ISB data and student comments submitted as part of the ISB. By creating their own strategy for how to share data across networks, ANU was able to maximize its impact.

University of Oxford

Another common obstacle to maximizing impact is ensuring an adequate participation rate of the group being studied. Often, students experience "survey fatigue," a term referring to a low response rate due to frequent and tedious surveys. University leaders and administrators are also affected – they must be given data at times and in formats that are both useful and actionable.

With these issues in mind, the University of Oxford sought to find a way to most effectively utilize their barometer data – which spans 38 colleges, four divisions, a number of faculties within each division, and many courses within each faculty. Starting with courses, Oxford used the data to identify those courses that needed particular attention, and these courses were then given the necessary support. On a university-wide scale, Oxford created a policy change that led to increases in student satisfaction with marking/grading feedback. Oxford used its results to help colleges and departments share best practices and to identify resources needed to make effective changes.

Externally, Oxford has leveraged its data for enhancing communication with prospective students, using it to explain differences between colleges. Student publications are also given some of the results and the changes they have brought about, which helps to demonstrate the utility of the survey and, thereby, to increase response rates. When multiple stakeholders are involved, preventing survey fatigue and ensuring that results are put to use is critically important.

ISB evolution and the future of data

As universities find ways to organize and use ISB data, the instrument itself is undergoing changes and innovations, including updated data collection methods and more autonomy in how data are visualized and presented.

Increasing numbers of students use mobile phones and tablets to participate in the survey, necessitating a tool that is both easier to read and answer, and engaging enough to compete. Shortening the time to completion, optimizing the display on handheld devices, and offering the ability to complete the survey over several sessions have all led to increased participation and completion rates.

Likewise, the development of an interactive tool that allows universities to tailor the data analysis to their interests and to visualize it from various angles has allowed institutions to take charge of the data. Finally, decreased time between collection and analysis has meant that results are quickly accessible and actionable.

As mentioned previously, there is a notable lack of use of ISB data in academic research and publications. Despite offering a trove of information that could significantly benefit higher education institutions' ability to serve their students, little academic research has been conducted that leverages the data. This is largely due to the confidentiality of the data, as i-graduate protects the data of its clients, the universities.

However, many universities that use the ISB see the potential for even greater understanding of the student experience if data were shared outside their institutions. The power of data comes not from the data themselves but from how they are used. In response, in recent years i-graduate has made an effort to put anonymized data in the hands of researchers and academics who are given permission to use this information in journal articles and scholarly publications.

ISB data have been requested and utilized by academics affiliated with universities around the world, including Harvard University in the United States, Deakin University in Australia, and the Università Cattolica del Sacro Cuore in Italy. The resulting research adds to the body of knowledge in international higher education.

Looking forward

As the ISB evolves to fit institutions' needs and to reflect changes in mobility and enrollment, its limitations are acknowledged and addressed – in particular, the need to complement data provided by the ISB, which only looks at "satisfaction" as an input, with other data to provide a more holistic view of the international student experience.

The potential uses of social media and online activity in understanding the student experience are enormous. Companies like Google and Facebook might be said to know more about students than any one survey could reveal. Nearly all higher education students use social media, and their behaviors can be used as indicators of their views and experiences. Online behavior analytics will complement rather than substitute for survey data gathered directly from students.

The advantage of using online behavior as an indicator of student experience and as a predictor of student preferences is that it is less likely to be influenced by the students' own biases. What students think and say they like is often different from what their behaviors actually indicate. In this way, using online activity rather than self-reporting alone might reveal a more accurate picture of preferences. Using data gathered in this manner presents some problems, however – in particular, related to privacy.

Overall, data will continue to play an important role in improving higher education. Data give deep insight into the motivations and experiences of students around the world, from where they choose to study, to what aspects of the student experience are going well, and where there are pain points.

From the university perspective, better understanding the factors that influence student satisfaction helps predict, and support, students most likely to struggle during their studies, as well as those most likely to become engaged alumni. Creating timely and actionable strategic plans related to all aspects of the student experience, from deciding where to study to alumni relations, benefits universities, students, and society alike.

Note

1 http://im.dev.virginia.edu/wp/managertoolkit/common-rating-errors/

References

Archer, W. (2015). *International Undergraduate Students: The UK's Competitive Advantage*. Retrieved from https://issuu.com/internationalunit/docs/international_undergraduate_student

Garrett, R. (2014). *Explaining International Student Satisfaction*. Retrieved from www.i-graduate.org/assets/2014-Explaining-Satisfaction.pdf

Lozano, Luis M., García-Cueto, Eduardo; Muñiz, J. (2008). Effect of the number of response categories on the reliability and validity of rating scales. *Methodology: European Journal of Research Methods for the Behavioural and Social Sciences, 4*(2), 73–79.

OECD (2015). *Education at a Glance 2015: OECD Indicators*. Retrieved from www.keepeek.com/Digital-Asset-Management/oecd/education/education-at-a-glance-2015_eag-2015-en#.V9sBYvkrLIU#page3

Shaftel, J., Nash, B., & Gillmor, S. (2012). *Effects of the Number of Response Categories on Rating Scales*. Roundtable presented at the annual conference of the American Educational Research Association, Vancouver, British Columbia April 15, 2012. Retrieved from https://aai.drupal.ku.edu/sites/cete.ku.edu/files/docs/Presentations/2012_04_Shaftel%20et%20al.,%20Number%20of%20Response%20Categories,%204-9-12.pdf

Chapter 10

Topic modeling

A novel method for the systematic study of higher education internationalization policy

Daniela Crăciun

Higher education internationalization represents a strategic priority for governments around the world, because of the academic, economic, socio-cultural, and political benefits associated with it. Nevertheless, how policy makers understand and operationalize the idea of internationalizing higher education systems differs greatly from country to country. Because of the sheer volume of policy texts and the plethora of policy measures that mingle under the umbrella concept of internationalization, researchers struggle to properly classify and make inferences about the process. This state of affairs raises a salient question: How can we systematically study internationalization policies without massive costs in terms of funding and time?

This chapter posits that using computer-assisted topic modeling techniques represents an innovative and efficient way to deal with this issue. Using an original database of national policies for the internationalization of higher education, the chapter demonstrates how topics can be automatically retrieved from documents while meeting validity and reliability standards. Specifically, this chapter shows how Latent Dirichlet allocation (LDA) can be applied to text corpora, using Python software, so as to provide a glimpse of how public policy documents can be efficiently processed, summarized, compared, and classified based on topic probabilities. This allows researchers to examine multiple cases while having limited resources and to discover new or understudied similarities between policies adopted by different countries.

The main goal of the chapter is to highlight a problematic area in higher education internationalization research and to demonstrate an innovative methodological approach for its resolution. Initially the chapter reviews scholarly literature highlighting the problems of defining internationalization in higher education. It argues that understanding internationalization is made difficult by the proliferation of different labels associated with the development of the process over time, by the coexistence of different scales of analysis (i.e., regionalization, internationalization, globalization), and by the plethora of policy measures that come under the umbrella concept of internationalization. In short, internationalization can be categorized as an essentially contested concept.

The chapter then argues that looking at existing national policies of internationalization may help to improve our understanding of the process, highlighting the role of the nation-state as a central actor in steering internationalization. The method of computer-assisted content analysis, and particularly topic modeling, is then introduced as a novel and innovative way to analyze and summarize large numbers of internationalization policies. Details on the setup of the research design are given in order to encourage scholars dealing with similar questions to adopt it. Certain preliminary findings from applying the topic modeling method on a database of internationalization policies are also presented. Finally, the chapter closes with some thoughts about the expected contributions of this innovative method for higher education research in general, and for internationalization research in particular. Considering the continuously evolving and dynamic nature of internationalization, the perfect reliability of the method – due to the fact that, unlike human coding, computer coding consistently applies the same measuring procedure over repeated trials – constitutes a key benefit.

Defining internationalization

What do we mean when we talk about internationalization? Answering this question is no simple task. Gaining a clear understanding of internationalization is difficult due to a number of factors. First, a multitude of policy measures come under the umbrella of internationalization, including international student mobility, collaborative research, the development of curricula and strategies for teaching and learning, or the establishment of cross-border institutional networks (Altbach, Reisberg, & Rumbley, 2009). Second, similar parallel processes such as "de-monopolization," "de-institutionalization," and "de-nationalization" (Kehm, 2003) have developed simultaneously and are not always easy to clearly separate from internationalization. Third, various scales of analysis coexist – institutional, national, regional, and global – and each one gives a different flavor to our understanding of internationalization. Finally, to underscore the historical development and ever-changing nature of internationalization, a proliferation of different labels has emerged, including "re-internationalization" (Teichler, 2009), "postinternationalization" (Brandenburg & de Wit, 2011), "globalized internationalization" (Jones & de Wit, 2014), "comprehensive internationalization" (Hudzik, 2011), and "intelligent internationalization" (Rumbley, 2015). Definitions of internationalization can be seen to have evolved over the years in various ways to reflect this reality: from focusing on a set of specific activities to be carried out by universities (Arum & van de Water, 1992) to viewing it as a dynamic process to be integrated in the wider set of organizational activities of higher education institutions (Knight, 1993); from focusing on internationalization as an institutional endeavor to viewing it as a result of broader developments and synergies between various national levels of authority with the power to steer internationalization (van der Wende, 2001); and from viewing internationalization as a limited function of a university's context (Sonderqvist, 2002) to viewing it as a broad and eclectic mix of policies and processes that evolve on various scales (Knight, 2003). A recent definition of internationalization highlights the fact that it is a planned process aimed at improving the quality and impact of higher education on all stakeholders. Specifically, internationalization is:

> the *intentional* process of integrating an international, intercultural or global dimension into the purpose, functions and delivery of post-secondary education, *in order to enhance the quality of education and research for all students and staff, and to make a meaningful contribution to society.*
>
> (de Wit, Hunter, Howard, & Egron-Polak, 2015, p. 29; emphasis in original)

This emphasis on internationalization as a planned activity is an important milestone in understanding the process, because it underscores the fact that 'internationalization does not just happen out of the blue' to a higher education institution or system, but is always intentional. How policy makers or institutional leaders understand and pursue internationalization differs from country to country (Graf, 2009; King, 2010; Matei & Iwinska, 2015) and from university to university (American Council of Education, 2012), depending on the specific needs of these entities. Against this background, internationalization can be understood as an umbrella term that subsumes various different measures that were designed to tackle specific issues (Callan, 2000), but is not a one-size-fits-all approach to reforming higher education.

This chapter argues that a viable way to understand the complex development of internationalization is to analyze, assess, and compare the policies and strategies intended to forward the process. While institutional polices are important, a first step is to look at national policies for internationalization because they provide the framework of rules and resources within which universities generally have to function.

The importance of the nation-state in internationalization

Understanding the role of the nation-state in the internationalization of higher education is a crucial issue in both academic literature and policy practice. The distinction between empirical evidence and normative issues is not always clear-cut. Nevertheless, it is hardly disputed that the development of modern higher education institutions is closely linked to the state:

> Their regulatory and funding context was, and still is, national; their contribution to national cultures was, and still is, significant; students tended to be, and still are, trained to become national functionaries; and universities played, and still play, a considerable role in what some have called the military-industrial complex of the nation state.
>
> (Enders, 2004, p. 365)

The importance of the national level cannot be overstated. In fact, research has shown that national policies and the national context are considered to play the most significant role in the internationalization of higher education (Enders, 2004; Graf, 2009; Luijten-Lub, van der Wende, & Huisman, 2005). Moreover, both higher education institutions (Egron-Polak & Hudson, 2014; European University Association, 2013) and supranational organizations (European Commission, 2013; Henard, Diamond, & Roseveare, 2012) expect and encourage the participation of the nation-state in the process. Having a well-defined and coherent national strategy has been shown to be an important ingredient in moving forward with internationalization efforts (British Council, 2011; Henard et al., 2012). As a result, there are calls for more centralized and broader strategic approaches to internationalization and for the harmonization of policies across sectors (i.e., labor market, migration, trade, economic development, foreign affairs) so as to address both national and institutional interests.

National internationalization plans are also important because they express a political commitment to internationalization, and not just political rhetoric. In other words, they can be considered part and parcel of the policy output of any government that promotes a supportive culture towards internationalization. Importantly, such plans push governments to operationalize their understanding of internationalization and thus help to clarify 'what we talk about when we talk about internationalization' in different contexts.

This chapter suggests that, in order to get a fuller and more nuanced picture of the reality of higher education internationalization around the world, a stock-taking and benchmarking exercise is needed. These endeavors are, however, resource-intensive. In an academic environment where descriptive inferences receive second billing to causal inferences, and in an economic environment characterized by austerity, few resources are available for this type of research. This situation raises the following question: how can we systematically study internationalization policies without massive costs in terms of time, money, and capacity? This chapter posits that using computer-assisted content analysis, and specifically topic modeling techniques, represents an innovative and effective way of summarizing, assessing, and comparing policy documents. This method is very well developed in domains like media studies and party politics to analyze messages from texts such as newspapers or party manifestos.

Research design basics for computer-assisted content analysis

As defined by Krippendorff (1980), a founding scholar of this scientific method, "content analysis is any research technique for making replicative and valid inferences from data to their context" (p. 21). Hence, content analysis can be applied to objectively quantify the existence of certain words, concepts, themes, sentences, phrases, idioms, or characters in texts, establishing a link between their content and their institutional, social, and cultural context (Berg, 2001). Computer-assisted content analysis achieves the same results, but documents are analyzed with the help of computers rather than human coders. This method is particularly useful for tackling the question raised by the chapter, as it can automatically summarize and reveal priorities of internationalization policies. The key components of any content analysis research design are: unitizing, sampling, recording/coding, reducing data, abductively inferring, and narrating the answer to the research question (Krippendorff, 2004). In what follows, these constitutive parts and their applicability to analyzing national policies for internationalization will be discussed in more detail.

"Unitizing" refers to systematically deciding which segments of texts can fruitfully inform the content analysis exercise. These units are entities that the researcher differentiates and considers as independent for the purpose of the research (Krippendorff, 2004). It is important to distinguish between two types of units: sampling units and coding units. The sampling units are essentially the texts that are to be analyzed (i.e., newspaper articles, policy documents, images). For this study, national plans and strategies for the internationalization of higher education serve as the sampling unit for the study. Meanwhile, coding units represent the entities that are to be categorized (i.e., paragraphs, phrases, words). As in the majority of computer-assisted content analysis research, the coding unit for this analysis is the "word."

"Sampling" in content analysis refers to the same process as in survey research but, instead of sampling people from a population, the researcher samples texts from a population of texts. In this context, the corpus of texts refers to national policy documents for the internationalization of higher education. As there is no reliable population list or repository of national higher education internationalization policy texts worldwide, from which documents could be selected using reliable sampling techniques, a census of all countries was conducted. The World Higher Education Database compiled by the International Association of Universities was used as a data-sourcing guide. This database regularly gathers information about higher education institutions, systems, and credentials worldwide, and is useful in tracing policies and laws adopted by governments.

"Recording/coding" refers to interpreting the unitized texts. For the current analysis, this task was carried out using automatic computer coding. Such an analysis assumes that texts are bags of words. This basically means that the order of the text is not important for the analysis and thus is discarded. The assumption is that "a simple list of words . . . is often sufficient to convey the general meaning of the text" (Grimmer & Stewart, 2013, p. 6). It cannot be emphasized enough that "[a]ll quantitative models of language are wrong – but some are useful" (Grimmer & Stewart, 2013, p. 3). For the research objective of this chapter, adopting a quantitative view of language is useful because it allows the researcher to considerably reduce the complexity of the texts. The assumption here is that "[p]olicy makers . . . may be interested in finding the needle in the haystack . . ., but social scientists are more commonly interested in characterizing the haystack" (Hopkins & King, 2010, p. 230). Classifications and comparisons are necessarily more useful in achieving the latter.

"Reducing data" serves to decrease the complexity and ease the interpretation of large volumes of texts. This component of the research design is crucial in achieving the intended goal of any study. Thus, the method of reducing data has to be chosen with the research objective in mind. In this case, the research makes use of Latent Dirichlet allocation (LDA), which is a generative probabilistic model for analyzing texts (Blei, Ng, & Jordan, 2003, p. 993). To put it in simple terms, LDA offers a way of automatically discovering topics within documents and, thus, making unknown categories known. This is achieved through three steps: (1) the researcher defines the number of topics/categories to be extracted from the text; (2) every word from each document is assigned (semi-)randomly to a topic by the computer; and (3) the LDA algorithm updates this (semi-)random assignment through an iterative process based on probabilities. As topic probabilities offer an explicit representation of the document, each document can be associated with multiple topics. This avoids the simplistic supposition that documents can be associated with a single topic. Because the statistical relationships are kept, documents – in this case, public policies for internationalization – can be easily clustered and compared with each other. As previously argued, national policies for the internationalization of higher education express and operationalize a state's understanding of the process. Following this assumption, we can infer that the position of the individual policies of internationalization in different clusters is representative of the position of the state with regard to internationalization.

Finally, making "abductive inferences" "bridges the gap between descriptive accounts of texts and what they mean, refer to, entail, provoke or cause" (Krippendorff, 2004, p. 85), while "narrating" ensures that the results are understood by others. Some preliminary results from a pilot test, conducted with a convenience sample of policies, are presented next in order to illustrate how the method works.

Analysis of preliminary results

The higher education internationalization policies of Australia, Estonia, Finland, Germany, Japan, Malaysia, the Netherlands, New Zealand, Spain, and the United Kingdom were selected for analysis. Before applying the LDA algorithm in Python, the documents had to be preprocessed. This entailed (1) transforming documents into .txt format, (2) cleaning texts (i.e., removing the cover page, table of contents, introductory statements, headers, footers, reference lists), (3) applying UNIX encoding (converting all characters from the texts into a recognizable and comparable form), (4) tokenizing text (breaking the text into units of analysis like words), (5) removing stop words (eliminating the most common words in a language that provide no content, i.e., "and," "the," "for," "in"), and (6) stemming (reducing the words to their root form, i.e., "education," "educating," "educational" becomes "educ*"). With the exception of the activities involved in cleaning the text, all other tasks can be automatically and reliably performed by computer by simply adding a line of code in the program.

After preprocessing the texts, the researcher only intervenes in the analysis of the documents to set the number of topics to be retrieved from the corpus and to interpret the results. Two trials were conducted in order to show how the LDA method works. For the first trial, the computer was given the task to find three topics from the texts and three words to characterize these topics (see Figure 10.1 for results).

It is important to remember that the computer did not know what the texts were about, but it has identified that they relate to internationalization (a word that features in all three topics), education, research, universities, and students. The words in each category seem to be overlapping, probably because of the reduced number of texts given as input. After seeing that the algorithm can correctly identify that the texts are about internationalization and education (which speaks to the validity of the method), the program was optimized by feeding this piece of information into the algorithm to fine-tune the results. This basically means adding a line of code in the program, before the LDA algorithm is applied, that removes all the words with the stems "internat*" and "educ*."

With these observations in mind, a second trial – meant to retrieve two topics with two characteristics words – was conducted. As can be seen from Figure 10.2, Topic 1 is about students and universities and Topic 2 is about students and research. The fact that students appear in both categories is not surprising methodologically or theoretically. From the previous trial presented, we can see that the word "student*" was picked up as relevant for multiple topics. From a theoretical perspective it is not surprising that the word "student*" was identified, because international student mobility is considered to be one of the most important aspects of internationalization, and students are the main stakeholders of higher education. So, it was expected that this term would figure prominently in the higher education internationalization policies of all countries.

RESULTS

TRIAL I (3 topics and 3 words)

TOPIC 1: educ* + intern* + student*

TOPIC 2: student* + educ* + intern*

TOPIC 3: intern* + research* + univers*

Figure 10.1 LDA results of first trial in pilot study

Source: author's compilation.

RESULTS

TRIAL II (2 topics and 2 words)

TOPIC 1: student + univers*

TOPIC 2: student + research

Result: [u'0.030*student + 0.024*univers', u'0.019*student + 0.015*research']

Figure 10.2 LDA results of second trial in pilot study

Source: author's compilation.

The results also show that some policy documents on internationalization focus more on institutional internationalization, while others focus more on the internationalization of research. Again, the internationalization literature supports this claim. Moreover, a separate computer-assisted content analysis of the corpus of texts using collocation analysis revealed similar results. Figure 10.3 shows a network graph of the highest-frequency terms that appear in proximity with each other in the documents (note that the only preprocessing task undertaken for this analysis was to clean the texts). In Figure 10.3, keywords from the policies are shown in dashed line containers and the words in proximity, known as collocates, are shown in continuous line containers. As becomes apparent, the results of the LDA analysis are reinforced and validated by the collocation analysis: students – especially international students, their mobility, and their numbers – followed by research, and institutions are at the core of these internationalization strategies.

In relation to reliability, the last line of Figure 10.2 gives the proportions in which words appear in each topic for the second trial. As can be seen, they are currently small. To amend and fine-tune the results, more documents will need to be analyzed and more attention paid to preprocessing the texts (i.e., adopting a less conservative list of stop words to be removed, and eliminating very rare words

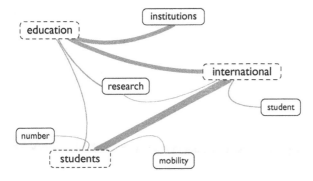

Figure 10.3 Network graph of national internationalization policies

Source: author's compilation.

and words that are uninformative for the analysis). These issues point to the fact that there is more work to be done before analyzing the worldwide census of national internationalization policies. Nevertheless, the results of this exercise are promising and the method can bring a number of contributions to the field of higher education internationalization research.

Contributions to next generation research in internationalization

Worldwide, higher education internationalization is talked about as a strategic priority for governments. Nevertheless, large-scale comparative research on the policies deployed by nation-states in order to strategically forward internationalization is scarce. With some notable exceptions, country-level research on internationalization typically focuses on in-depth case studies or small-n comparative research. Internationalization, however, does not occur in a vacuum. It only occurs at the confluence of cooperation and competition between nation-states, institutions, and individuals. Therefore, studies that have a narrow geographical scope – while providing valuable insights into the multidimensional fabric of the process – are limited in their ability to map the global reach of internationalization. If we are to make sense of the intricate landscape of national internationalization policies, a broader and more systematic approach is needed. This chapter proposes a novel methodology for researching higher education internationalization, which is in line with the dynamic of the process.

The chapter also brings a number of contributions to the field of higher education research, both for scholarly research and policy practice. It puts forward a methodology for analyzing not only higher education internationalization, but also other higher education research areas. The methodology is replicable by other researchers or analysts and within different policy fields. Considering the number of procedural documents that are created at every level in higher education, this type of methodology could provide invaluable insights into issues such as cooperation between departments or student (dis)satisfaction with university services. Moreover, this method provides perfect reliability of results, as the same procedures or algorithms are applied consistently and systematically to all documents by the computer. Computer-assisted content analysis can help to provide a clearer picture about how nation-states compare in their focus, objectives, and rationales for internationalization. It can help researchers and policy makers to discover trends and issues emerging in national and institutional strategies for internationalization in a timely manner.

Considering the current policy-making environment in which we are striving to learn from best practices and design evidence-based policies, benchmarking exercises have acquired new importance. However, benchmarking exercises like the one proposed in this chapter, while undoubtedly useful, are resource-intensive. What sets this method of research apart from others is that it allows researchers with limited resources in terms of time, money, and capacity to investigate multiple (and complex, text-heavy) cases.

References

Altbach, P. G., Reisberg, L., & Rumbley, L. E. (2009). *Trends in Global Higher Education: Tracking an Academic Revolution*. Report prepared for the UNESCO 2009 World Conference on Higher Education. Paris: UNESCO.

American Council of Education. (2012). *Mapping Internationalization on U.S. Campuses*. Washington, DC: ACE.

Arum, S., & van de Water, J. (1992). The need for a definition of international education in U.S. universities. In C. Klasek (Ed.), *Bridges to the Futures: Strategies for internationalizing higher education* (pp. 191–203). Carbondale: Association for International Education Administrators.

Berg, B. L. (2001). *Qualitative Research Methods for the Social Sciences* (4th ed.). Boston: Allyn & Bacon.

Blei, D. M., Ng, A. Y., & Jordan, M. I. (2003). Latent Dirichlet allocation. *Journal of Machine Learning Research, 3*, 993–1022.

Brandenburg, U., & de Wit, H. (2011). The end of internationalization. *International Higher Education, 62*, 15–17.

British Council. (2011). *Global Gauge*. Education Intelligence Report Series. London: British Council.

Callan, H. (2000). Higher education internationalization strategies: of marginal significance or all-pervasive? The international vision in practice: a decade of evolution. *Higher Education in Europe, 25*(1), 15–23.

de Wit, H., Hunter, F., Howard, L., & Egron-Polak, E. (2015). *Internationalisation of Higher Education*. Brussels: European Parliament.

Egron-Polak, E., & Hudson, R. (2014). *Internationalization of Higher Education: Growing Expectations, Fundamental Values*. Paris: International Association of Universities.

Enders, J. (2004). Higher education, internationalisation, and the nation-state: recent developments and challenges to governance theory. *Higher Education, 47*, 361–382.

European Commission. (2013). *Communication from the Commission to the European Parliament, the Council, the European Economic and Social Committee and the Committee of the Regions: European Higher Education in the World*. COM(2013) 499. Brussels: European Commission.

European University Association. (2013). *Internationalisation in European Higher Education: European Policies, Institutional Strategies and EUA Support*. Brussels: EUA.

Graf, L. (2009). Applying varieties of capitalism approach to higher education: comparing the internationalization of German and British universities. *European Journal of Education, 44*(4), 569–585.

Grimmer, J., & Stewart, B. M. (2013). Text as data: the promise and pitfalls of automated content analysis methods for political texts. *Political Analysis, 21*(3), 1–31.

Henard, F., Diamond, L., & Roseveare, D. (2012). *Approaches to Internationalisation and Their Implications for Strategic Management and Institutional Practice: A Guide for Higher Education Institutions*. Paris: OECD.

Hopkins, D. J., & King, G. (2010). A method of automated nonparametric content analysis for social science. *American Journal of Political Science, 54*(1), 229–247.

Hudzik, J. K. (2011). *Comprehensive Internationalization: From Concept to Action*. Washington, DC: NAFSA.

Jones, G., & de Wit, H. (2014). Globalized internationalization: implications for policy and practice. *IIE Networker*, Spring, 28–29.

Kehm, B. M. (2003). Internationalization in higher education: from regional to global. In R. Begg (Ed.), *The Dialogue Between Higher Education Research and Practice* (pp. 109–119). Amsterdam: Kluwer Academic Publishers.

King, R. (2010). Policy internationalization, national variety, and governance: global models and network power in higher education states. *Higher Education, 60,* 583–594.

Knight, J. (1993). Internationalization: management strategies and issues. *International Education Magazine, 9*(1), 21–22.

Knight, J. (2003). Updated internationalization definition. *International Higher Education, 33,* 2–3.

Krippendorff, K. (1980). *Content Analysis: An Introduction to its Methodology.* London: Sage Publications.

Krippendorff, K. (2004). *Content Analysis: An Introduction to its Methodology.* Thousand Oaks, London/New Delhi: Thousand Oaks.

Luijten-Lub, A., van der Wende, M., & Huisman, J. (2005). On cooperation and competition: a comparative analysis of national policies for internationalisation of higher education in seven European countries. *Journal of Studies in International Education, 9*(2), 147–163.

Matei, L., & Iwinska, J. (2015). National strategies and practices in internationalisation of hIgher education: lessons from a cross-country comparison. In A. Curaj, L. Deca, E. Egron-Polak, & J. Salmi (Eds.), *Higher Education Reforms in Romania* (pp. 205–226). London: Springer.

Rumbley, L. E. (2015, April 17). Intelligent internationalisation: a 21st century imperative. *University World News.* Retrieved from www.universityworldnews.com/article.php?story=20150414062211377

Sonderqvist, M. (2002). *Internationalisation and Its Management at Higher Education Institutions: Applying Conceptual, Content and Discourse Analysis.* Helsinki: Helsinki School of Economics.

Teichler, U. (2009). Internationalization of higher education: European experiences. *Asia Pacific Education Review, 10*(1), 93–106.

van der Wende, M. (2001). Internationalisation policies: about new trends and contrasting paradigms. *Higher Education Policy, 14*(3), 249–259.

Chapter 11

Engaging in dialogue with the world

What English-language academic journals tell us about the internationalization of China's humanities and social sciences

Li Mengyang

Introduction

Social thinking, or "systematic inquiry into the human condition" (Manicas, 1987, p. 7), dates to antiquity in all societies. However, the key ideas out of which the modern fields of humanities and social sciences (HSS) were constituted came from Europe. These fields expanded into other parts of the world mainly through colonialism and imperialism (Keim, 2010). Today, the center-periphery structure (Altbach, 1998), fueled by the prevalence of the English language, is still powerful in explaining disparities in the international knowledge system. The direction of internationalization remains predominantly from the metropole to the periphery, especially in soft disciplines.

However, there are tendencies toward pluralization of research capacity (Marginson, 2010) in an era of globalization. Questions about Euro-American dominance in the HSS and calls for alternative discourses have emerged since the 1960s. Today there seems to be a revival of such currents, with concerns expressed about the homogenization of HSS, as well as questions about the universalism of Western theories and approaches (e.g., Castro, 2013) and the epistemological value of multiple perspectives (e.g., Al Zeera, 2001). Nevertheless, arguments against the homogeneity of HSS have in turn provoked fears about the fragmentation of the disciplines into localized, nationalized, or indigenized knowledges (Keim, 2010). Indeed, for researchers in non-Western societies, it is a significant challenge to construct an interpretative framework that is both drawn from local contexts and able to dialogue with the existing 'global' framework. There is a long way to go. This chapter looks into the case of China, a giant non-Western society, to explore recent changes in the internationalization of its HSS and the relationship between these evolving disciplines and China's longstanding cultural struggles.

A shift in the internationalization of China's humanities and social sciences

The humanities and social sciences as disciplines in China can be traced back to the late 19th and early 20th centuries, when China looked to the West for knowledge to 'save the nation.' From then on, the emphasis of HSS has largely been on importing theories, methods, academic systems, and practices from the outside. Though never formally colonized, China's academic development was shaped by foreign influences from Germany, France, Britain, Japan, the United States, and (after 1950) from the Soviet Union (Altbach, 1989). Since China's reform and opening up in the 1980s, the country has turned again to Western approaches for standards (Huang, 2010). Despite the fact that China has rich cultural heritages, they are seldom incorporated into modern HSS research. However, along with China's rising economy and higher education sector, when it comes to internationalization, there appears to be a shift toward a more balanced dynamic between importing the world to China and exporting China to the world (Yang, 2014).

On the policy level, the discourse of internationalization in China has changed from an emphasis on 'bringing in' and 'connection of tracks' (which means to connect the academic system of China with the track of Western countries) to 'reaching out,' 'going out,' or 'going global' (Feng, Beckett, & Huang, 2013; Wang, 2014). Every five years, the National Planning Office of Philosophy and Social Sciences publishes a Five-Year Plan guiding the development of China's philosophy and social sciences.[1] The *11th Five-Year (2006–2010) Plan* stated China's aim "to implement [a] going-out strategy, positively absorb outstanding cultural achievements from abroad, introduce outstanding Chinese cultural achievements to other parts of the world, and improve the international influence of China's philosophy and social sciences" (National Planning Office of Philosophy and Social Sciences, 2006, Bill 3). It was the first time that China's national policy explicitly used the phrase 'going out' concerning HSS development. The following *12th Five-Year (2011–2015) Plan* (National Planning Office of Philosophy and Social Sciences, 2011) continued to focus on a 'going-out' strategy, and initiated further exploration into measures to expand the export of cultural products and services. In November 2011, the Ministry of Education issued a specific guideline entitled *The "Going-Out" Plan for Philosophy and Social Sciences in Higher Education* to encourage Chinese research and researchers 'going global.'

On a practical level, scholarly publishing is a major means of knowledge dissemination in academia. Given that English has become the dominant language for scholarly publication around the world, the Chinese government, universities, academic organizations, and publishers have been working together to publish translations of outstanding Chinese research both at home and abroad, to encourage publication by Chinese scholars in leading international journals, and to establish China's own English-language scholarly journals. Since 2006, a series of projects has been launched, such as the 'China Book International Initiative,'

'China Classics International Publication Project,' and 'Chinese Academic Research Translation Project.' The 'Chinese Academic Research Translation Project,' for example, has funded the publication of more than 500 books and journals in foreign languages (mainly in English) since its establishment in 2010, covering most of the HSS disciplines.

Chinese universities and research institutes are increasingly using publication in journals indexed in the Science Citation Index (SCI), Social Sciences Citation Index (SSCI), and Arts & Humanities Citation Index (A&HCI) as a criterion in academic recruitment and assessment. However, the overall international visibility of Chinese HSS scholars is still limited, especially compared with *problem* their peers in the hard sciences and engineering. For example, in 2015, there were 296,800 articles authored by Chinese scholars published in SCI journals, accounting for 16.3 percent of the global total and ranking second among all nations. Meanwhile, Chinese scholars published 12,700 articles in SSCI journals, which comprised 4.44 percent of the global total, and ranked China sixth in the world (Institute of Scientific & Technical Information of China [ISTIC], 2016). This disparity is largely due to the fact that the HSS disciplines are more dependent on different languages, discourses, paradigms, and ideologies across cultures when compared with hard sciences and engineering (Yang, 2014). In fact, there is resistance towards publishing in international journals from some Chinese HSS scholars. One argument is that not publishing in such journals avoids pandering to 'orientalist discourse' – in other words, this avoids catering to the interests of Western journals by ignoring domestic cultural contexts and concerns through self-colonialism (Flowerdew & Li, 2009). By this argument, establishing English-language scholarly journals in China is considered as a means of serving domestic needs while simultaneously enhancing international influence (Yang, 2012).

On a theoretical level, what China can bring to global academic development is a fundamental issue. The contemporary disciplinary system that categorizes knowledge into sciences, humanities, and social sciences comes from the West. Traditional Confucianism has a different system of organizing knowledge based on *Jing* (Confucian classics), *Shi* (historical records), *Zi* (philosophical writings), and *Ji* (literature collections). Different approaches to organizing knowledge come from differences in cultural thinking. Ancient Greek thinkers endeavored to explore the outside world. The inner logic of Western learning is 'seeking knowledge.' By contrast, traditional Chinese thinkers chose an inward-looking path. The Confucian worldview sees individuals as part of the world and people can understand the world perfectly if they understand themselves well. There is no severe dichotomy between knowledge and practice in Chinese thought. The inner logic of Chinese learning is 'seeking for [what] should be' (Fang, 2002; Yang, 2013).

However, the internationalization process in China during the 20th century encouraged the adoption of the Western disciplinary system and research paradigm. In the first half of the 20th century, elite Chinese scholars embraced science and democracy and started a revolt against Confucianism. During the Cultural

Revolution (1966–1976), Chinese cultural traditions further experienced cata-strophic condemnation and destruction (Huang, 2010). Traditional Chinese ways of organizing knowledge are seldom visible in today's teaching and research. But traditional Chinese ways of thinking are still influential in Chinese society. This leads to a paradox: while policy is encouraging developing Chinese dis-courses in HSS research, Chinese cultural thinking is extremely under-theorized in modern research. Westernization of the Chinese social sciences is still common in China, which implies using Western social science theories and methods to explain Chinese issues (Deng, 2010).

Furthermore, unlike former colonies, where the import of HSS was initiated and conceptualized as a means for Western countries to export their knowledge to the colonies (Okamoto, 2010), China and Chinese intellectuals selectively chose, absorbed, and transformed the original Western concepts into Chinese contexts (Qi, 2014). The primary aim of HSS internationalization in China since the late Qing dynasty has been to make China a powerful country again. Western research paradigms, theories, and methods were imported for their usefulness to achieve these ends. This leads to a second paradox: while China has learned from Western HSS for many years, a deep understanding of Western scientific rational-ity and its cultural localities is still lacking (Yang, 2013).

As the Western academic model has become institutionalized in China, poten-tial theoretical development of China's HSS lies in the dialogue between Chinese and Western scholarship. The two above-mentioned paradoxes reveal that a deep and comprehensive understanding about Western humanities and social sciences, Chinese cultural thinking, and their encounters is highly needed. As Alatas (2010) has posited, calling for alternative discourses (to Euro-American discourses) does not reject Western knowledge, but calls for genuine non-Western systems of thought, theories, and ideas that are based on non-Western cultures and prac-tices. The following section uses China's English-language journals as an example to explore the efforts China is making to engage in dialogue with the world.

China's English-language academic journals in the humanities and social sciences

Establishing English-language academic journals, as noted above, is part of China's overall 'going-out' strategy. Therefore, government plays an impor-tant role in the development of such journals. But there is a dilemma. While the Chinese government seeks to have more voices from China in the international cultural arena, it also wants to maintain ideological control at a certain level.

On the one hand, the government has provided significant funding to sup-port the development of English-language journals. For example, the 'Chinese Academic Research Translation Project' has been funding 10 journals, including *China Economist, Social Sciences in China, Journal of Modern Chinese History*, and 7 HSS journals of the *Frontiers in China* series, to the sum of around USD 7,300 for every issue (Xu, 2014). On the other hand, the government has been regulating journal publishing. The General Administration of Press and Publications (GAPP) is responsible for the administration of publishing in China. GAPP strictly controls the domestic uniform serial publication number (abbreviated as CN). As such, it is extremely difficult for a new publication to acquire a CN number. Therefore, many English-language journals have resorted to applying for an ISSN (International Standard Series Numbers) or ISBN (International Standard Book Numbers) number. By the end of 2014, China had 42 copyrighted English-language HSS journals and another 14 English-language HSS journals organized by Chinese institutions, but under the copyright of foreign publishers. All of the 14 foreign-owned journals and 15 of the 42 Chinese-owned journals do not have a CN number (Li & Lv, 2015). Journals without CN numbers are not officially recognized; thus they are often excluded from China's domestic evaluation, and very few of them receive funding from the government. To some extent, the strict control of CN numbers has led to the outflow of certain high-quality journals, and limited the development of others.

Among the 42 journals, 34 (80 percent) were established in or since 2000; 23 (61 percent) have 'China' or 'Chinese' in their journal titles; and 11 (26 percent) are in the field of economics, which is the HSS discipline with the most English-language journals. Universities, academic organizations, publishers, and governmental or quasi-governmental agencies are the major hosts of English-language journals in China. Journals managed by governmental or quasi-governmental agencies usually rely solely on Chinese resources for funding, personnel, authorship, and publishing (Li & Lv, 2015). For example, *China International Studies* is hosted by the China Institute of International Studies (CIIS), which is the think tank of China's Ministry of Foreign Affairs. However, most of the English-language journals are managed by universities, academic organizations, and publishers. These journals usually rely on both domestic and foreign resources, through establishing an international editorial board, inviting reviewers from different countries or regions, and paying attention to diversified authorship. Many journals choose to cooperate with international publishers for overseas publishing and marketing (Xu, 2014) – for example, *Social Sciences in China* cooperates with Taylor & Francis, and *China & World Economy* cooperates with Wiley-Blackwell.

None of China's English-language journals is included in A&HCI. Only 3 of the 42 journals are indexed by SSCI. They are *China & World Economy, Journal of Sport and Health Science*, and *Annals of Economics and Finance*. In addition, the *Chinese Journal of International Law* (managed by Wuhan University, but co-published and owned by Oxford University Press), the *Chinese Journal of International Politics* (managed by Tsinghua University, but co-published and owned by Oxford University Press), and *China Agricultural Economic Review* (managed by China Agricultural University, but co-published and owned by Emerald) are also SSCI indexed journals. Overall, the international influence of China's HSS English-language journals is still very limited. This is first because many Chinese researchers do not possess satisfactory proficiency in English (Flowerdew & Li, 2009), and lack full knowledge of the requirements expected in the international academic community as well as the required familiarity with the extant literature (Yang, 2012). The Chinese styles of argumentation and use of English in some of these journals also make them difficult for foreign readers to understand (Xu, 2014).

At the same time, there are voices that question whether indexation in SSCI and A&HCI should be the criteria or target for China's HSS English-language journals (e.g., Zhu, 2009). Journals indexed in SSCI and A&HCI are highly centralized in Europe and North America (e.g., Gingras & Mosbah-Natanson, 2010). Following the discourses of major international citation indices bears the danger of sacrificing academic autonomy. By using Western standards only, developing English-language journals might again result in a 'bringing-in' rather than reciprocal exchanges. But it is unrealistic and irrational to refuse Western influence and develop something completely brand new. A reasonable path for China's English-language journals is to be both internationalized and indigenized, although, with relatively little international influence, many journals are making valuable contributions.

With respect to internationalization, as mentioned above, most journals adopt international management models. The review process of English-language journals provides an opportunity for Chinese scholars to experience international academic requirements and English writing conventions, and to build a relationship with scholars from other parts of the world. It can help stimulate academic rigor and originality in China. For example, the *Annals of Economics and Finance* aims to "set the highest research standard for economics and finance in China" (*Annals of Economics and Finance*, n.p.). The *Fudan Journal of the Humanities and Social Sciences* requires its papers to "have theoretical and methodological approaches," and encourages authors to "engage in the international scholarly dialogue by offering comparative or global analyses and discussions" (*Fudan Journal of the Humanities and Social Sciences*, n.p.).

In social science research, indigenization means to integrate reflections on the local culture and/or society and/or history into one's approaches (Yang, 2013). Indeed, many journals seek to provide Chinese perspective in HSS research. For example, the SSCI indexed publication *China & World Economy* positions itself as "a truly international journal that provides a unique Chinese perspective on international issues in economics that are related to China" (*China & World Economy*, n.p.). More proactively, English-language journals are making attempts to establish a platform for dialogue across cultures. For instance, *Frontiers of Education in China*, co-published by Higher Education Press and Brill, works to "combine Chinese points of view with international perspectives, creating a platform for a deepening understanding of Chinese education," with the aims to "stimulate mutual investigation and multi-dimensional dialogue" and "explore the global significance of China's educational traditions and contemporary patterns" (Frontiers of Education in China, 2010).

Toward cultural self-awareness and cultural dialogue

Internationalization has been characterized as driven by four rationales: political, economic, academic, and cultural/social (Knight, 1997). Internationalization of higher education in China is now very much a top-down activity aimed at supporting the policy agenda of enhancing global competitiveness (Hammond, 2016). The current shift in the internationalization of China's humanities and social sciences has an obviously political rationale. Nevertheless, academic development has its own rules. The humanities and social sciences have an inherent cultural dimension in a context where China has been struggling with tensions between Westernization and indigenization since the late 19th century. The cultural rationale is fundamental for understanding internationalization in China. When it comes to culture, there are different predictions about the direction of diversified cultures in the era of globalization. Some have argued that the endpoint of mankind's ideological evolution is Western liberal democracy (Fukuyama, 1992) and globalization will bring homogenization of culture. Huntington (1996) is more realistic in predicting the fragmentation and clash of civilizational blocs as national cultures and regionalization persist. His standpoint is one of concern for the future of Western civilization confronting a rising Asia and divided Islamic countries.

But we can draw different inspiration from Chinese culture. Throughout its long history, China's large population has developed a culture that values human relationships highly. In the Chinese view of the world, civilizations can coexist through 'harmony in diversity.' Today, 'pure' cultures do not exist. Even though Western culture has spread globally with great prestige, it has also absorbed a great deal from other cultures. A new dynamic, holistic, multifaceted vision is needed when examining intercultural and inter-civilization relations (Fei, 2015). History has shown how reciprocity across cultures has nurtured knowledge development (Hayhoe & Pan, 2001). In HSS research, awareness of the importance of a multiplicity of perspectives and pluralistic epistemologies (Polkinghorne, 1983) is the first step toward genuine cultural dialogue. Fei Xiaotong, an eminent Chinese sociologist and anthropologist, proposed the concept of "cultural self-awareness," which provides an insightful response from a non-Western society:

> Cultural self-awareness means that those who live within a specific culture have a true understanding of it, know where it comes from, how it developed, which its unique features are, and how it is evolving. Cultural awareness does not mean "cultural regression" or bringing back the past; it advocates neither a total "Westernization" nor a "hanging on to tradition." This kind of self-knowledge is to increase the capacity for deliberate and conscious choices in the process of cultural transformation that occurs

under new circumstances and in a new age. Acquiring this self-awareness is not easy and will take a long time because it means first of all knowing one's own culture and then knowing the many cultures it encounters. After that, it may be possible to find one's place in this culturally diverse world, and through conscious adaptation absorb the strengths of others, and together build a commonly acceptable order in which all cultures can coexist, flower, and grow.

(Fei, 2015, p. 50)

China's recent changes in internationalizing its HSS disciplines demonstrate efforts in countering Euro-American hegemony and facilitating dialogue across cultures in HSS research, but it takes time to see the effectiveness.

Note

1 In China's policy documents, "philosophy and social sciences" is used to refer to "humanities and social sciences."

References

Alatas, S. F. (2010).The call for alternative discourses in Asian social sciences. In UNESCO (Ed.), *World Social Science Report 2010* (pp. 68–72). Paris: Unesco Publishing.

Altbach, P. G. (1998). *Comparative Higher Education: Knowledge, the University, and Development*. London: Alex Publishing Corporation.

Altbach, P. G. (1989). *From Dependence to Autonomy: The Development of Asian Universities*. Dordrecht: Kluwer Academic.

Al Zeera, Z. (2001). Paradigm shifts in the social sciences in the East and West. In R. Hayhoe J. & Pan (Eds.), *Knowledge Across Cultures: A Contribution to Dialogue Among Civilizations* (pp. 55–74). Hong Kong: Comparative Education Research Centre.

Annals of Economics and Finance. (n.d.). *Introduction*. Retrieved June 12, 2017 from http://aeconf.com/

Castro, N. (2013). Isn't anthropology already a multiversalist discipline? Assessing the status of anthropology in Asia. In M. Kuhn & K. Okamoto (Eds.), *Spatial Social Thought Local Knowledge in Global Science Encounters* (pp. 33–42). Stuttgart: ibidem Press.

China & World Economy. (n.d.). *Introduction*. Retrieved June 12, 2017 from http://onlinelibrary.wiley.com/journal/10.1111/(ISSN)1749-124X/homepage/ProductInformation.html

Deng, Z. (2010).Westernization of the Chinese social sciences: the case of legal science (1978–2008). In UNESCO (Ed.), *World Social Science Report 2010* (pp. 182–183). Paris: Unesco Publishing.

Fang, Z. (2002). *Between Chinese Learning and Western Learning: Toward a Re-Interpretation of Modern Chinese Learning*. Baoding: Hebei University Press.

Fei, X. (2015). *Globalization and Cultural Self-Awareness*. Beijing: Foreign Language Teaching and Research Publishing/Heidelberg: Springer.

Feng, H. Y., Beckett, G. H., & Huang, D. (2013). From "import" to "import–export" oriented internationalization: the impact of national policy on scholarly publication in China. *Language Policy, 13*(12), 251–272.

Flowerdew, J., & Li, Y. (2009). English or Chinese? The trade-off between local and international publication among Chinese academics in the humanities and social sciences. *Journal of Second Language Writing, 18*, 1–16.

Frontiers of Education in China. (2010). Exploring the global significance of Chinese education: a new start for *Frontiers of Education in China*. *Frontiers of Education in China, 5*(1), 1–2.

Fudan Journal of the Humanities and Social Sciences. (n.d.). *Introduction.* Retrieved June 12, 2017 from www.springer.com/social+sciences/journal/40647

Fukuyama, F. (1992). *The End of History and the Last Man.* New York: Free Press.

Gingras, Y. & Mosbah-Natanson, S. (2010). Where are social sciences produced? In International Social Science Council (Ed.), *World Social Science Report 2010* (pp. 149–153). Paris: Unesco Publishing.

Hammond, C. (2016). Internationalization, nationalism, and global competitiveness: a comparison of approaches to higher education in China and Japan. *Asia Pacific Education Review, 17*(4), 555–566.

Hayhoe, R. & Pan, J. (2001). A contribution to dialogue among civilizations. In R. Hayhoe, & J. Pan (Eds.), *Knowledge Across Cultures: A Contribution to Dialogue Among Civilizations* (pp. 1°24). Hong Kong: Comparative Education Research Centre.

Huang, H. (2010). China's historical encounter with Western sciences and humanities. In M/Kuhn & D. Weidemann (Eds.), *Internationalization of the Social Sciences: Asia-Latin America Middle East-Africa-Eurasia* (pp. 21–44). New Brunswick: Transaction.

Huntington, S. (1996). *The Clash of Civilizations and the Remaking of World Order.* New York: Simon & Schuster.

Institute of Scientific & Technical Information of China, ISTIC (2016). *Statistical Data of Chinese S&T Papers in 2015.* Retrieved June 12, 2017 from http://conference.istic. ac.cn/cstpcd/newsrelease.html

Keim, W. (2010). The internationalisation of social science: distortions, dominations and prospects. In International Social Science Council (Ed.), *World Social Science Report 2010* (pp. 169–171). Paris: Unesco Publishing.

Knight, J. (1997). Internationalization of higher education: a conceptual framework. In J. Knight & H. de Wit (Eds.), *Internationalization of Higher Education in Asia Pacific Countries* (pp. 5–19). Amsterdam: EAIE.

Li, C., & Lv, C. (2015). Internationalization of China's English-language academic journals in the humanities and social sciences. *Journal of Tsinghua University (Philosophy and Social Sciences). 30*(4), 168–183.

Manicas, P. (1987). *A History and Philosophy of the Social Sciences.* Oxford: Blackwell.

Marginson, S. (2010). *Global Creation: Space, Mobility and Synchrony in the Age of the Knowledge Economy.* New York: Peter Lang Publishing.

National Planning Office of Philosophy and Social Sciences. (2006). *The 11th Five-Year (2006–2010) Plan for National Philosophy and Social Sciences Development.* Retrieved from www.npopss-cn.gov.cn/GB/219555/219556/14587978.html

National Planning Office of Philosophy and Social Sciences. (2011). *The 12th Five-Year (2011–2015) Plan for National Philosophy and Social Sciences Development.* Retrieved from www.npopss-cn.gov.cn/GB/219468/14820244.html

Okamoto, K. (2010). Internationalization of Japanese social sciences: importing and exporting social science knowledge. In M. Kuhn & D. Weidemann (Eds.), *Internationalization of the Social Sciences: Asia–Latin America–Middle East–Africa–Eurasia* (pp. 45–66). New Brunswick: Transaction.

Polkinghorne, D. E. (1983). *Methodology for the Human Sciences: Systems of Inquiry.* Albany: State University of New York Press.

Qi, X. (2014). *Globalized Knowledge Flows and Chinese Social Theory.* New York: Routledge.

Wang, L. (2014). Internationalization with Chinese characteristics: the changing discourse of internationalization in China. *Chinese Education and Society, 47*(1), 7–26.

Xu, Y. (2014). Current situation, problems, and suggestions for China's social science English-language scholarly journals. *Journal of World Education, 19*, 54–57.

Yang, R. (2012). Scholarly publishing, knowledge mobility and internationalization of Chinese universities. In T. Fenwick & L. Farrell (Eds.), *Knowledge Mobilization and Educational Research: Politics, Languages and Responsibilities* (pp. 185–167). New York: Routledge.

Yang, R. (2013). Indigenised while internationalised? Tensions and dilemmas in China's modern transformation of social sciences in an age of globalisation. In M. Kuhn & K. Okamoto (Eds.), *Spatial Social Thought Local Knowledge in Global Science Encounters* (pp. 43–62). Stuttgart: ibidem Press.

Yang, R. (2014). China's strategy for the internationalization of higher education. *Frontiers of Education in China, 9*(2), 151–162.

Zhu, J. (2009). Academic appraisement, academic periodical and academic internationalization: a proper thought over the upsurge of internationalization of humanities and social sciences. *Journal of Tsinghua University (Philosophy and Social Sciences). 24*(5), 126–137.

Chapter 12

Toward humanistic internationalization

Does the current Western theory of internationalization have Protestant capitalist roots?

Bryan McAllister-Grande

In *The Protestant Ethic and the Spirit of Capitalism*, Max Weber (1930) controversially asserted that modern capitalism originated with the Calvinistic spirit of 'work.' Early Protestants, he argued, found spiritual enlightenment in the secular world by doing good (and profitable) jobs. Weber also asserted that key concepts of the Protestant Reformation (1500s–1680s), such as ideas of predestination, proof, and reason, morphed into secular and modern concepts of capital, individualism, science, and property rights.

This chapter revives this provocative thesis to critique the origins of Western and American internationalization theory during and since the Cold War. The chapter argues that key concepts of modern, Western internationalization theory – such as autonomy of institutions, institutional 'cultures,' individual intercultural growth, integration, infusion of global perspectives, and process – owe something to a Cold War Protestant ethic.

The dominant theory of internationalization in the West – the infusion/integration model

Since the Cold War, Western educational institutions (and American institutions especially) have adopted a dominant 'infusion' or 'integration' theory of internationalization. The infusion/integration model is typically defined as "the process of infusing intercultural, international, and global perspectives into the curriculum, campus, and delivery of education" (an amalgam of definitions by Harari, 1981; Knight, 2004; Leask, 2015, NAFSA, n.d.).

Although definitional and theoretical nuances exist, this general theory is widely used – both in the 'developed' world and in the 'developing' world. Universities, private schools, and corporate providers all tend to prescribe to this theory.

What about this theory could be wrong or dogmatic? Does it not have decades of research and practice behind it? Additionally, when a scholar or pundit attacks such a theory, he or she risks seeming anti-internationalization or overly critical of his or her peers, institutions, and leaders. In a time of rising nationalism and ethnocentrism, perhaps it would be better to leave the theory alone. Yet, this theory contains some unrecognized assumptions that are too rarely discussed. First, the theory itself is not just a science or a theoretical model. It has a complex Cold War history. Second, the theory assumes that institutions are autonomous from larger historical processes and ideologies of knowledge and power and that global knowledge can be infused into existing Western frameworks without altering those Western frameworks themselves. Third, the theory has a circular and self-renewing logic, not unlike the endless Protestant spirit of capitalism. Internationalization, defined in the manner of process, seems to never begin and never end.

Knight (2004) specifies that internationalization is a process operating primarily at the institutional and individual levels. Such a theory contains unexamined assumptions about society, power, science, and values. Although other levels (international, regional, national, etc.) impact internationalization, most of what is worthy studying, practicing, and examining, according to Knight, happens at the level of the individual or the institutional.

The theory thus gives strong preference to empirical data collection and best practice ideals. If internationalization occurs primarily at the university level – and not at any larger level – then the Western social scientist, using the tools of science, is the leading authority on internationalization. Similarly, if institutions are largely working autonomously and competitively, then a best practices approach seems apt and natural.

This is not the only way to study and practice internationalization. What if international education professionals also viewed internationalization through the lens of other forces that operate beyond (or at least in tandem with) the individual and institutional levels of analysis? What if they considered culture, religion, history, ideology, or nation-building as the central lenses through which to understand internationalization? These larger structural forces are what this chapter is concerned with.

Although I take a critical approach, this chapter is written from an Anglo-American, white Protestant point of view and therefore works from within a tradition of national, ethnic, and patriotic critique. Indeed, this chapter contains the assumption that it is usually from within the lens of one's own culture and one's own nation-state that the 'international' or 'global' can be usefully understood.

In the first part of this chapter, I consider some of the historical antecedents and assumptions of the popular infusion/integration theory. The second part of the chapter recovers a somewhat lost humanistic/pragmatic theory of internationalization as a kind of "door" to further thinking in the field. The pragmatic or humanistic theory, developed in the early part of the twentieth century, does not privilege empirical data or practices. Rather, it seeks to understand knowledge as part of distinct cultural and differing epistemological traditions.

Finally, this chapter proposes a 'humanistic/pragmatic' definition of internationalization. I define humanistic/pragmatic internationalization as:

> An understanding of the foundations of knowledge and of the academic disciplines; understanding how to think in complex deductive systems; and the skills required to go beneath the surface of immediate experience to historical, philosophical, and future-oriented conceptions of goodness, wealth, and wisdom.

Instead of 'infusing' global perspectives into the university, a humanistic/pragmatic theory of internationalization would seek to understand the origins and goals of different global perspectives. I will explain more about the definition below.

The Cold War roots of the infusion/integration model

If we are to take a humanistic and historical point of view, the infusion/integration model is not just a science or a scientific theory. It is also a value, and one that was solidified during the Cold War. During the Cold War, American organizations such as the National Association of Foreign Student Advisors (NAFSA), the Ford Foundation, the Institute of International Education (IIE), and a now-defunct organization called Education and World Affairs (EWA) began pushing for the infusion/integration model (House Committee on Education and Labor, 1966; Vestal, 1994). These organizations had connections to the nation-state and to a Protestant leadership class.

In the early 1960s, these organizations began asserting an infusion/integration model of internationalization grounded in 'Western' frameworks. It was hardly the only model available at the time. Other models, some more pragmatic, philosophical, and radical, were also on the table. In landmark reports such as *The University and World Affairs* (1961), *The College and World Affairs* (1964), and *Higher Education and World Affairs* (1968), EWA endorsed an infusion/integration model, defined as "a process by which men come to understand themselves and their own destinies through understanding their identity with and differences from human beings in other cultures and societies" (Education and World Affairs, 1961, p. vii). This education must "understand these cultures in the same manner . . . as those of the West," or through an inductive and infusion-based approach (Education and World Affairs, 1961, p. 5). This nationalist version of internationalization espoused a continuous process of infusing other cultural perspectives into existing 'Western' frameworks. Many American universities and colleges went along with this model, because they assumed they would be getting significant funding and attention from the (failed) International Education Act of 1966 (Vestal, 1994).

The other, related factor to the acceptance of the infusion model was a major shift in the American academy toward universalizing knowledge over contextualizing it. It is difficult to overstate this shift to what Reisch (2005) calls the "icy slopes of logic." Before the Cold War, the field now known as the sociology of knowledge was not a separate, esoteric field practiced by French or critical theorists. It was an 'ethos,' and it was widely assumed that knowledge – including science and mathematics – was socially and historically conditioned, not value-free. Owing much to Émile Durkheim and Weber, as well as to John Dewey, Franz Boas, Ruth Benedict, Edward Sapir, and many others, the contextual and social nature of knowledge was a given (Jewett, 2012; Kloppenberg, 1986).

This was a transnational dialogue of pragmatism and democratic socialism that crossed to Chinese thinkers such as Hu Shih and to Latin American thinkers, as well (Flores, 2014; Grieder, 1970). Even students were highly aware that their curricula had deep religious, nationalist, and ideological roots and that what we now call 'disciplines' had their roots in religious absolutes (McAllister-Grande, 2017). Indeed, 'science' was widely contested terrain, with overlaps to art, poetry, and the very meaning of democracy (Jewett, 2012).

From the 1960s through the 1980s, however, the universalism of the general education/liberal education program, the prominence of 'Civilization' (Western, 'Oriental,' etc.) courses, the dominance of positivist and institutional theories of science, and the infusion/integration model of internationalization, all became normative. This is when the now-common dichotomy between 'Western' and 'non-Western' as a curricular and organizing framework entrenched itself in the academy and when infusing 'non-Western perspectives' into the existing curriculum became commonplace.

Of course, the infusion/integration model is not the only current theory of internationalization in the West. Other scholars have questioned the model, and a rich selection of alternatives is available. My claim, however, is that the dominant Western internationalization model, championed primarily by American non-governmental organizations, is still the infusion/integration model. This model is increasingly popular among the American Council on Education and Association of American Colleges and Universities internationalization laboratories and collectives. Even in the last few years of critical internationalization dialogue, there has been a surprising non-reflexivity about the relationship between internationalization theories and national or corporate agendas. I do not mean to suggest these agendas consciously direct local internationalization efforts (as they often did in the Cold War), but rather that agendas (and funding) are interwoven and centralized and therefore provide an organizing logic that is difficult to challenge or argue against. It is a "habitus" (Bourdieu, 1977) that is taken to be the given 'way things work.' By definition, the infusion model even 'integrates' these 'alternative' perspectives on internationalization into a unified whole, thus swallowing them up rather than truly comparing them.

Knight, who is the leading theorist of the infusion/integration model, has herself recognized some of the challenges and pitfalls of the model. She has identified what she calls "unintended consequences" such as problems of quality, *problem* Western dominance, commercialism, and inequalities among nations and peoples (Knight, 2009).

Knight, however, does not adequately recognize values and assumptions that underpin the theory itself. She is focused on the outcomes and empirical practices, but not on the foundations. In the next part of the chapter, I examine some of the values and assumptions of the infusion/integration model.

Institutional theory assumptions

During the Cold War, institutional theory (Peters, 1999) dominated Western social and political science as well as educational theory. According to institutional theory, universities and other institutions, including academic disciplines (science, social science, etc.), are autonomous, rational 'cultures.' Each institution and each discipline has its own 'culture' with its own particular rules and methods. Indeed, even educational science is a separate 'culture.' In Cold War institutional theory, these autonomous 'cultures' were understood to be separate from larger historical processes and ideologies. These 'cultures' were thus filled with rational actors and logical processes that could be isolated and studied as separate and unique variables. If we return to the Weber thesis, this is but an extension of Weber's argument that Protestantism was rationalized into 'capital' that can be isolated and produced.

Although institutional theory is less dominant in the West today, it and neo-institutional theory pervade the Western view of internationalization. First, institutional theory helped to create the idea that the best place to understand any phenomenon was at the individual and institutional levels – at the level of the institutional and disciplinary 'culture,' individual experience, and practice. In institutional theory, universities and schools are assumed to be self-contained systems (and systems of other self-contained systems) with rational organizational structures. Nothing is connected except perhaps by correlation or circumstance. Such an assumption may be helpful and interesting, but certainly these so-called autonomous institutions and disciplines and 'cultures' are part of the state (Loss, 2012) and to larger "imagined communities" tied to nationalism, philosophy, religious movements, and history (Anderson, 2006).

Institutional theory also contributed to the Western idea of 'international education' itself. Not only was 'international education' itself a separate 'culture,' but it was composed of a number of autonomous 'parts' which, when combined together, added up to the 'whole.' All of these parts (study abroad, international students, area studies, partnerships, technical assistance, the general curriculum, graduate and professional schools) could be broken down into sub-parts and sections, it was thought. Each was believed to have a logic – incoming, outgoing, function, value, input, output, etc. – which was considered mostly rational and instrumental and which could then be combined into a 'whole,' which made up the 'world.'

Rarely was the university or international education considered as embedded in a larger philosophy or agenda, such as Protestantism, capitalism, Anglo-American culture, or the nation-state. Only in the mirror opposite of institutional theory – Marxist dialectical materialism – were the university, the curriculum, and knowledge considered to be utterly embedded into something larger and more powerful. Power was almost entirely missing from early international education theories and concepts based in institutional theory, mostly because early international education theorists viewed their work and theories as non-ideological and 'free.'

Institutional theory had a formative influence on the Western foundations of the international education field. Institutional theory was not just a method. It was, itself, something like an ideology, which conditioned how the arts and sciences, knowledge, education, and international education functioned and operated. Think of something as simple but widespread as the idea of 'changing the culture of the institution.' Or think of the concept of 'paradigm shifts' (Kuhn, 1962) – if only we shifted 'paradigms,' things would be better! This ignores larger structures of power, influence, and culture that easily transcend the 'cultures' and 'paradigms' of individual disciplines and institutions.

Although the international education field in the West has overcome some of this thinking, the field as a whole has moved to a post-institutional (or post-positivist) model of thinking, just as social and educational science has transitioned to post-positivism and neo-institutionalism. "Comprehensive Internationalization" (Hudzik, 2014) or "Internationalization Remodeled" (Knight, 2004) still considers the 'parts' separately and operationally; it still considers the "institutional" as where "the real process of internationalization is taking place" (Knight, 2004, p. 5). The basic assumptions of individualism and autonomy remain primary.

Institutions and individuals are important. Yet, largely unconsciously, we in Western international education have placed far too much emphasis on the individual and institutional. Individuals (people) and institutions are also part of history. This chapter is not suggesting, as classic Marxist theory might posit, that they are determined by history. Rather, this chapter simply points out that the Cold War contributed to a dramatic overemphasis on individual and institutional freedom at the expense of ideological, philosophical, and historical critique.

Teleological assumptions

To deal with ideological, philosophical, and historical questions, one must deal with questions such as 'What have nations and creeds considered to be good or desirable?' or 'What do nations and creeds want?' This can also be called the study of 'teleology' – or ends.

By 'teleology,' I do not mean anything normative. Rather, 'telos' here refers to any kind of ends, purposes, desires, or goals. What are the ultimate goals of internationalization? Of knowledge? Of universities and educational institutions?

From my perspective, the infusion/integration model of internationalization contains an unquestioned assumption about teleology. And, that unquestioned assumption is that there is no final goal. In the infusion/integration model, there is seemingly no end and no beginning. In the infusion/integration model, inter- *problem* nationalization is such a vague and value-less proposition that it contains no past *of* and no future. It only refers to the present – to what is happening right now on a day-to-day basis. The infusion/integration model is far too obsessed with daily practice and work.

The infusion/integration model is usually accompanied by a logic of 'process,' wherein everything is defined as a 'process.' Global learning objectives or strategic goals are created, perspectives integrated, outcomes assessed, and the 'process' restarts. This model is successful, because following positivist and institutional modeling, it views internationalization as a progressive science toward more cosmopolitan directions, and away from earlier, ethnocentric positions. Indeed, this is the way that most process-logic models of intercultural development work: as a continuous process of individual growth. *yes, and*

Similarly, universities continue to 'integrate global perspectives' and 'internationalize' without much structural change occurring. There is no beginning and no end to their internationalization. The process can never really end as long as there are more global perspectives to integrate. It is a circular logic, or telos, that continually self-renews into infinity.

The same appears to be true about the infusion/integration internationalization theory itself. Every five or ten years or so, it is 'remodeled.' The 'new' model is not much different from the 'old' model. It includes new variables, but the foundations and overall structure remain largely unchanged. It is, in this sense, a self-renewing system characteristic of the Protestant ethic.

These assumptions – rarely discussed – resemble the old Protestant (and not just Protestant) dream of "pure reason": knowledge that is static and self-renewing (Kant, 2003), rather than knowledge that is epistemologically radical or open-ended (Bevir, 2015). These teleological assumptions and circular logic can be viewed as an extension of what Weber called the "spirit of capitalism" (capitalism and profit as ends in themselves).

Moving beyond the infusion/integration model by recovering a lost way of thinking

A pre–Cold War definition of internationalization could help the Western states move beyond the infusion/integration model – or, at the very least, help us question our assumptions more critically. One of the exciting features of Progressive-era thought (roughly 1880–1930) in the West was its hope for a 'via media' between democracy and socialism, and likewise, between Protestant-capitalist thought and Marxist thought (Kloppenberg, 1986). That lost 'via media' (which obviously never fully materialized in the West, except perhaps in some European states) had its own utopian flaws, of course, but one of the things it excelled in was thinking comparatively, contextually, and systematically.

why findings are important #1

Again, I am defining this older, humanistic/pragmatic internationalization as:

> An understanding of the foundations of knowledge and of the academic disciplines; understanding how to think in complex deductive systems; and the skills required to go beneath the surface of immediate experience to historical, philosophical, and future-oriented conceptions of goodness, wealth, and wisdom.

A humanistic definition of internationalization would first involve what I call "understanding of the foundations of knowledge and of the academic disciplines." This means a curriculum for all students, regardless of ability, that would teach students about the origins of knowledge in all cultures and societies. It would seek to teach the 'internationalization' of knowledge (which has been going on for a long time) as a historical phenomenon intimately related to power, statehood, quests for freedom, and ideas of justice as these topics developed over time and in different contexts. Additional topics such as the development of science, the humanities, philosophy, and religion would be included and related to these big ideas. This is a daunting task, of course – but not an impossible one. Talented teachers, scholars, and practitioners could devise exciting ways to teach these historical and cultural origins of knowledge.

A more humanistic internationalization might also include an "understanding of how to think in complex deductive systems." Deduction here refers to the method of deducing particulars from universals rather than the other way around (induction). Deduction is a lost art in American education especially. Deduction looks at wholes, not parts. It assumes that there are big human principles and ideas, such as freedom, autonomy, community, harmony, wealth, and industry – which exist and have existed for many centuries, and that in many ways determine or influence everything else in a respective nation or culture (art, science, religion, philosophy). Thinking in complex, deductive systems means thinking comparatively, historically, and contextually about the origins of knowledge – about Chinese theories of language, for instance, or Arabic ideas of mathematics, and how these ideas were connected to values, goals, and ideas.

The last component of the definition, "the skills required to go beneath the surface of immediate experience to historical, philosophical, and future-oriented conceptions of goodness, wealth, and wisdom," is the most challenging to explain. My thesis here, related to the above critique, is that the current, dominant model of internationalization in the West has a self-renewing, value-free teleology. Therefore, it seems to ignore, or even hide, its assumed conceptions of goodness, wealth, and wisdom by creating internationalization itself as an end goal. Everything is related to the current moment – the empirical and capitalist 'now.' In contrast, a more humanistic definition might pull out these assumed conceptions of goodness (being and acting as a good person or good society), wealth (defined broadly as any kind of wealth, not just monetary), and wisdom (knowing, understanding) in more transparent forms. What have cultures, religions, and nations historically wanted, and why? What does this say about their values? How were their science and art created around these desires and goals?

In essence, then, what I am suggesting is actually more radical than a reform of Western internationalization. It is a reform of Western education back to its classical ideals and away from Cold War positivism and institutional theory. In classical education, deduction and induction were ideally balanced, as were personal and general knowledge, knowledge of 'self' and 'other,' contemplation and action, knowledge of particulars and universals, and knowledge of different conceptions of justice and goodness. Again, this classical ideal had its own flaws. However, it excelled at many things, including balance, comparison, humanistic thinking, and thinking in terms of goals and values over time.

[handwritten margin note: going against the norm.]

Conclusion

It is time for the infusion/integration model to be fully reimagined or even discarded. It has a Cold War history, and a cold logic, that the higher education and international education fields in the West have failed to properly grapple with. Otherwise, internationalization models will never include hopes, dreams, desires, and goals, and thus overlook actual humanity.

Note

My thanks to Eduardo Contreras, Jr., and to the editors of this book, for their insightful comments on earlier drafts of this chapter. All opinions and errors are my own, however.

References

Anderson, B. (2006). *Imagined Communities: Reflections on the Origin and Spread of Nationalism* (rev. ed.). London/New York: Verso.

Bevir, M. (2015). What is radical historicism? *Philosophy of the Social Sciences 25*(2), 258–265.

Bourdieu, P. (1977). *Outline of a Theory of Practice* (Cambridge Studies in Social Anthropology No. 16). Cambridge/New York: Cambridge University Press.

Education and World Affairs. (1961). *The University and World Affairs.* New York: Ford Foundation.

Education and World Affairs. (1964). *The College and World Affairs.* New York: Ford Foundation.

Education and World Affairs. (1968). *Higher Education and World Affairs.* New York: Education and World Affairs.

Flores, R. (2014). *Backroads Pragmatists: Mexico's Melting Pot and Civil Rights in the United States.* Philadelphia, PA: University of Pennsylvania Press.

Grieder, J. (1970). *Hu Shih and the Chinese Renaissance: Liberalism in the Chinese Revolution, 1917–1937* (Harvard East Asian Series, No. 46). Cambridge, MA: Harvard University Press.

Harari, M. (1981). *Internationalizing the Curriculum and the Campus: Guidelines for AASCU Institutions.* Washington, DC: American Association of State Colleges and Universities.

House Committee on Education and Labor. (1966). *International Education: Past, Present, Problems and Prospects*. Washington, DC: U.S. Government Printing Office.

Hudzik, J. (2014). *Comprehensive Internationalization: Institutional Pathways to Success*. Abingdon, UK: Routledge.

Jewett, A. (2012). *Science, Democracy, and the American University: From the Civil War to the Cold War*. Cambridge, UK: Cambridge University Press.

Kant, I. (2003). *Critique of pure reason* (rev. 2nd ed.). Houndmills, Basingstoke/New York: Palgrave Macmillan.

Kloppenberg, J. (1986). *Uncertain Victory: Social Democracy and Progressivism in European and American thought, 1870–1920*. New York: Oxford University Press.

Knight, J. (2004). Internationalization remodeled: definition, approaches, and rationales. *Journal of Studies in International Education, 8*(1), 5–31.

Knight, J. (2009). Internationalization: unintended consequences? *International Higher Education, 54*, 8–10.

Kuhn, T. (1962). *The Structure of Scientific Revolutions*. Chicago: University of Chicago Press.

Leask, B. (2015). *Internationalizing the Curriculum*. Abingdon, UK: Routledge.

Loss, C. (2012). *Between Citizens and the State: The Politics of American Higher Education in the 20th Century*. Princeton, NJ: Princeton University Press.

McAllister-Grande, B. (2017). The inner revolution: freedom, humanism, and education at Harvard, Princeton, and Yale, 1930–1960. Doctoral dissertation, Harvard University, Cambridge, MA.

NAFSA. (n.d.). Internationalization. Retrieved from www.nafsa.org/About_Us/About_International_Education/Internationalization/

Peters, G. (1999). *Institutional Theory in Political Science: The "New Institutionalism."* London/New York: Pinter.

Reisch, G. (2005). *How the Cold War Transformed Philosophy of Science: To the Icy Slopes of Logic*. Cambridge, UK/New York: Cambridge University Press.

Vestal, T. (1994). *International Education: Its History and Promise for Today*. Westport, CT: Praeger.

Weber, M. (1930). *The Protestant Ethic and the Spirit of Capitalism*. London: G. Allen & Unwin, Ltd.

Chapter 13

Rhizomatic knowledge in the process of international academic mobility

Ana Luisa Muñoz-García

Chapter synopsis

This chapter explores the major discourses constructed by Chilean academics who received their PhDs outside Chile, both about their experiences abroad and the process of returning to their country, in order to ascertain how international movement affects the construction of knowledge in academia. Chile, the only South American country that belongs to the Organisation for Economic Co-operation and Development (OECD) (OECD & World Bank, 2010), is a particularly interesting and relevant site of research. Despite belonging to an organization that pertains to the most industrialized societies in the world, and despite the increasing process of internationalization during the past decade, Chile invests less in research and development than any other country in the OECD (OECD, 2014). This contradiction in investment priorities raises questions about research policies and the systemic conditions of Chilean academia.

The Chilean government has funded more than 7,000 PhD fellowships in the period stretching from 2008 to 2014 from the National Commission of Science and Technology (CONICYT), (CONICYT, 2014). This number is equivalent to 70 percent of all PhD holders living in Chile in 2012 (OECD, 2013). A third of the fellowships were awarded to students completing doctoral degrees at foreign universities, mostly in England, the United States, and Spain (CONICYT, 2014). Therefore, contemporary studies show that in 2018 Chile will have more than 8,000 researchers with doctorates, which is 10 times more than in 2014 (Gonzalez & Jiménez, 2014). It is important to note that discussion about internationalization in the Chilean literature has focused primarily on the discourse of advancing human capital, which situates the country within the main narrative of the knowledge economy (CONICYT, 2008; Consejo-Asesor-Presidencial, 2008; CSE, 2011; Escudey & Chiappa, 2009; Eyzaguirre, Marcel, Rodríguez, & Tokman, 2005; Rojas & Bernasconi, 2009), and there is little discussion about internationalization processes and academic mobility outside this perspective.

Thus, the main argument of this chapter is that in the process of internationalization, knowledge construction in academia operates as a rhizomatic process. Adopted from the work of Gilles Deleuze and Félix Guattari (1987), the concept of the rhizome indicates a systematic movement that does not have a precise beginning or end and operates in between layers and power dynamics. To think of knowledge rhizomatically is to view it as unfinished, multiple, and open, and to recognize the existence of different powers that interconnect and split apart knowledge construction constantly (Campbell, 2008). In the present analysis, I use the concept of rhizomatic knowledge both to escape traditional, rational, and logical approaches to knowledge, and to explain systematic movement in the construction of knowledge: a movement that is neither linear nor has beginning or end, a movement that is crucial for understanding the results of this study.

Rhizomatic knowledge

Rhizomatic knowledge is a conceptualization in which knowledge, power, place/space, and mobility are connected. A rhizome is a form of plant-life that spreads, such as mushrooms or crabgrass, without a central root, point of origination, or logical pattern. Deleuze and Guattari (1987) explain that:

> A rhizome has no beginning or end; it is always in the middle, between things, interbeing, *intermezzo*. The tree is filiation, but the rhizome is alliance, uniquely alliance. The tree imposes the verb "to be" but the fabric of the rhizome is the conjunction, "and . . . and . . . and . . ." This conjunction carries enough force to shake and uproot the verb "to be." Where are you going? Where are you coming from? What are you heading for? These are totally useless questions.
>
> (1987, p. 25)

As we will see, the feeling of working, thinking, and existing 'in between' frequently emerges in the reflections of Chilean academics who have studied abroad. Thus, to think of knowledge rhizomatically is to view it as "unfinished, multiple, and 'open' and to recognize that beneath official histories and divisions there exist other powers, actualized through other kinds of encounter and invention, tracing divergent, entangled lines of composition that both interconnect and split apart constantly" (Campbell, 2008, p. 9).

Deleuze and Guattari (1987) also argue that a rhizome might become broken, shattered at a given place, but it will again grow out of one of its old lines, or along new lines. They claim:

> Every rhizome contains lines of segmentarity according to which it is stratified, territorialized, organized, signified, attributed, etc., as well as lines of deterritorialization down which it constantly flees. There is a rupture in a rhizome whenever segmentary lines explode into a line of flight, but the line of flight is part of the rhizome.
>
> (1987, p. 9)

The authors use the example of the orchid and the wasp to describe movements of deterritorialization and processes of reterritorialization to show how the two species are always connected, that is, caught up in one another.

The orchid deterritorializes by forming an image, a tracing of a wasp; but the wasp reterritorializes on that image. The wasp is nevertheless deterritorialized, becoming a piece in the orchid's reproductive apparatus. But it deterritorializes the orchid by transporting its pollen. Wasp and orchid, as heterogeneous elements, form a rhizome.

(Deleuze & Guattari, 1987, p. 10)

The processes of territorialization, deterritorialization, and reterritorialization can help explain the process of internationalization that scholars in this study have experienced. These academics and their construction of knowledge have become territorialized: organized as sets of guidelines, principles, frameworks, outcomes, which may constitute lines of segmentarity. The notion of deterritorialization enables the possibility that these lines of segmentarity may rupture or explode into lines of flight, shifting the way in which we look at global discourses on what internationalization means. In other words, in the process of internationalization, knowledge has become territorialized into a global discourse, but the global discourse also deterritorializes those constructions, resulting later in reterritorialization when those scholars return to their local contexts. In addition, this study posits that the process is not linear in nature. Territorialization, deterritorialization, and reterritorialization are a continuous process where flows are never smooth but always disjunctive, and where flows look different from every angle (Rizvi, 2007).

Researching movement

This analysis is based on a qualitative phenomenological study that aimed to understand the common and shared experiences of Chilean scholars who have completed a doctorate abroad and returned to Chile. In the phenomenological approach, the researcher describes and interprets the meaning of the lived experiences of the subjects in order to develop a composite description of the basic nature of the experience for all of the individuals in the study (Creswell, 2007). This research was based on 41 semi-structured interviews with Chilean professors of the social sciences and humanities. Three research universities were selected as sites of research: a public university and a private university, both located in Santiago, and a third public university located in southern Chile. These institutions were selected based on their commitment to research, affiliation (private or public), and geographic location (metropolitan or situated in the provinces). All of the participants were working as academics in one of the three chosen universities, had completed their doctorate in the past 15 years, and had returned to Chile at least two years prior to the start of the study. The group of academics was intentionally diverse in terms of gender, with 16 females and 25 males in the sample. Interview questions were organized around four different issues: social and educational background, experience abroad, the process of returning to Chile, and experience in the academic world after returning. For the analysis, the interviews were transcribed and translated. To ensure confidentiality and participants' protection, pseudonyms were used to identify the respondents. The information was analyzed using Hyper Research software, coded, and organized into themes that emerged from the data. This methodological approach allowed for the identification and understanding of multiple realities that were connected with the expansion of scholarships for Chileans to undertake doctoral studies abroad.

Finally, this research also included the analysis of documents and discussions related to academic mobility coming from the Chilean Congress, media, websites, historical documentaries, and government sources. Besides setting the scene, these resources provide valuable data that complement, contrast, and aid in the interpretation of the interview data. The documents are used to answer 'why' questions related to academics' lived experiences during their time abroad and at home; hence, they connect individuals' lived experiences and constructed biographies with the broader context of academic mobility and the process of academic internationalization.

Landing in the process of constructing knowledge

For multiple reasons, Chilean academics who received their education abroad describe the process of returning to their home country as complex. While most participants in this study were abroad for four years, some studied abroad for as little as two years, while a few participants pursued international study for as many as 10 years. As thinkers, these individuals have constantly been going back and forth between the different ways they have imagined (and currently imagine) academia. This is a fundamentally non-linear process: past, present, and future merge in a narrative that disrupts linear temporality. (rhizomatic)

After returning to Chile, one of the common issues that these participants experienced was to feel as if they were 'landing in between.' First, some participants mentioned feeling divided between two countries. Second, participants in this study struggle with a constant process of negotiation between what is considered 'more of the same' and 'thinking otherwise' in academia. Third, upon their return to Chile, many participants encountered a conservative academic environment, where, at best, they confronted difficulties communicating what they had learned abroad, and at worst they experienced what they called peer surveillance and difficulty finding a job. The following analysis focuses first on the feeling of being divided between two countries, followed by participants' negotiation of 'thinking otherwise,' and finally, participants' strategies for dealing with a conservative academic environment. The section concludes with thoughts related to the processes of deterritorialization and reterritorialization.

Between here and there

'Between here and there' is a narrative that participants used to express the idea of feeling divided between Chile (home) and their doctoral host countries, and to explain the ways in which academics deal with the complexities of returning, primarily during the first few months or years in Chile. Many participants utilized this 'between here and there' narrative to contexualize their ongoing search within their home country for academic spaces and experiences akin to what they had had abroad, as well as their experiences negotiating and confronting a conservative academic environment.

I guess on personal terms, just being abroad changes one's perspective. There, I missed Chile, here I miss Spain. It is like being divided. One cannot truly imagine what it will be like until one does it.

(Andrea, Assistant Professor in Social Science,
public university)

I returned to Chile in 2010. It was a hard process, because in personal terms I arrived in Chile last year. My soul stayed there [France] for a little while, and I really returned just last year (laughs). It took me two years to really land in this country.

(Monica, Adjunct Professor in Psychology,
private university)

Both Andrea's and Monica's narratives challenge linear thinking about time and space. Their statements also challenge a linear way of understanding the literature of academic mobility. The process of returning goes beyond moving from one place to another. It implies a process of deterritorialization and reterritorialization, where arriving to a specific place means encountering the collection of interwoven stories of which that place is made. Based on an analysis of place and space, Massey (2005) noted that "there is an imagination that going home means going back in both space and time, back to the old familiar things, to the way things used to be" (p. 124). However, space travels in the same way that time travels. Places change and go on with or without people, who themselves are in constant movement. Massey (2005) continues: "For the truth is that you can never simply 'go back' to home or to anywhere else. When you get 'there' the place will have moved on just as you yourself will have changed" (Massey, 2005, p. 124). Therefore, in order to make sense of the process of academic mobility, there is a need to think of space and time as interrelated and as a product of their interrelations. Applying Massey's perspective, Matus and Talburt (2009) consider how the static-passive construction of space and time in the process of movement of scholars becomes problematic because there is dissociation and de-politicization of the past in relation to the present, where the past no longer acts in the present, maintaining the neutrality of institutional spaces. Therefore, in order to make sense of the process of academic mobility, there is a need to think of space and time as imbricated and as a product of the interrelations of the process of movement of academics.

Until recently, institutions such as universities have taken for granted ideas of time and space, which allow the reproduction of practices and essentialization of subjectivities. This becomes problematic because it positions universities as empty receptacles and academics as independent of the content of those spaces. In other words, academic spaces such as universities create and recreate what it means to 'be' an academic and the ways in which knowledge should be produced.

Between the same and otherwise

None of the participants in this study ever imagined pursuing their doctoral degrees in Chile. By that, they believed that the doctoral programs in the social sciences and humanities fields that they wanted to study were not available in Chile. Or, if those programs did exist, these programs would have offered the same professors and topics of research as during their undergraduate or master's programs. In their words, it would have been 'more of the same.' Thus, they experienced knowledge construction abroad as a more open, creative, and critical process which impacts the ways these scholars consider what their experience would have been like within their home country.

> Studying abroad opens your mind, and it gives you the life experience of a different socio-cultural dynamic, something that would not have happened if I had stayed in Chile . . . The academic circle here is homogeneous.
> (Ana María, Assistant Professor in Social Work, private university)

> I feel that theories travel and have a temporality, and I am convinced of that. I feel that Chile is a very conservative country. So, I could not experience anything of what I needed to experience. I needed to know theories and people who performed that theory and those are things that I would never imagine. One of the things that Chile has is how predictable we are. We know perfectly how many languages you can speak in the discipline. I wanted something else. I think that during that time, I could not explain the neoconservative issue of Chile but I felt it inside. I needed to do my PhD in another country, because I was assured that I did not know what would happen. If I stayed here I would know what would happen in advance.
> (Daniela, Associate Professor in Education, private university)

The quotes above present a discourse of 'moving there' (out of the country) in order to be able to think differently – the idea that place may determine the construction of knowledge. As other studies have shown in relation to scholars who move, "new countries, institutions and environments have made a major difference to their practices of thought but in different ways" (Kenway & Fahey, 2006). Traveling and being abroad produce what Kenway and Fahey (2009, p.11) call "a wider intellectual horizon," a space where it is possible to transgress disciplinary surveillance, thus allowing scholars to develop a different relationship with knowledge. In this study, academics discussed the limits to what might be said and done within the academia, and what might not in the process of doing knowledge which affect their academic work, which diminish their contribution within universities and disciplines. This type of discussion was placed mostly when these participants talked about research funding where the language used in their proposals must fit specific disciplinary regulations.

For these academics, thinking otherwise involves wrenching concepts away from their usual configurations outside of the system of understanding in which they have a home, far from the "structures of recognition that constrain thought to the already-known" (Grosz, 1995, p. 129). This strong connection between place, knowledge, and experience challenges the ways knowledge, place, and mobility are widely understood, and it requires new ways of understanding place and knowledge (Massey, 2005). This raises an important question about whether space creates a place to change your point of view, and would suggest a constant need to travel to keep up to date in knowledge. More importantly, however, this connection creates a backdrop for understanding what it means for academics to return home after 'thinking otherwise' abroad.

> [Abroad] I think differently. For example, I became more liberal. My perspective is wider. I also feel free, so free. I had the feeling of being free and anonymous as well. That was a nice feeling, I remember. Nobody cared about what I did. I returned with that thought, but I think that this university made me go backwards again concerning that. All the freedom I had there, the idea of being a free thinker, I do not have it here today. I became conservative again because of this university. We have to fit the model of this university, indeed. I remember, I was more liberal, more tolerant too.
>
> (Gustavo, Assistant Professor in Anthropology,
> public university)

During the years these scholars studied abroad, they had the opportunity to question and challenge different issues related to their histories, their politics, and even their own identities. The feeling that they changed, but that their country did not change in the same way, makes it more difficult now for them to handle the way people think back home. In an analysis of the critical implications that traditional understandings of time have on intellectual practices of travel, Matus and Talburt (2009) point out that "institutional discourses and policies ignore the geopolitics of intellectual practices and their effect on other geographies, other people, and other cultures" (p. 8). According to Matus, there is an "idealized process of coming back," which seems problematic because "expectations about the institutional meanings of their returning processes show the dissonances between what has happened to them in time and what is not absorbed by the place they inhabit" (Matus, 2009, p. 11).

The results of this study lead us to a critical question about how the experience of going abroad complicates the politics of the construction of knowledge within universities when, for these participants, being abroad meant not only experiencing different kinds of knowledge, but also different ways of knowing, and being exposed to different conditions for possibilities of being and becoming.

Between negotiation and resistance

The process of returning to Chilean academia takes different forms depending on the institution within which one operates. The discourse of negotiation and resistance was most strongly present in interviews with academics working in a religiously affiliated private university; however, it also appeared in interviews with those at public universities.

Gustavo is an academic who studied in Germany and works in a private university in Santiago. In different parts of the interview, he mentioned how free and liberal he became while he was studying abroad, only to indicate that any sense of himself as a 'free thinker' was diminished upon his return to Chile. When asked how he negotiates the fact he felt more liberal abroad and considers that his freedom was reduced when he came back, he says:

> I think that you do not negotiate it. It is a gradual process . . . I think that there are little things that make you more conservative, and this university encourages you to be more conservative . . . They ask it implicitly.
>
> (Gustavo, Assistant Professor in Anthropology,
> private university)

The process of negotiation (or non-negotiation) became relevant to understanding the complexities of returning after studying abroad. Sidhu (2006), who examines the operations of power and knowledge in international education under the conditions of globalization from an interdisciplinary approach, considers that relations between power and space shape the process of internationalization. With the assumption that knowledge is caught up in relations of power in different spaces, and is therefore neither neutral nor impartial, Sidhu (2006) says: "Not everything is visible or sayable; rather, a set of rules determines what can be said, written, communicated, and legitimated as institutional practice, knowledge, and 'truth'" (Sidhu, 2006, p. 27).

Such results beg the question of how opportunities to think and construct knowledge may be deterritorialized, and how between the dual tyrannies of immediacy and newness, knowledge may become "challenged, renewed, and transformed" (Sidhu, 2006, p. 302). Academic work is imbricated on issues of success and efficiency imposed by the imperatives of time and speed. These tyrannies that surround intellectual work prevent scholars from engaging reflexively about the ways knowledge is produced. Kim (2010) suggests that academics who are mobile undertake a certain detour from the common trajectories within the system and therefore do not become totally alienated by the university order. Based on this idea, the results of this study invite a "spatialized reading" (Sassen, 2001) of the internationalization processes and the flow of scholars.

According to Grosz (1995), who questions fundamental assumptions within various systems of contemporary knowledge, there is a presumption of the atemporal and transgeographic value and validity of knowledge by its most uncritical supporters. In this sense, the genesis of knowledge usually becomes irrelevant to the information that is produced, even though knowledge is produced at specific times and places. Similar to this critical analysis developed by Grosz, the data in this study speak loudly for the argument that knowledge reflects the social and historical context in which it is constructed.

Conclusion

This chapter aimed to draw attention to two related but distinct points. First, academic mobility is characterized by multiple aspects that completely escape mainstream conversations about human capital development, the main frame within which discussions about internationalization in Chile are positioned. Second, naturalized ways of understanding mobility within time and space, and depicting it as something linear, are inadequate to the task of understanding academic mobility. This study challenges linear understandings of mobility and the construction of knowledge via the migration process: one does not simply go, live abroad, return, and become an academic in one's home country.

To understand the results of this study, Deleuze and Guattari (1987) give us a theoretical grounding from which to rethink practices described by the participants. 'Going back' to their country in the knowledge construction process means going back in both space and time. The notions of territorialization, deterritorialization, and reterritorialization can usefully help us to understand the process of internationalization that forms the context for the experiences and discourses of existing 'in between,' as described by scholars in this study. These academics and their experiences of constructing knowledge have become territorialized: organized as sets of guidelines, principles, frameworks, and outcomes, which may constitute lines of segmentarity. The notion of deterritorialization enables the possibility of these lines of segmentarity rupturing or exploding into lines of flight, shifting the way in which we look at global discourses the meaning of internationalization. Based on Deleuze and Guattari (1987), a rhizome might break or shatter at a given place, but it will again grow on one of its old lines, or on new lines. Creating knowledge within an internationalization process demands understanding knowledge in a rhizomatic way. This takes our thinking about academic mobility across space and time to new levels of complexity and authenticity more appropriate to the realities of the 21st-century global knowledge society.

References

Campbell, N. (2008). *The Rhizomatic West: Representing the American West in a Transnational, Global and Media Age*. Lincoln, NE: University of Nebraska Press.

CONICYT. (2008). *Capital Humano Avanzado: Hacía una Política Integral de Becas de Postgrado*. Santiago, Chile: Comisión Nacional de Ciencia y Tecnología. Retrieved from www.bcn.cl/catalogo/busqueda_resultado?busqueda=Capital+humano+avanzad o+%253A+hacia+una+pol%25C3%25ADtica+integral+de+becas+de+postgrado+%252F &opcionesbusqueda=TITULO&frase_exacta=&alguna_palabras=&sin_palabras=&pag ina=1&mindate=+&maxdate=+&sort=+&b=1

CONICYT. (2014). *Brain Exchange: Departamento de Estudios y Gestión Estratégica*. Santiago, Chile: Comisión Nacional de Ciencia y Tecnología. Retrieved from www.conicyt. cl/wp-content/uploads/2014/07/Resumen-Ejecutivo-Brain-Exchange-2014.pdf

Consejo-Asesor-Presidencial. (2008). *Los Desafos de la Educación Superior Chilena: Informe del Consejo Asesor Presidencial para la Educación Superior*. Santiago, Chile.

Creswell, J. (2007). *Qualitative Inquiry and Research Design: Choosing Among Five Approaches*. Thousand Oaks, CA: Sage.

CSE. (2011). *Indice and Estadisticas 2011*. April 2012: CSE. Retrieved from www.cned. cl/public/Secciones/SeccionIndicesEstadisticas/indices_estadisticas_sistema.aspx

Deleuze, G., & Guattari, F. (1987). *A Thousand Plateaus: Capitalism and Schizophrenia*. Minneapolis, MN: University of Minnesota Press.

Escudey, M., & Chiappa, R. (2009). *El Desarrollo Científico-Tecnológico y la Gestión de la Investigación*. Santiago, Chile: CNA-Chile.

Eyzaguirre, N., Marcel, M., Rodríguez, J., & Tokman, M. (2005). Hacia la economía del conocimiento: el camino para crecer con equidad en el largo plazo. *Estudios Publicos, 97*, 5–57.

Gonzalez, H., & Jiménez, A. (2014). Inserción laboral de nuevos investigadores con grado de doctor en Chile. *Journal of Technology Management & Innovation, 9*(4), 132–148.

Grosz, E. (1995). *Space, Time and Perversion: Essays on the Politics Body*. New York: Routledge.

Kenway, J., & Fahey, J. (2006). The research imagination in a world on the move. *Globalisation, Societies and Education, 4*, 261–274.

Kim, T. (2010). Transnational academic mobility, knowledge, and identity capital. *Discourse: Studies in the Cultural Politics of Education, 31*(5), 577–591.

Massey, D. (2005). *For Space*. Thousand Oaks, CA: Sage Publications.

Matus, C. (2009). Time as becoming: women and travel. *Journal of Curriculum Theorizing, 25*(3), 7–21.

Matus, C., & Talburt, S. (2009). Spatial imaginaries: universities, internationalization, and feminist geographies. *Discourse: Studies in the Cultural Politics of Education, 30*(4), 515–527.

OECD. (2013). *Reviews of National Policies for Education: Quality Assurance in Higher Education in Chile 2013*. Paris: OECD.

OECD. (2014). *Education at a Glance 2014: OECD Indicators*. Paris: OECD.

OECD & World Bank. (2010). *Reviews of National Policies for Education: Becas Chile Scholarship Program*. Paris: OECD.

Rizvi, F. (2007). Transnational academic flows. In D. Epstein, R. Boden, R. Deem, F. Rizvi, & S. Wright (Eds.), *Geographies of Knowledge, Geometries of Power: Framing the Future of Higher Education* (pp. 299–304). New York/London: Routledge.

Rojas, A., & Bernasconi, A. (2009). El gobierno de las universidades en tiempo de cambio. In N. Fleet (Ed.), *Desafíos y Perspectivas de la Dirección Estratégica de las Instituciones Universitarias* (pp. 183–214). Santiago, Chile: Grafica, LOM.

Sassen, S. (2001). Spatialities and temporalities of the global: elements for a theorization. In A. Appadurai (Ed.), *Globallization* (pp. 260–278). Durham, NC: Duke University Press.

Sidhu, R. (2006). *Universities and Globalization: To Market, to Market.* Mahwah, NJ: Lawrence Erlbaum.

Chapter 14

A changing narrative for international students?

The potential influence of Brexit and Trump

Charles Mathies and Leasa Weimer

International education has often been framed, in a Western perspective, as an active competition to maintain or secure intellectual and human capital (e.g., brain gain/brain drain; (Ziguras & McBurnie, 2015). While there is competition for attracting both students and staff, in this chapter we focus solely on international students. Although international higher education is more than just students moving across borders, student mobility is an important manifestation of how higher education has become more international (Caruso & de Wit, 2015). Indeed, student mobility is considered to be a foundation of how the internationalization of higher education is understood, because it is tangible and an easily recognized aspect by relevant stakeholders (Rumbley, 2012).

The motivation for the recruitment and retention of international students is often framed in economic terms (Ziguras & McBurnie, 2015). While this is certainly not the only rationale for hosting international students, and also not without criticism, it is a dominant view held by many governments and nongovernmental organizations, such as the World Bank and the Organisation for Economic Co-operation and Development (OECD). Questions arise, though, as to whether this rationale will continue to be the dominant justification for international student mobility at a time when an emerging populist narrative, which is gaining political power, embraces nationalism, anti-immigration, and anti-globalization attitudes. The role of, and acceptance of, immigrants in many national contexts is clearly under criticism and, in turn, this discourse has impacts on international higher education and specifically on international students.

The dominant discourse for international students

The primary rationale to host international students for most nation-states has long centered on the economic impact they bring to local communities and higher education institutions (HEIs), often in the form of tuition fees and personal spending (housing, meals, etc.) (Ziguras & McBurnie, 2015). Prime examples of such benefits are international student mobility programs, which regularly claim financially relevant outcomes, such as the amount of revenue they generate through tuition, fees, and local consumer spending. Diplomacy, cultural benefits, and academic rationales have also been used as fundamental arguments to explain the raison d'être of national programs for international student mobility, but even these programs and initiatives are regularly quantified and measured to understand the economic impact of hosting international students.

Recently, though, the economic rationale by governments for hosting international students has expanded beyond simple revenue generation to include improving a country's ability to compete in the global economy. The modern global economy has been marked by a shift from industry to knowledge-based pursuits where societies value and use knowledge as a raw material (Castells, 1996; Guruz, 2011). Knowledge, as embodied in individuals (i.e., human capital), requires training and education, and results in developing a qualified skilled worker (OECD, 2014). Having a highly skilled workforce is seen as a key aspect for economic development (OECD, 2014). This has often been framed as part of a neoliberal, market-based, or 'new public management' movement, with higher education as one of the systems being reformed in a larger shift of government perspectives and priorities (Olssen & Peters, 2005). This movement has been championed by groups like the World Bank and the OECD, as their 'agenda-setting' documents offer up policy options promoting an interconnected global knowledge economy (Robertson, 2005). This has had a powerful effect, as many national governments and ministries of education have adopted the positions of these external groups to justify significant changes to their educational systems with an aim to better compete within the global knowledge economy (Robertson, 2005). However, in many countries, this has led to an escalation of tensions among HEIs, ministries, and governments, as these changes have typically accompanied large-scale reductions in public funding and increasing regulation through the use of performance indicators and metrics (Ferlie, Musselin, & Andresani, 2008; Guruz, 2011).

As there is an increasing need for skilled workers to compete in the modern global economy, many nation-states actively recruit international students and enact measure to retain them in-country after graduation, because they can provide a competitive advantage as they increase the available supply of skilled workers (Caruso & de Wit, 2015; Weimer, 2012; Ziguras & Law, 2006). It is important to note, however, that many stakeholders (particularly government and industry) have expressed concerns about international students staying and fully integrating into the host country (Shumilova, Cai, & Pekkola, 2012). Such concerns include inadequate language skills, limited previous work experience in the local labor market, and not having the 'right' networks to connect professionally with employers (Shumilova et al., 2012). There are also arguments about whether students can be considered 'skilled' because they have not, in most cases, demonstrated their abilities in the labor market (King & Sondhi, 2016). However, the counter-arguments are that training (educating) international students within national borders is not only easier and more affordable than importing skilled workers trained elsewhere, but that they are also more readily employable, as they were trained (educated) with that country's labor market in mind (Ziguras

& Law, 2006). In short, the neoliberal agenda aimed at opening up cross-border trade and a global economy strongly supports the idea that international students are a needed strategic economic resource (Britez & Peters, 2010).

Challenges to the dominant discourse for international students

The dominant discourse for international students is being challenged by an emerging populist narrative that espouses anti-immigration and anti-globalization sentiments. While the economic and dominant rationale for international students is largely constructed to recruit and train highly skilled labor to help the host country compete in the global economy, the populist narrative has the ability to disrupt this by advocating for legislation that potentially limits the number of international students and restricts post-graduation opportunities. The space limitations of this chapter do not allow a full and in-depth treatment of the populist movement (see Mudde & Rovira Kaltwasser, 2017); however, we do highlight specific aspects that may directly impact international students and their choice of where to study.

Anti-immigration sentiment

Populism takes different forms according to a country's political history and culture (Greven, 2016; Inglehart & Norris, 2016). This is clearly evidenced by the 2016 election of Donald Trump in the United States and the 2016 Brexit vote in the United Kingdom. However, there are similarities in populist rhetoric across countries that directly impact the internationalization of higher education and, more specifically, challenge the economic rationale for international students. Populist parties use negative political communication and deconstruct 'political correctness,' thereby opening the door to the identification and ostracism of the 'other' (Greven, 2016). This rhetoric creates and perpetuates an 'us vs. them' mentality, subsequently leading to an anti-immigration attitude, rejecting multiculturalism and cosmopolitan ideals. The 'other' (minorities and/or migrants) is identified according to the national context. For example, Trump's discourse identifies that it is undocumented Mexicans and Muslims who should be feared; in continental Europe, with the recent influx of refugees, there has been pushback against opening borders for asylum seekers; while in the United Kingdom there are fears about European integration (i.e., euro-skepticism) and explicitly in relation to the free movement of the 'other' into the country.

Nationalism and anti-globalization sentiment

The right-wing populist movement adheres to an anti-globalization narrative and at the same time idealizes the nation-state (Greven, 2016). This discourse seeks to protect vulnerable citizens from the competitive global market and return the nation to its 'post-war' characteristics of growing prosperity, security, and sense of shared community (Inglehart & Norris, 2016). Trump's campaign motto "Make America Great Again" provides an illustrative example of this form of nationalism. De Vries and Hoffmann (2016) found, in a study across the 28 European Union (EU) member states, that the primary rationale for citizens turning to populist parties was fear of globalization, while the protection of traditional values (in comparison to progressive values) played only a minor role.

A new reality?

The populist discourse against immigration and globalization is now the new reality in many countries, and specifically in the United States and United Kingdom. We speculate that the current economic discourse for international students will be shaped and altered by this developing narrative. This will undoubtedly create additional tensions, beyond the current ones, amongst HEIs, ministries, and governments. How these tensions will resolve will likely take many years. However, there are enough pieces of evidence to begin hypothesizing how this could unfold.

First, with increasing anti-immigration sentiment comes the potential for changes in national immigration legislation, which may lead to a decrease in the number of international students studying in a country. However, there does not necessarily need to be a change in legislation to impact the number of international students studying in a country. There is a great deal of conjecture that international students will not find countries with strong populist movements attractive to study in, and that perception alone may be enough to decrease the number of international students selecting those specific destinations.

As the populist movement normalizes xenophobic discourse, international students will be challenged by these types of attitudes and may experience discrimination firsthand. Lee and Rice (2007) developed a conceptual framework called 'neo-racism' to explain some of the challenges international students experience in the current global society, specifically discrimination. They draw from previous research focused on 'new racism' where discrimination was not solely based on biological race, but on cultural attributes and national origin (Barker, 1981). Applying their framework, Lee and Rice (2007) found that some hardships faced by international students were due to their foreign national status. Neo-racism operates in a global society where beliefs about cultural order and hierarchy exist and perpetuate discrimination against those coming from parts of the world considered 'inferior', thus fueling the "principles of exclusion and nationalism" (Lee & Rice, 2007, p. 389). Building on neo-racism research, Lee, Jon, and Byun (2017), while studying international student experiences in South Korea, developed the notion of 'neo-nationalism,' which focuses more on individuals' national identity rather than race and can play out in many different ways. For example, they found that Asian students in South Korea experienced more discrimination than students coming from Europe, North America, or other regions.

The United States and United Kingdom are particularly interesting case studies, as they host (in absolute terms) the most international students in the world. They are English-speaking countries for both academia and the labor market. The United States currently hosts over one million international students, while the United Kingdom hosts approximately half a million international students (Institute of International Education [IIE], 2016); combined, they account for more than 41 percent of all students studying abroad globally (OECD, 2016). A UK study, conducted prior to the Brexit vote, surveyed approximately 44,000 prospective international students and found over 82 percent of EU nationals and 35 percent of all respondents would see the United Kingdom as less attractive for study and immigration if the United Kingdom were to leave the European Union (Hobsons Solutions, 2016). As for the United States, a good deal was written in the weeks following the November 2016 election of Trump suggesting that the once welcoming environment for international students in the United States was changing and not as attractive (Altbach & de Wit, 2016). The result, as Altbach and de Wit (2016) submit, is that the image of Americans and British not welcoming foreigners will make these countries less attractive as host destinations, regardless of the reputation and quality of their HEIs.

A change in immigration law represents a structural change and would have a lasting impact (i.e., reductions in the U.K. and U.S. cases) on the number of international students studying within a country. However, if there is only an environmental change and little or no change in immigration legislation, there is a good chance the number of international students studying in the United States and the United Kingdom will rebound fairly quickly. For the United Kingdom though, this does not look to be the case, as roughly six months after the Brexit vote the government proposed a dramatic cut in student visas (Fazackerley, 2016).

Second, while globalization offers a dynamic backdrop for internationalization to thrive, it also presents some significant challenges, as not everyone benefits from the global knowledge economy. The reality of the global knowledge economy is that it displaces manufacturing and services jobs (e.g., low or non-skilled employment) away from developed countries (Guruz, 2011). There are individuals left behind and many have mobilized behind anti-globalization rhetoric and populist candidates. These are citizens who identify as 'us' (Greven, 2016) and advocate for protecting their national labor markets from foreigners and returning jobs to local unemployed people. However, it is unlikely that developed countries operating in the interconnected global knowledge economy can detach themselves from the global economic order.

This creates a situation where the politics of the populist movement are in conflict with economic realities. Enacting new legislation in line with the populist agenda has direct and significant economic impact for developed countries (e.g., the negative economic projections for the United Kingdom for leaving the European Union). To overcome these economic realities requires a significant amount of political will to enact policies in line with populist sentiment. Evidence from both the United Kingdom and the United States indicates that global economic (as well as some legal and political) entanglements make it difficult to move forward with many of the populist agenda items

Two realities, in particular, make it difficult to advance the populist agenda: most developed countries are experiencing declining birth rates and the need for skilled workers in the global knowledge economy is increasing (Guruz, 2011). Coupling these realties together suggests not only that there will be space for international students in most national labor markets, but they will be needed to meet economic development demands. This implies that one of two things will likely happen. International students will simply go elsewhere (to countries without a strong populist movement) to study, as the demand by students desiring to study abroad is increasing. Or international students will be exempted (in whole or part) from more restrictive immigration legislation due to the economic realities of given countries. Specifically, international students will be viewed favorably due to the income they generate for the host economy and that economy's labor market needs for highly skilled workers. As such, international students will become part of a 'protected' class in many contexts, due to the economic needs of the nation-state. This appears to be occurring in the United Kingdom with Prime Minister May's concession not to include international students in immigration totals (Elliot & Zeffman, 2017).

This brings us to a third hypothesis, related to who exactly will be part of a 'protected' class of international students. Choudaha, Orosz, and Chang's (2012) taxonomy of international students is a useful place to start. They categorize international students into four groups within two dimensions of academic preparation (high/low) and financial resources (high/low). The "highfliers" (high/high) typically do not encounter difficulties in choosing where to study, due to their high level of academic preparation and ability to pay tuition, fees, and living expenses. However, viewing the taxonomy through the lens of neo-racism (Lee & Rice, 2007) could lead to a third dimension, placing individuals in two groups (high or low) of desirability based on culture and national origin. Adding this third dimension suggests that not all highfliers would be welcomed, regardless of their academic ability or ability to pay, as those who are identified as the 'other' would either be denied entry (via immigration legislation) or face discrimination (within the host country environment).

If this third dimension develops, it implies two things. First, regardless of whether it is based on structural (legislation) or environmental factors, this third dimension will supersede both the academic and economic ability of international students in determining where they study. For example, the highfliers cannot overcome the structural barriers and likely will not want to experience the environment in the host country. Second, aligned with the literature on the populist movement (Greven, 2016; Inglehart & Norris, 2016), the specific international students who will be impacted changes based on the national context. This implies that the populist movement could significantly impact international student choice, but it will be individually tailored for each country based on national environment, legislation, and history.

Conclusion

We operate in a connected global economy. While countries may become more isolationistic, global collaboration and competition will continue. Globalization cannot be undone; it may slow down, but it will not fade away. The same is true for the global flow of international students. While some countries may enact restrictive immigration policies (i.e., visa schemes), reduce the number of study spots for international students, implement higher tuition fees, or develop a negative environment, the flows of international students will continue. Although a few countries (e.g., Canada, Australia) are likely to experience growth in international students due to the populist movement in other countries, it is not clear if there will be space globally for all the displaced students (Altbach & de Wit, 2016). The result is that many students who want to study internationally may not be able to do so.

Overall, a great deal of further research on this topic is needed. For example, in countries experiencing a recent surge in populist thinking, comparing the rationale (discourse) for international student recruitment over time would indicate if there is a shift in narrative. Neo-racism and neo-nationalism also provide unique lenses through which to study how populist attitudes may shape the micro-level of the international student experience. Finally, research on the various forms of capital and how students use it to overcome (or not) the barriers to studying internationally could shed light on the student experience.

Olson (2016) argues that there are two types of internationalization of higher education: exclusionary and inclusionary. Exclusionary internationalization is targeted, competitive, strategic, and economically focused, while inclusionary internationalization is collaborative, uniting, and equality-focused. The recruitment and retention of international students is principally exclusionary under the dominant rationale, but it has the potential of becoming even more exclusionary as the 'other' is further ostracized. On the other hand, the change in discourse may give space for renewed thinking and opportunities for action with more inclusionary practices. This will likely occur in two places. First, in countries that are experiencing populist movements, HEIs will be in a position to develop inclusionary practices, as this is not only where the international students live, study, and work (local environment) but the HEIs often possess a reputation, history, and culture of encouraging a diverse community. Second, for countries that are not currently major players in recruiting international students, there may be opportunities to attract additional students. To do so, though, will require significant investments of resources (human, financial, and time) by governments and HEIs. In summary, while the populist movement adds a new dimension of challenges, it also creates opportunities for international education to become more inclusionary. Whether this will happen remains to be seen, but there are reasons to remain optimistic about the future of international education at a time of an emerging populist narrative.

References

Altbach, P., & de Wit, H. (2016, November 11). Now we have the (temporary?) end of American internationalism. *University World News, 436*. Retrieved from www.universityworldnews.com/article.php?story=20161110203906750

Barker, M. (1981). *The New Racism: Conservatives and the Ideology of Tribe*. London: Junction Books.

Britez, R., & Peters, M. (2010). Internationalization and the cosmopolitical university. *Policy Futures in Education, 8*(2), 201–216.

Caruso, R., & de Wit, H. (2015). Determinants of mobility of students in Europe: empirical evidence for the period 1998–2009. *Journal of Studies in International Education, 19*(3), 265–282.

Castells, M. 1996. *The Information Age: Economy, Society and Culture*, Vol. 1, *The Rise of the Network Society*. Oxford: Blackwell.

Choudaha, R., & de Wit, H. (2014). Challenges and opportunities for global student mobility in the future: A comparative and critical analysis. In B. Streitwieser (Ed.) *Internationalisation of Higher Education and Global Mobility (Oxford Studies in Comparative Education)* (pp. 19–33). Oxford: Symposium Books.

Choudaha, R., Orosz, K., & Chang, L. (2012). *Not All International Students Are the Same: Understanding Segments, Mapping Behavior*. New York: World Education Services.

de Vries, C., & Hoffmann, I. (2016). *Fear not Values. Public Opinion and the Populist Vote in Europe*. Gütersloh: Bertelsmann Stiftung. Retrieved from www.bertelsmann-stiftung.de/fileadmin/files/user_upload/EZ_eupinions_Fear_Study_2016_ENG.pdf

Elliot, F., & Zeffman, H. (2017, April 20). May forced to soften key target on migrants. *The Times*. Retrieved from www.thetimes.co.uk/article/may-forced-to-weaken-key-target-onmigrants-qfmgp5fgq

Fazackerley, A. (2016, December 12). UK considers plan to nearly halve international student visas. *The Guardian*. Retrieved from www.theguardian.com/education/2016/dec/12/uk-halve-international-student-visa-tougher-rules

Ferlie, E., Musselin, C., & Andresani, G. (2008). The steering of higher education systems: a public management perspective. *Higher Education, 56*, 325–348.

Greven, T. (2016). *The Rise of Right-Wing pPopulism in Europe and the United States: A Comparative Perspective*. Berlin: Friedrich-Ebert-Stiftung. Retrieved from www.fesdc.org/fileadmin/user_upload/publications/RightwingPopulism.pdf

Guruz, K. (2011). *Higher Education and International Student Mobility in the Global Knowledge Economy* (2nd ed.). Albany, NY: SUNY Press.

Hobsons Solutions (2016). *Hobsons International Student Survey*. London: Hobsons Solutions.

Inglehart, R. F., & Norris, P. (2016). *Trump, Brexit and the Rise of Populism: Economic Have Nots and Cultural Backlash*. Harvard Kennedy School of Government Faculty Research Working Paper Series. Retrieved from https://papers.ssrn.com/sol3/papers.cfm?abstract_id=2818659

International Institute of Education (IIE) (2016). *Project Atlas Global Mobility Trends*. New York: IIE.

King, R., & Sondhi, G. (2016). *Gendering International Student Migration: A Comparison of UK and Indian Students' Motivations and Experiences of Studying Abroad* (Working

Paper No. *84*). Falmer, UK: Sussex Centre for Migration Research at the University of Sussex.

Lee, J., Jon, J. E., & Byun, K. (2017). Neo-racism and neo-nationalism within East Asia: the experiences of international students in South Korea. *Journal of Studies in International Education*, doi:10.1177/1028315316669903

Lee, J. J., & Rice C. (2007). Welcome to America? Perceptions of neo-racism and discrimination among international students. *Higher Education, 53*, 381–409.

Mudde, C. & Rovira Kaltwasser, (2017). *Populism: A Very Short Introduction*. Oxford: Oxford University Press.

OECD. (2014). *Measuring the Digital Economy: A New Perspective*. Paris: OECD Publishing.

OECD. (2016). *Trends Shaping Education 2016*. Paris: OECD Publishing.

Olson, J. (2016). Imagining internationalisation as a "first responder" to the new mobility in European higher education. In L. Weimer (Ed.), *Imagine . . . EAIE Conference Conversation Starter 2016* (pp. 11–16). Amsterdam: EAIE.

Olssen, M. & Peters, M. (2005). Neoliberalism, higher education and the knowledge economy: from the free market to knowledge capitalism. *Journal of Educational Policy, 20*(3), 313–345.

Robertson, S. (2005). Re-imagining and rescripting the future of education: global knowledge economy discourses and the challenge to education systems. *Comparative Education, 41*(2), 151–170.

Rumbley, L. (2012). So many data, so little clarity: the ongoing challenges of making sense of academic mobility in Europe. In J. Beelen & H. de Wit (Eds.), *Internationalisation Revisted: New Dimensions in the Internationalisation of Higher Education* (pp. 125–133). Amsterdam: Centre for Applied Research on Economics and Management, School of Economics and Management of the Hogeschool van Amsterdam.

Shumilova, Y., Cai, Y., & Pekkola, E. (2012). Employability of international graduates educated in Finnish higher education institutions. *VALOA-Project*. Career services, University of Helsinki. Retrieved from www.helsinki.fi/urapalvelut/valoasurvey/#/1/

Weimer, L. (2012). Economics of the international student market. *Journal of the European Higher Education Area, 3*, 84–98.

Ziguras, C., & Law, S. (2006). Recruiting international students as skilled migrants: the global "skills race" as viewed from Australia and Malaysia. *Globalisation, Societies, and Education. 4*(1), 59–76.

Ziguras, C., & McBurnie, G. (2015) *Governing Cross-Border Higher Education*. London: Routledge.

Part III

New topics

Chapter 15

Warp and weft[1]
Weaving internationalization into institutional life

Fiona Hunter and Neil Sparnon

Internationalization in higher education is increasingly seen as an essential component in the delivery of institutional missions (de Wit, Hunter, Howard, & Egron Polak, 2015), which, predictably, has given rise to lively academic debates around its meaning and application. In turn, these discussions have led to the development of associations, publications, and organizations that advocate for the better understanding and application of internationalization agendas, and provide opportunities for further discussion, research, and the sharing of best practice.

Yet, while it is possible to discern the development of themes, approaches, and schools of thought that have led to a degree of convergence and coherence over the last three decades, the literature constantly laments the gap between the rhetoric and the reality of the internationalization of higher education (Davies, 1995; McNay, 2012; Middlehurst, 2008; Middlehurst & Woodfield, 2007; Nolan & Hunter, 2012). On the one hand, we have grand statements of vision and mission, endless strategic plans, and institutional policies that identify internationalization as a key pillar of institutional development. On the other, we have fragmented activities, lack of comprehensive understanding, conflicting priorities, the collection of memoranda of understanding that never see the light of day, and missed opportunities and unmet targets.

This chapter is an attempt to bridge this gap between rhetoric and reality. It draws extensively on our experience as higher education managers, researchers, and consultants supporting different institutions around the world in their internationalization and strategic planning efforts. In the first section, we consider how and why the gap between the rhetoric and reality of internationalization has emerged and consider its practical consequences. In the second, we examine how the definition of internationalization itself has expanded over recent years to provide a rationale through which this gap might be bridged. Third, we present a framework to build this bridge that may be used by a broad range of institutions regardless of their histories, circumstances, ambitions, and current state of development. We close by musing on why the current political and economic climates make this approach particularly timely.

The effective delivery of institutional internationalization strategies is not easy and this chapter does not pretend otherwise. It requires leaders to assess their institutional priorities, strategies, structures, and established ways of working in a purposeful and critical manner if they are to weave internationalization into the day-to-day fabric of the institution. This takes time and is rarely unopposed. The rewards for success, however, are considerable. Our experience is that successfully bridging the gap between rhetoric and reality can not only lead to the delivery of the internationalization strategy per se, but also harness it as an engine for institutional growth and renewal.

Internationalization rhetoric and reality: mind the gap

The dominance of economics as the driver for internationalization

As the internationalization of higher education has grown in scope and scale, much has been written around what exactly is meant by internationalization and why universities internationalize; what the rationales are; what the expected benefits might be; and what the activities are that characterize it. There have also been attempts to classify and list the many activities that fall under internationalization.

These debates have underlined the fact that, at its heart, internationalization is a dynamic and evolving combination of diverse, sometimes competing, rationales that emerge from the many activities in which modern universities engage. These include academic activities – teaching, learning, research and outreach – social and political engagement, as well as the extent to which universities can be income generators and economic engines for regional and national growth.

While in theory, and to varying degrees, all these activities might be present, it is the economic dimension that has become the dominant driver of institutional internationalization strategies. Originating in the United Kingdom, the United States, and Australia in the 1990s, this dominance is now spreading to Europe and the rest of the world as universities focus on international student recruitment, the employability of graduates for the global labor market, recruiting global talent for the knowledge economy, cross-border delivery of education, and the development of articulation programs, branch campuses, educational hubs, virtual learning, and MOOCs as means to generate income or position themselves globally (de Wit et al., 2015).

The demise of non-economic rationales for internationalization

The consequences of this dominance are several. For example, the academic case for internationalization – improving the quality of education and teaching and learning, enhancing standards, building partnerships and alliances, and developing the international and intercultural competences of students and staff – remains strong and continues to be advocated in the literature. Indeed, a 2015 European Parliament report on internationalization argued that the internationalization of higher education is an intentional process that involves all students and staff with the aim of enhancing the quality of education, research, and service to society (de Wit et al., 2015). How often is this rationale deployed within institutional senior management teams, however? How often is it considered a sufficient rationale in and of itself, if the financial returns are insufficient?

The detachment of internationalization from institutional life

Second, the dominance of the economic rationale for internationalization has, to some degree, detached these activities from the wider aspects of institutional life. This detachment has meant that practical questions around exactly how institutions should involve all students, engage academic and administrative staff, and use internationalization as a lever for continuous improvement, have gone largely unexplored. As Huisman (2013) states, the literature tends to focus more on general trends, or higher education institution outputs in internationalization, and rarely addresses issues around internal strategic management challenges, institutional inner workings, and micro-dynamics. Consequently, we know very little about the impact of internationalization on internal planning processes in universities, the creation and adaptation of structures, the development of new policies and procedures, the level of staff engagement, the provision of professional development, and the identification of necessary resources to realize quality enhancement goals.

The rise (and rise) of the institutional international office

Third, the emerging dominance of the economic rationale for internationalization has had the effect of raising the status of international offices, and has led to a significant growth in their size and scope, as well as in the seniority of their managers (Taylor, 2012). Reflecting their initial status as specialisms, the management and structures associated with internationalization activities have evolved over the last 25 years so that there is now a spectrum of options from which institutions can choose. Early developments focused on specialist units that supported all aspects of university activity under the general banner of 'international.' These offices tended to be small and often struggled with the scope of activity they adopted as their own. Moreover, they risked engendering tension with other organizational units onto whose territory they were perceived as encroaching, either by taking over specific tasks or by requiring alignment with international rather than local practice. Nevertheless, the scope of international offices has continued to expand and can embrace a very broad range of activities from international marketing, prospective student enquiries, admissions, and managing overseas offices, to partnerships, exchanges and study abroad, staff travel, student welfare, and

English language support, as well as the more strategic functions such as international policy development, alumni services, and public relations (Fielden, 2012; Rumbley, 2016).

In itself, the growth of international offices is not a bad thing. The size and scope of the modern international office is a reflection of the importance of internationalization in many institutions. Moreover, there is no 'right' form of international office – the appropriate form and function of institutional internationalization structures should be dependent on clearly identified and articulated institutional priorities, which will in turn be influenced by factors such as institutional reputation, current academic strengths and weaknesses, the current financial position, as well as shifting local concerns and circumstances. All reflect a move away from ad hoc arrangements towards a more strategic, planned, and directed approach, which coordinates international affairs across the institution and manages their administration efficiently. In turn, these developments reflect a growing need for effective leadership and management of international activities. As Taylor (2012, p. 34) reminds us:

> Internationalization has emerged as a key management function within most universities. Some of the traditional features of internationalization remain, notably the importance of personal contacts, but internationalization is now characterized by increasingly professional management, by careful strategy and planning, by institutional centralization and control, and by the application of new forms of HE management.

There are, however, consequences of this growth. As the size and scope of international offices has grown, so has the tendency to view internationalization as a detached specialization. In turn, this has exacerbated the tension around the purpose of internationalization. On the one hand, the level of resources and expertise devoted to internationalization underlines its central place in institutional strategy; on the other, the degree of specialization means that the impact of internationalization is limited. As Taylor (2012, p. 9) again notes:

> On one hand internationalization is recognized as a core function within the university with clear strategic importance: on the other hand, many staff working in the International Offices still feel themselves to be somewhat detached from the mainstream of the university. This appears to confirm the view, that, in professional terms, the work of the International Office is still evolving in terms of status and recognition.

The consequences of the gap

Collectively these consequences have had the effect of creating a gap between the rhetoric and reality of internationalization in many institutions. This manifests itself in numerous ways, such as the creation of multiple, often duplicate, systems for marketing, recruitment, admission, orientation, and other aspects of the student life cycle, when international expectations and needs cannot be met by local systems; or the use of dedicated staff and resources, which inevitably limits the extent to which the benefits of internationalization, particularly in terms of academic and community life, is felt by the rest of the institution.

The question arises as to how these negative consequences might be mitigated. It is to this question we now turn.

A rationale for bridging the gap – the evolving definition of internationalization

Key to bridging this gap is to return internationalization strategy and activities to the wider context of institutional strategic planning and the activities that deliver it. This rationale has become more apparent in the ongoing discussions around the definition and functions of internationalization, which have gradually widened their scope to embrace all aspects of institutional activity.

While early definitions focused primarily on "the multiple activities, programs and services that fall within international studies, international educational exchange and technical cooperation" (Arum & van de Water, 1992, p. 202), this expanded quickly to the "process of integrating an international and intercultural dimension into the teaching, research and service functions of the institution" (Knight, 1994, p. 3). Expansion continued beyond the institutional level to "the process of integrating an international, intercultural or global dimension into the purpose, functions or delivery of higher education" (Knight, 2004, p. 11). This has undoubtedly become the most widely known and commonly used definition.

However, it is interesting to note that van der Wende introduced the notion of internationalization as an institutional response as early as 1997 when she defined internationalization as "any systematic effort aimed at making higher education responsive to the requirements and challenges related to the globalization of societies, economy and labor market" (van der Wende, 1997 p. 18). This definition implied the need for outward-facing institutions able to scan their external environment, gather the appropriate intelligence, and make decisions to adapt and innovate their programs, policies, and practices in the face of rapid external change.

As internationalization has evolved and matured, so have the activities and tasks that fall under its ambit. Early years saw a focus on the mobility component of internationalization, known as "internationalization abroad" but, by the turn of the 21st century, a growing number of practitioners felt the necessity to address the needs of the 90 percent of non-mobile students (at that time, the European Commission's target for Erasmus mobility was 10 percent). The concept of 'internationalization at home' was born and defined as "any internationally related activity with the exception of outbound student and staff mobility" (Crowther et al., 2001 p. 8). This has since been revised to focus specifically on the experience of all non-mobile students and is now defined as "the purposeful integration of international and intercultural dimensions into the formal and informal curriculum for all students in domestic learning environments" (Beelen & Jones, 2015).

This reference to the informal curriculum implies that internationalization might involve more than academic processes. Leask (2015, p. 9), however, retooled her own definition of internationalization of the curriculum to make this evolution explicit. Internationalization, she argues, is the "incorporation of international, intercultural and/or global dimensions into the content of the curriculum as well as the learning outcomes, assessment tasks, teaching methods and *support services* of a program of study."

As the definitions of internationalization at home and internationalization of the curriculum expand, our understanding of these dynamics increasingly overlaps in their purpose and scope. While the purpose of both phenomena is to reach 100 percent of students and embed internationalization within the core formal and informal curriculum, they also indicate, particularly in the case of the curriculum, that there is a role for support services in the successful delivery of internationalization (Rumbley, 2015).

Arguing that "as the international dimension of higher education gains more attention and recognition, people tend to use it in the way that best suits their purpose" (de Wit, 2002, p. 114), a recent revision of Knight's intentionally neutral definition sought to close the gap between rhetoric and reality by providing an overarching purpose to internationalization to encourage institutions to reflect more on their own rationales for engaging in it. This new definition states that internationalization is "the intentional process . . . to enhance the quality of education and research for all students and staff, and to make a meaningful contribution to society" (de Wit et al., 2015).

Two elements of this definition demand attention. First, by embracing "all students and staff" it seeks to reflect the growing awareness that internationalization must become more inclusive and less elitist; both for students – in that it should focus on the internationalization of the teaching and learning process (with mobility as an optional but integral part) – and for staff, by emphasizing that successful internationalization is critically dependent on the active engagement of everyone, academics and administrators. Second, "intentional" highlights that internationalization is a planned process – one that not only requires reflection and decision about the future direction of the institution, but also, and most critically, that it should lead to action and institutional change (de Wit et al., 2015).

Hudzik's definition of comprehensive internationalization moves us a step further by embracing "a commitment, confirmed through action, to infuse international and comparative perspectives through the teaching, research and service missions of higher education" (Hudzik, 2011, p. 6). He insists that a comprehensive approach is one that needs to be embraced at all levels of the institution from the institutional leadership to the students and across all academic and administrative units.

Further steps along this journey are evident in the work of Brandenburg and de Wit, who argue that recent developments mean there is now "the shared feeling that international education no longer can be seen as a fragmented list of activities executed by international offices and a small group of motivated internationalists among staff and students. Internationalization should on the contrary be integrated, broad and core" (Brandenburg & de Wit, 2011).

The culmination of this discussion re-emphasizes that internationalization is not a goal in itself to be viewed in isolation from the rest of the institution, nor judged solely in terms of income generation. Rather, it has a contribution to make to academic quality and student life. It should be linked to academic objectives, rather than solely quantitative indicators; to the curriculum, teaching and learning, and research; and be able to demonstrate outcomes and impact. In short, it should be managed alongside other activities through the institutional strategic planning process.

Warp and weft: strategic planning and internationalization

Our approach to internationalization is to place it within the wider context of the institutional strategic plan and the mechanisms through which the strategic plan is delivered. This context is defined by our recommended approach to strategic planning, where institutions are encouraged to view themselves in a holistic manner, in which all activities have a contribution to make to the delivery of strategic objectives, and which also recognizes there is a hierarchy of objectives within a strategic plan.

Drawing on common understandings of strategic planning in higher education, we argue that there are four key components underpinning a strategic planning framework in higher education. These are:

- A – a statement of purpose, commonly expressed through vision and mission statements;
- B – an articulation of the key academic activities through which this purpose is pursued and ultimately delivered;
- C – an indication of supporting functions which enable these activities, and
- D – a discussion of how appropriate resources will be deployed to support them.

This framework represents a hierarchy of priorities. The aims set out in A should be relatively stable – they represent the *raison d'être* of the institution and the institution will ultimately be judged on the extent to which it is able to deliver them. The academic activities identified in B can change as circumstances require, but should be constantly evaluated against the extent to which they enable the aims that A indicates are to be achieved. If they do not, they should be either changed or deleted. Support functions in C should be managed with the objective of enabling the delivery of the academic activities set out in B, while the resources listed under D (usually understood to mean finance, but also human resources and physical estate) enable the functions and activities in C and B. As such, the underlying structure of the strategic plan might be depicted as shown in Figure 15.1. In this type of model, all elements of the plan are interrelated and geared towards delivery of the institutional mission. Meanwhile, it is crucial to recognize that the principal activities through which institutions of higher education deliver their missions are academic.

Where does internationalization lie within this framework? In short – in sections, B, C, and D. It is confined neither to section A – where it may have the

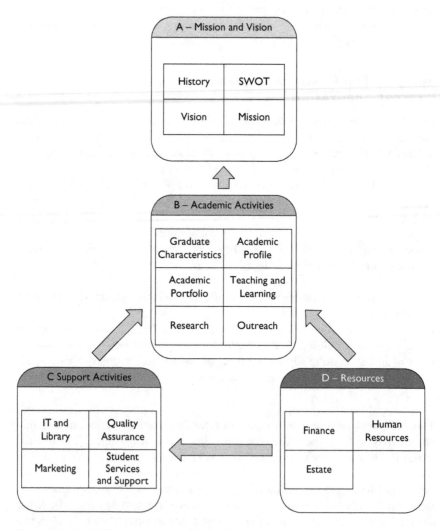

Figure 15.1 The ABCD structure of institutional strategic plans

effect of expanding or indeed subsuming the institutional mission and becoming an end in itself – nor to section D, where the economic rationale is so dominant that it potentially undermines the extent to which internationalization can contribute to support activities and academic life in general. This is not to say that internationalization cannot, indeed should not, contribute to income generation; rather, that its contribution should be balanced across the wider spectrum of institutional activities.

What does placing internationalization within this framework mean in practice? Within our four constituent sections (A, B, C, and D), institutions should identify core elements that can be drafted appropriately to deliver institutional mission. Within section B, institutions should define graduate characteristics; academic teaching and learning; research; and outreach strategies. At all times institutions should ask themselves how each articulated characteristic, course, approach to teaching and learning, research, and outreach project is not only consistent with institutional mission, but actively contributes to its delivery.

In this context, internationalization becomes an additional dimension that enhances the quality of academic activity. If, for example, the intention is that students should be able to deal with multiple perspectives arising from diverse information sources, advocates of internationalization would argue that their capacity to do so is strengthened by an ability to communicate in several languages and to have experienced these perspectives for themselves. The implications for course content (languages and overseas placements), teaching and learning, research and outreach follow not only across the rest of section B, but also across sections C and D. Let us further consider this example through the lens of languages and overseas placements.

In section C (support activities), institutions should consider library and information technology (IT) provision, quality assurance, marketing, and student support services. In our example, if academic provision actively promotes languages and placements, then these services should overtly support them. Quality assurance systems should not only include these dimensions in course development, delivery, monitoring, and accreditation, but also the possibility of joint and dual programs, student exchanges, study abroad, international placements, or service learning. Marketing can include countries and institutions that are considered especially beneficial and likely to welcome exchanges of staff, students, and ideas as well as promoting the international dimensions of study at the institution domestically. Student support services can not only prepare students for the international dimensions of their studies – for example, with medical advice and travel arrangements – but can facilitate social activities and mentoring arrangements.

Section D continues this pattern. Recognizing the need to promote language acquisition and exchange, institutional human resource activities might actively seek to recruit new staff with language skills, not only into academic departments, but also across the entire institution. They might also offer developmental programs focused on language and intercultural skill-building and adjust policies in relation to incentives, appraisal, and promotion accordingly. Financial resources should be deployed, and the physical estate managed, to facilitate the delivery of not only the agreed academic program but also the support services that enable them. For example, financial incentives might be used to encourage language acquisition among staff, as well as targeted scholarships for students; dining areas, social spaces, and classrooms might be managed to increase social interactions between staff and students from different cultural and linguistic backgrounds.

The overall effect of this approach is to weave internationalization into the warp and weft of the day-to-day life of the institution. Using our previous model, it may it may be usefully depicted as shown in Figure 15.2.

This approach should not be considered definitive on the question of whether institutions develop a single, comprehensive institutional strategy or

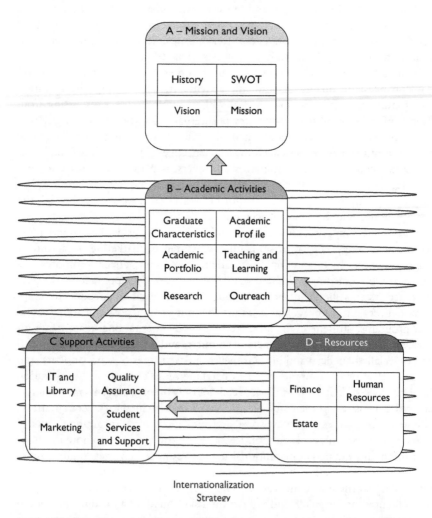

Figure 15.2 Warp and weft: integrating internationalization into institutional strategic plans

a separate strategy for internationalization. Fundamental to our approach is to understand that, whatever the model chosen, collectively the actions for internationalization are embedded across the full spectrum of institutional activities, with the resulting model both coherent and comprehensive. Of course, this model does little to settle the ongoing discussion around the appropriate size and scope of institutional international offices. An institutional response to this question should be determined by its history, size, external circumstances, and the extent of its collective internationalization activities. In some senses, the nature and size of the international office is of less importance than a recognition of the role that internationalization plays across all aspects of institutional activity. How to support these activities then becomes a matter of institutional preference.

Conclusion: getting real about internationalization

Some might consider that placing internationalization at the service of institutional strategic planning is to return it to a second-tier status from which it has only recently emerged. We argue the exact opposite. Indeed, at a time of increasing nationalism, when concerns around identity, immigration, and economic protectionism have led certain countries to adopt policies that bring into question the very concept of internationalization in higher education as it has come to be understood, we feel that this approach actually strengthens internationalization.

Internationalization cannot be viewed solely as an income-generating activity detached from the wider activities of, and the rationale for, higher education institutions. To do so is to place internationalization at the mercy of economic fluctuations that might lead to its sudden demise, just as easily as the favorable economic and political circumstances of the last three decades have led to its unprecedented growth.

At this time of uncertainty, it is more important than ever to restore internationalization to its rightful place as a cross-functional dimension of institutional activities. From there, it not only has the capacity to enhance quality, but it can also act as a gear-shift in the engine of change for institutional growth and renewal that the institutional strategic plan represents. In turn, placing internationalization within the wider context of the institutional strategic plan and defining practical actions in support of other activities gives real meaning to internationalization, enhancing its role and value and embedding it more securely in the warp and weft of institutional life.

Note

1 The terms 'warp' and 'weft' are used in the production of textiles, specifically those that are woven. In the literal sense, they are the technical terms for the two types of thread used to create a finished woven product. The warp is the tightly stretched lengthwise core of a fabric, while the weft is woven between the warp threads to create various patterns. www.wisegeek.org/what-are-warp-and-weft.htm

References

Arum, S., & van de Water, J. (1992). The need for a definition of international education in U.S. universities. In C. Klasek (Ed.), *Bridges to the Futures: Strategies for Internationalizing Higher Education* (pp. 191–203). Carbondale, IL: Association of International Education Administrators.

Beelen, J., & Jones, E. (2015). Redefining internationalisation at home. In A. Curaj, L. Matei, R. Pricopie, J. Salmi, & P. Scott (Eds.), *The European Higher Education Area: Between Critical Reflections and Future Policies* (pp. 59–72). New York: Springer.

Brandenburg, U. and de Wit, H. (2011) Has international education lost its way? *Chronicle of Higher Education*, November 15. Retrieved from www.chronicle.com/blogs/worldwise/has-international-education-lost-its-way/28891

Crowther, P., Joris, M., Otten, M., Nilsson, B., Teekens, H., & Wächter, B. (2000). *Internationalisation at Home: A Position Paper*. Amsterdam: EAIE.

Davies, J. L. (1995). University strategies for internationalisation in different institutional and cultural settings: a conceptual framework. In P. Blok (Ed.), *Policy and Policy Implementation and Internationalisation of Higher Education* (pp. 3–18) (EAIE Occasional Paper, No. 8). Amsterdam: EAIE.

de Wit, H. (2002). *Internationalization of Higher Education in the United States of America and Europe: A Historical, Comparative, and Conceptual Analysis*. Westport, CT: Greenwood Press.

de Wit, H., Hunter, F., Howard, L., & Egron Polak, E. (2015). *Internationalisation of Higher Education*. European Parliament. Brussels: Directorate-General for Internal Policies.

Fielden, J. (2012). The management of internationalisation in universities. *Internationa lisation of European Higher Education. An EUA/ACA Handbook*. Retrieved from www.handbook-internationalisation.com/en/handbuch/gliederung/#/Beitragsdetailansicht/164/398/The-Management-of-Internationalisation-in-Universities

Hudzik, J. K. (2011). *Comprehensive Internationalization: From Concept to Action*. Washington, DC: NAFSA: Association of International Educators.

Huisman, J. (2013). The need for more emphasis on intra-organisational dynamics in strategic management of internationalisation. In H. de Wit, F. Hunter, L. Johnson, & H. G. van Liempd, *Possible Futures: The Next 25 Years of the Internationalisation of Higher Education* (pp. 1–27). Amsterdam: EAIE.

Knight, J. (1994). *Internationalization: Elements and Checkpoints* (CBIE Research, No. 7). Ottawa: Canadian Bureau for International Education (CBIE).

Knight, J. (2004). Internationalization remodelled: definition, approaches and rationales. *Journal of Studies in International Education*, 8(1), 5–31.

Leask, B. (2015). *Internationalizing the Curriculum*. London: Routledge.

McNay, I. (2012). *Leading Strategic Change in Higher Education - closing the implementation gap*. Leadership and Governance in Higher Education – Handbook for Decision-Makers and Administrators, 4. Berlin: Raabe Academic Publishers.

Middlehurst, R. (2008). Developing institutional internationalisation policies and strategies: an overview of key issues. In M. Gaebel, L. Purser, B. Wachter, & EAIE (eds.), *Internationalisation of European Higher Education*. Berlin: Dr. Josef Raabe Verlag.

Middlehurst, R., & Woodfield, S. (2007). *Responding to the Internationalisation Agenda: Implications for Institutional Strategy*. York, UK: Higher Education Academy.

Nolan, R., & Hunter, F. (2012). Institutional strategies and international programs: learning from experiences of change. In D. Deardorff, H. de Wit, J. Hale, & T. Adams, *The SAGE Handbook of International Higher Education* (pp. 131–146). Thousand Oaks, CA: SAGE Publications.

Rumbley, L. (Ed.). (2015). Internationalisation at home. *2015 Winter Forum*. Amsterdam: EAIE.

Rumbley, L. (Ed.). (2016). The new international officer. *2016 Winter Forum*. Amsterdam: EAIE.

Taylor, J. (2012). *Structuring Internationalisation: The Role of the International Office. Internationalisation of European Higher Education, An EUA/ACA Handbook.* Berlin: Dr. Josef Raabe Verlag.

van der Wende, M. (1997). Missing links: the relationship between national policies for internationalisation and those for higher education in general. In T. Kalvermark & M. van der Wende (Eds.). *National Policies for the Internationalisation of Higher Education in Europe* (pp. 10–31). Stockholm: Hogskoleverket Studies, National Agency for Higher Education.

Chapter 16

Rearticulating the publicness of higher education in a global world

Hiro Saito

Over the past two decades, globalization has prompted strategic responses from many universities around the world. To name but a few, these responses include: the establishment of overseas offices to expand pools of applicants, the development of summer programs targeting foreign students, and efforts to break into and climb up world university rankings. Today, more and more universities are intensifying these internationalization efforts in pursuit of profit and prestige, as they are increasingly subjected to economic and status competition in the emerging global field of higher education.

At the same time, globalization has created opportunities for policymakers, university leaders, and other stakeholders to critically rethink the missions and policies of universities. What roles can, and should, universities play in the contemporary world facing unprecedented global problems, such as climate change, pandemics, and armed conflicts and terrorism? How should curricula be revised to better prepare students for meeting these challenges of globalization? What kinds of international collaboration are possible and desirable for producing innovative research on those global problems – where the goals are ultimately solutions, rather than profits or prestige? By posing these questions, universities can respond, not only strategically but also critically, to globalization.

Nevertheless, these critical questions have yet to be fully examined in the burgeoning research field of internationalization of higher education (IHE). Apart from a few recent exceptions (de Wit, Hunter, Howard, & Egron-Polak, 2015; Marginson, 2016), IHE research has so far focused on the strategic responses of universities, because economic and status competition preoccupies policymakers, university leaders, and other stakeholders, pushing aside critical questions regarding the implications of internationalization for citizens and societies. To expand the scope of IHE research to illuminate the critical questions, in this brief chapter I propose a synthesis of IHE research with another growing research field, that of public engagement (PE) in higher education.

Specifically, I argue that PE research enables IHE researchers to examine the critical responses of universities as conterminous with the problem of how to rearticulate universities' publicness – both as providers of public goods in the form of knowledge and as loci of critical debates in public spheres – in response to the globalization of the economy, governance, human and cultural flows, and social problems, among many other things. This synthesis of IHE and PE research also offers insights into how various stakeholders of higher education might be able to work around the negative effects of the internationalization of higher education – most notably the isomorphism promoted by world university rankings – and redefine the missions and policies of universities at global, national, and local levels.

Economic and status competition in the emerging global field

Simply put, IHE research examines a variety of organizational responses of universities in an institutional environment that has become increasingly global. These organizational responses aim to internationalize teaching, research, and other components of universities that used to be firmly grounded in the nation-state (Altbach, 2016). The ongoing process of internationalization includes: the expansion of study abroad programs; the creation of overseas branch campuses and study centers; the establishment of twinning, double, and joint degree programs across national borders; faculty exchange and research collaboration with overseas partner universities – among many other activities that take the globe, rather than the nation-state, as a primary frame of reference (Knight, 2006).

IHE research has shown that these internationalization efforts on the part of universities have been largely driven by competition for profit and prestige. First, profit has become a key imperative for universities around the world since the 1995 General Agreement on Trade in Services (GATS) officially designated higher education as a tradable service in the global market (Verger, 2009). To be sure, such commercialization of higher education remains uneven across different regions of the world and among different types of higher education institutions; however, the GATS and other trade agreements set in motion the formation of the global market for higher education, in which not only traditional non-profit universities but also new for-profit universities and educational service providers compete for students and their tuition payments (Knight, 2004).

Second, universities also compete for prestige as a "positional good" (Marginson, 2006). For a long time, a higher education system was organized hierarchically within each country – for example, Cambridge and Oxford in England, the Ivy League schools in the United States, and national universities in Asia were regarded as the most prestigious in their respective countries because these universities were associated with ruling national elites. Given the advancement of communication technologies and the growth of transnational flows of students, however, the reputations of universities began to travel across national borders, giving rise to a global, albeit still fragmented, field of competition for prestige. This globalization of status competition then began to accelerate in the 2000s with the emergence of world university rankings (Pusser & Marginson, 2013).

Given that the emerging global field of higher education is driven primarily by the logics of profit and prestige, many universities have adopted strategic orientations toward internationalization. Here, profit and prestige, two forms of capital around which strategic responses of universities are organized, feed into each other: profit allows universities to invest in faculty and facilities to boost their prestige, whereas prestige allows universities to make profit by attracting students, donors, and top researchers with the ability to obtain substantial research funding.

Accordingly, IHE research has focused on the strategic responses of universities and even taken a tone of consultancy, e.g., evaluating "academic excellence," "world-class university" status, and other initiatives by policymakers and university leaders to increase the prestige of their institutions, and offering recommendations on how to successfully implement these initiatives (Altbach & Balán, 2007; Salmi, 2009). To be sure, IHE research has made some critical observations on the internationalization of higher education – for example, how the dominance of English as the de facto lingua franca gives "unfair" advantages to research universities in North America and elsewhere in the English-speaking world, how the global field of economic and status competition reinforces the hegemony of universities in the "West," and how world university rankings exert pressure for "unhealthy" homogenization among higher education institutions (Altbach, 2016; Marope, Wells, & Hazelkorn, 2013; Pusser & Marginson, 2013). Nevertheless, these critical observations remain incipient in the field of IHE research partly because, I suspect, it is difficult for IHE researchers to radically call into question the very object of their study – the internationalization of higher education – upon which their careers depend. In fact, since IHE researchers often take the role of consultant to various stakeholders of higher education, they have played a "performative" role in legitimating the reality of economic and status competition in higher education vis-à-vis the strategic responses of universities.

Rethinking public engagement at the global level

To help IHE research to fully develop critical perspectives, I propose to turn to another growing field of higher education research, that of public engagement (PE). This field began to develop in the early 2000s, as more and more researchers became concerned about the ongoing commercialization and vocationalization of higher education, as witnessed by growing pressure for profit-driven research collaboration with industry and for practical training to prepare students for the job market and the corporate world. This commercialization and vocationalization of higher education was set in motion by the worldwide ascendancy of the knowledge economy, organized around the systematic use of scientific and technological innovations to drive economic growth. Given the emergence of the global knowledge economy, universities began to incorporate the logic of capitalism, restructuring research and teaching activities to produce more private goods and thereby departing from their traditional identity as public institutions (Gumport, 2002; Slaughter & Leslie, 1997). This prompted a significant number of critically minded researchers to reclaim the publicness of higher education by promoting socially engaged scholarship, community-university partnerships, and civic engagement by faculty and students (Chambers & Burkhardt, 2005; Fitzgerald, Burack, & Seifer 2012; Saltmarsh & Hartley, 2011).

Specifically, PE research sees universities as public in a twofold sense: they are producers of knowledge as a public good, and they are loci of public spheres (Burawoy, 2005; Calhoun, 2006; Marginson, 2011). Universities continue to freely share knowledge produced by their faculty with their publics – members of local communities and other citizens – through outreach activities, in spite of the growing pressure for the commercialization of university-based research. Universities also operate as crucial infrastructures of critical and democratic debates on public issues, given their commitment to free thinking and rational discourse. While PE research has so far focused on universities in North America, initiatives to make universities more publicly engaged seem to be gaining momentum in different regions of the world, as evidenced, for example, by the growing membership and activities of the Talloires Network, a transnational coalition of universities committed to incorporating a greater degree of public engagement in teaching and research (Watson, Hollister, Stroud, & Babcock, 2011).

I argue that PE research offers a promising point of departure for fully developing critical perspectives on the internationalization of higher education, for the focus on the publicness of higher education helps IHE researchers shed light on the non-strategic "civic" responses of universities that cannot be subsumed under economic and status competition. Take, for example, the growing practice of "international service learning," defined as:

A *structured academic experience in another country* in which students (a) participate in an organized service activity that addresses identified community needs; (b) *learn from direct interaction and cross-cultural dialogue with others*, and (c) reflect on the *experience* in such a way as to gain further understanding of course content, a deeper understanding of *global and* intercultural issues, a broader appreciation of the *host country* and the discipline, and an enhanced sense of their own responsibilities as citizens, locally and *globally*.

(Bringle & Hatcher, 2010, p. 19; emphasis in original)

International service learning thus synthesizes service learning with study abroad and international education to facilitate students' personal, intellectual, and civic development as members of a globally interconnected world. To be sure, international service learning faces various challenges of its own, most notably the risk of reproducing power relations between the "West" and the rest (Larsen, 2016); however, when carefully planned through collaboration between faculty and students from both sending and receiving countries, international service learning becomes maximally effective, producing a transnational community of learners who are non-strategically committed to changing the world for the better.

Moreover, in the area of research, the growth of faculty exchange and interaction across national borders has expanded the capabilities of universities to collectively study phenomena which are fundamentally global in scope, including but not limited to, climate change, pandemics, armed conflicts and terrorism, and illegal trafficking of humans, drugs, and weapons. To address these global problems, nongovernmental organizations (NGOs) have already formed transnational networks, serving as organizational infrastructures of "global civil society" (Fraser, 2007; Guidry, Kennedy, & Zald, 2000). Importantly, universities are part and parcel of this global civil society; for example, universities produce knowledge of global problems through their international research collaboration and foster public debates at the global level through international symposia, seminars, and many other discursive occasions open to the public (Kennedy, 2015). Although these transnational initiatives may be driven by the strategic orientation of universities to enhance their international reputations, they also serve as vehicles for individual faculty members and professional associations to express their civic concerns and facilitate the formation of transnational public spheres in tackling global problems (Saito, 2015b).

In sum, international service learning and international research collaboration on global problems offer two prime examples of universities' non-strategic civic responses to globalization. These responses are in no small part motivated by critically minded university leaders, faculty, and other stakeholders who wish to counteract the dominant trends in the internationalization of higher education driven by economic and status competition. Indeed, I suggest that the internationalization of higher education is essentially two-pronged: increased international flows and connections among students and faculty create opportunities for universities not only to pursue profit and prestige, but also to contribute to the public good at the global level.

How to work around negative effects of internationalization

Thus, PE research can foreground the non-strategic civic responses of universities, but it is only the first step in fully developing critical perspectives on the internationalization of higher education. The next and more important step is to rearticulate the publicness of higher education not only at the global level, but also at national and local levels. Even though IHE researchers speak of the importance of a "glonacal" approach (Marginson & Rhoades, 2002), their research focuses on the global-national – the nexus that, by definition, pertains to "internationalization" – and downplays the national-local and local-global. Nevertheless, rethinking the publicness of higher education at the national-local and local-global nexuses is indispensable for illuminating a full range of critical responses to globalization by universities.

First, the focus on the national-local nexus helps to shift the unit of analysis from the university to the higher education system (Hazelkorn, 2015). This shift is crucial in critiquing the economic and status competition that pits one university against another. In particular, world university rankings produce isomorphic effects forcing higher education institutions to emulate the unidimensionally defined world-class research university (Marope, Wells, & Hazelkorn, 2013). This unidimensional status competition at the global level risks harming entire ecosystems of higher education in different countries that have developed within unique historical, socioeconomic, political, and cultural contexts. In turn, within each national ecosystem of higher education, different types of higher education institutions, ranging from nationally well-known research universities to locally embedded community colleges, serve different pools of students whose needs vary according to their socioeconomic status and geographical location, among other factors. The focus on the national-local nexus thus prompts policymakers, university leaders, and other stakeholders to think critically about how to preserve an ecosystem of higher education – and specifically, internal heterogeneity that makes the system adaptive and resilient – against isomorphic effects exerted by the internationalization of higher education (Altbach, Reisberg, & de Wit, 2017).

Second, the focus on the local-global nexus allows various stakeholders of higher education to consider multiple levels of publicness of their institutions. No matter how much the activities of universities become internationalized, universities cannot but be physically embedded in certain geographical spaces. This is an important reminder for the most internationalized, often world-class, universities. Does internationalization have to be pursued at the expense of public engagement at the local level? How can, and should, world-class universities balance, and even meaningfully integrate, their public engagement at the local and global levels? By contrast, universities at the other end of the spectrum, such as small to midsize universities in rural areas, face different questions. Internationalization is rightly a low priority for them, and the local is the most important level of their public engagement. Nevertheless, even rural areas in many countries today are affected by economic and political globalization; for example, foreign migrant workers stay in rural towns for seasonal farming and other temporary jobs, and regime changes abroad and international conflicts generate negative externalities on local businesses and municipalities. Attention to the local-global nexus thus helps leaders and faculty at these universities critically reflect on how they can best serve their local publics, including temporary residents of foreign origin, when their locales are increasingly penetrated by the global.

To fully advance this second step in developing critical perspectives on the internationalization of higher education, however, policymakers, university leaders, and other stakeholders in non-English-speaking countries face particularly difficult challenges created by the dominance of English as the de facto lingua franca. English has achieved this dominant status due to the legacy of British imperialism and the hegemony of the United States, reinforced by world university rankings that privilege English-language publications (Altbach, 2016;

Marginson, 2006). Here, the dominance of English can undermine the public engagement of universities in non-English-speaking countries at the national and local levels, where ongoing debates on public issues are conducted in non-English native languages. For example, more and more universities in East Asia have been pushing their faculty members to publish in internationally recognized English-language journals and to teach in English, so that they can climb up in world university rankings (Ishikawa, 2016). This effectively discourages faculty members from speaking to their local and national publics who communicate in non-English native languages.

Thus, it is crucial to keep in mind the publicness of universities at multiple levels – global, national, and local – because doing so helps various stakeholders of higher education in non-English-speaking countries to articulate critical responses to the isomorphic effects of the internationalization of higher education. In particular, the focus on the national-local and local-global nexuses, I suggest, can help different national ecosystems of higher education, and different types of higher education institutions within each ecosystem, to define and defend their unique missions and policies in terms of their distinct public contributions.

Conclusion

In this brief chapter, I have proposed a synthesis of IHE and PE research to develop critical perspectives on the internationalization of higher education. Paying attention to public engagement allows IHE researchers to foreground the non-strategic civic responses of universities to globalization, such as international service learning and research collaboration, and to critically examine the "dark side" of the internationalization of higher education – namely, economic and status competition and resultant isomorphism, driven by the emergence of the global knowledge economy and world university rankings. Specifically, I have suggested that IHE researchers focus on the national-local and local-global nexuses to illuminate the publicness of higher education, not only at the global level but also at the national and local levels. By so doing, IHE researchers can help policymakers, university leaders, and other stakeholders of higher education to reimagine the global field of higher education as a set of overlapping ecosystems, where heterogeneous institutions respond to the needs of their distinct publics, rather than as a unidimensional hierarchy based on zero-sum competition for profit and prestige.

In conclusion, to consolidate critical perspectives on the internationalization of higher education vis-à-vis its pubic implications, I suggest that IHE researchers take a reflexive look at their own performative role in shaping the practices and institutions of higher education: they may think that they simply describe and explain what is happening to the field of higher education, but they are in fact shaping the field by providing policymakers, university leaders, and other stakeholders with conceptual models and empirical findings as rationales for justifying their decisions (cf. Saito, 2015a). Once IHE researchers fully recognize their performative involvement in the field of higher education, they can then begin to rethink and transform their own practices of research, teaching, and consultancy to intervene in the reality of the internationalization of higher education. In short, given the feedback loop between theory and practice, future generations of IHE researchers, collectively promoting critical perspectives, have a chance to reorient the practices of the internationalization of higher education to the question of how higher education institutions can best serve their distinct publics in an increasingly global world.

References

Altbach, P. G. (2016). *Global Perspectives on Higher Education*. Baltimore, MD: Johns Hopkins University Press.

Altbach, P. G., & Balán, J. (2007). *World Class Worldwide: Transforming Research Universities in Asia and Latin America*. Baltimore, MD: Johns Hopkins University Press.

Altbach, P. G., Reisberg, L., & de Wit, H. (2017). *Responding to Massification: Differentiation in Postsecondary Education Worldwide*. Hamburg: Körber Foundation.

Bringle, R. G., & Hatcher, J. A. (2012). International service learning. In R. G. Bringle, J. A. Hatcher, & S. G. Jones (Eds.), *International Service learning: Conceptual Frameworks and Research* (pp. 3–28). Sterling, VA: Stylus Publishing.

Burawoy, M. (2005). For public sociology. *American Sociological Review, 70*(1), 4–28.

Calhoun, C. (2006). The university and the public good. *Thesis Eleven, 84*(1), 7–43.

Chambers, A. C., & Burkhardt, J. C. (Eds.). (2005). *Higher Education for the Public Good: Emerging Voices from a National Movement*. San Francisco: John Wiley & Sons, Inc.

de Wit, H., Hunter, F., Howard, L., & Egron-Polak, E. (2015). *Internationalisation of Higher Education*. Brussels: European Union.

Fitzgerald, H., Burack, C., & Seifer, S. D. (Eds.). (2012). *Transformations in Higher Education: Handbook of Engaged Scholarship: Contemporary Landscapes, Future Directions, Vol. 1, Institutional Change*. East Lansing: Michigan State University Press.

Fraser, N. (2009). *Scales of Justice: Reimagining Political Space in a Globalizing World*. New York: Columbia University Press.

Guidry, J., Kennedy, M., & Zald, M. (Eds.). (2000). *Globalizations and Social Movements: Culture, Power, and the Transnational Public Sphere*. Ann Arbor: University of Michigan Press.

Gumport, P. J. (2002). Universities and knowledge: restructuring the city of intellect. In Brint, S. (Ed.) *The Future of the City of Intellect: The Changing American University* (pp. 47–81). Stanford, CA: Stanford University Press.

Hazelkorn, E. (2015). *Rankings and the Reshaping of Higher Education: The Battle for World-Class Excellence*. New York: Palgrave Macmillan.

Ishikawa, M. (Ed.). (2016). *Sekai daigaku ranking to chi no joretsuka: daigaku hyōka to kokusai kyōsō wo tou [World University Rankings and Hierarchization of Knowledges: Questioning Evaluation of Universities and International Competition]*. Kyoto: Kyoto University Press.

Kennedy, M. (2015). *Globalizing Knowledge: Intellectuals, Universities, and Publics in Transformation*. Stanford, CA: Stanford University Press.

Knight, J. (2004). Internationalization remodeled: definition, approaches, and rationales. *Journal of Studies in International Education, 8*(1), 5–31.

Knight, J. (2006). *Higher Education Crossing Borders: A Guide to the Implications of the General Agreement on Trade in Services (GATS) for Cross-Border Education*. Paris: UNESCO.

Larsen, M. (Ed.) (2016). *International Service Learning: Engaging Host Communities*. New York: Routledge.

Marginson, S. (2006). Dynamics of national and global competition in higher education. *Higher Education, 52*(1), 1–39.

Marginson, S. (2011). Higher education and public good. *Higher Education Quarterly, 65*(4), 411–433.

Marginson, S. (2016). *Higher Education and the Common Good*. Melbourne: Melbourne University Publishing.

Marginson, S., & Rhoades, G. (2002). Beyond national states, markets, and systems of higher education: a glonacal agency heuristic. *Higher Education, 43*(3), 281–309.

Marope, P. T. M., Wells, P. J., & Hazelkorn, E. (Eds.) (2013). *Rankings and Accountability in Higher Education: Uses and Misuses*. Paris: UNESCO.

Pusser, B., & Marginson, S. (2013). University rankings in critical perspective. *Journal of Higher Education, 84*(4), 544–568.

Saito, H. (2015a). Cosmopolitics: towards a new articulation of politics, science and critique. *British Journal of Sociology, 66*(3), 441–459.

Saito, H. (2015b). The possibility of global public sociology. *ISA eSymposium for Sociology, 5*(3). Retrieved from www.sagepub.net/isa/resources/ebulletin_pdf/EBul-HiroSaito-Dec2015.pdf

Salmi, J. (2009). *The Challenge of Establishing World-Class Universities*. Washington DC: World Bank Publications.

Saltmarsh, J., & Hartley, M. (Eds.). (2011). *"To Serve a Larger Purpose": Engagement for Democracy and the Transformation of Higher Education*. Philadelphia, PA: Temple University Press.

Slaughter, S., & Leslie, L. L. (1997). *Academic Capitalism: Politics, Policies, and the Entrepreneurial University*, Baltimore, MD: Johns Hopkins University Press.

Verger, A. (2009). *WTO/GATS and the Global Politics of Higher Education*. London: Routledge.

Watson, D., Hollister, R., Stroud, S. E., & Babcock, E. (2011). *The Engaged University: International Perspectives on Civic Engagement*. New York: Routledge.

Chapter 17

Providing refugees with access to online education

A new frontier for the internationalization agenda

Thomas Greenaway

Contextualization

The United Nations High Commissioner for Refugees (UNHCR) reported in 2017 that there were 65.3 million "persons of concern" worldwide, and 21.3 million of these were refugees (UNHCR, 2017). These figures have doubled in the last decade (UNHCR, 2014). The majority of refugees have fled Somalia, Afghanistan, and Syria, and for the most part are hosted by neighboring countries (Ethiopia, Pakistan, Turkey, Lebanon, Jordan, and Iran), themselves some of the world's poorest countries, without resources to provide refugees with amenities beyond their immediate needs (UNHCR, 2016). The number of "university-qualified" refugees worldwide is not known. There are estimates that there are 70,000 such Syrian refugees in Lebanon, 20,000–30,000 in Turkey, and some 25,000 in Jordan (Hahn, 2014; Watenpaugh, Fricke, & King, 2014; Watenpaugh, Fricke, King, Gratien, & Yilmaz, 2014). However, these figures could have increased after these estimates were published.

The current situation for refugees regarding access to higher education

The need for refugees to gain access to higher education is incredibly important. This is true both for their own personal development and psychological wellbeing (Crea, 2016), as well as for the future of the societies that they will live in; whether as permanent residents in their host country or as returnees to their country of origin. Butler (2015) has warned of the creation of a "lost generation" of young people who will not have the skills necessary to contribute and sustain a civil society in whichever country they eventually reside. Yet, in spite of the recognized importance of educating refugees, only 1 percent of refugees have access to higher education (Global Education Monitoring Report, 2016). Furthermore, until recently the subject of refugee education has featured little in the discourse on the internationalization of education.[1]

Barriers to access

The barriers that refugees face regarding access to higher education are considerable. The first is that of physical location, as refugees may be based somewhere that does not have an institution of higher learning within feasible distance. Second, they may have a history of disrupted education, where they may not have either the requisite academic skills or experience even they have the will to pursue an education. Third, they may lack the documentation to prove that they are qualified to study. Finances can also be a problem. For example, in Lebanon the fees for higher education are much higher than in Syria, making enrollment much more difficult for refugees who have limited (or no) means of financing their study (Watenpaugh, Fricke, & King, 2014). Finally, there can be linguistic challenges if the refugee is now residing in a country where they are not proficient in the language of instruction used in the local universities.

Recognizing these barriers for access, Kiron Open Higher Education (KOHE) and Jesuit Worldwide Learning: Higher Education at the Margins (JWL), amongst others (see Table 17.1), have sought to provide refugees with access to higher education through online courses. This form of education aims to circumvent the traditional barriers for education listed above. However, as a form of distance learning, online higher education has its own impediments, not least a high attrition rate (as discussed below). Refugees also have distinct needs as learners that providers must be aware of and be willing to accommodate. Before looking specifically at the work of KOHE and JWL, this chapter presents research on the challenges that regular students encounter with distance learning, noting that studies focusing on refugees and distance learning are still sparse. This is followed by a consideration of the challenges that refugees encounter while studying a higher education course.

The challenges of online education

There are several benefits of online education. It provides students with the opportunity to access the same content multiple times. It allows for flexible learning, such that students can often choose their own study times. It is not location-specific, so, theoretically, a student can be anywhere in the world, provided they have access to the internet for their study (Welsh & Dragusin, 2013). However, online courses, and particularly massive open online courses (MOOCs), also have low retention rates. Studies have shown that the completion rate for a MOOC can range from 5 percent to 15 percent of the students who initially enroll (Jordan, 2015; Onah, Sinclair, & Boyatt, 2014).

Qualitative studies into the possible causes of low retention rates by Chung (2015) and Khalil and Ebner (2014) found that students reported several impediments to the completion of their online courses. These included lack of time, low motivation, feelings of isolation from the learner community, and a lack of interactivity within the online courses. Students also mentioned hidden costs, limited access to technology, and insufficient background knowledge as reasons for not completing courses. Hidden costs could be particularly important for refugee students studying online (e.g., payment for certain textbooks or computer software), because they may not have the financial support or library resources that institution-based students would likely have.

Some work has been carried out by Moser-Mercer (2014) on the subject of refugees completing MOOCs. She found that the students faced three main challenges. One such challenge was technological, in relation to access to the internet and sufficient computer software to complete the course. Contextual difficulties were also relevant, which Moser-Mercer (2014) related to the individual situation of the refugee, and whether they had the time and support (both financial and academic) for their study. Finally, linguistic challenges were identified; since the students were not proficient in English for academic purposes, they struggled to understand linguistic nuances in the online materials. Crea and McFarland (2015) also found, in a similar context, that refugees who embarked on online education might have restricted resources, which could impose significant limitations on their ability to study.

The final barrier that refugees faced over online learning was accreditation of their work. Although MOOCs have been around since 2008 (Powell, 2013), accreditation has been slow; for example, by 2016 only two universities in the United Kingdom offered MOOCs that were accredited (Havergal, 2016). Table 17.1 (below) shows that each of the organizations providing access to online higher education to refugees relies on partners to accredit the work done by the their students. As will be seen in the case of KOHE, accreditation is not always straightforward.

The additional needs of refugees in higher education

In addition to the challenges that refugees may confront when undertaking online learning, studying itself may present further difficulties. According to Stevenson and Willott (2010), refugee students at UK universities were likely to need pastoral care, due to the upheaval experienced through leaving one country and then resettling in another. Refugee students have also been found to be more successful if they have strong peer support and social networks, and isolation (which is common in online learning) can lead to students leaving university prematurely. Stevenson and Willott (2010) also found that refugee students had difficulties in adapting to the academic practices required by Western universities. Even if they had prior experience of higher education, it was likely to have involved different cultural contexts and expectations, and they required more targeted support – a finding which was also supported by research on refugee students in the United States (Hirano, 2015). Finance can also be an issue for refugees, who may not have the means to fund their studies. Challenges in this area include knowing whether financial support is available, or how to access it (Gateley, 2015). Finally, and perhaps the most challenging aspect for providers, refugees may be unwilling to seek help for fear of stigmatization, or due to an understandable reluctance to reflect on past experiences (Hannah, 1999; Kaprielian-Churchill, 1996). Clearly, the task of providing online higher education to refugees is complex. The challenges that students face with respect to online learning need to be considered in tandem with the particular needs of refugee students in order to provide a learning environment that successfully empowers such students to complete higher education qualifications.

There are several organizations that are now providing higher education access to refugees internationally through online learning (see Table 17.1). Although relatively modest in size, they have employed some innovative methods in order to reach refugee populations, and have demonstrated new forms of international collaboration within higher education institutions. Below, we will look at what KOHE and JWL have accomplished in higher education provision to populations in post-conflict situations, the limitations of their work, and the challenges that lie ahead.

The case of Kiron Open Higher Education

Kiron Open Higher Education (KOHE)[2] was set up in order to provide refugees with access to free online education through publicly available MOOCs. The name of the organization was inspired by the Greek mythical figure Chiron, a symbol of wisdom and learning. KOHE initially raised money through crowd funding, securing more than €500,000 in its first two months (Startnext, 2016). This enabled it to set up an online platform and to begin recruiting students. KOHE targets refugees, but it does not require its students to prove their refugee status, nor does it require any proof of linguistic proficiency, or to pass a test of academic ability. KOHE offers students access to MOOCs in four subject areas (see Table 17.1). In the KOHE model, students study for two years as Kiron students, before being enrolled with one of 41 academic partners for the final two years, where they are then awarded a bachelor's degree upon successful completion. Academic partners include universities such as Bards College Berlin, Berlin University of Applied Sciences, and RWTH Aachen University.

Advantages of the KOHE model

The KOHE approach has many advantages. It does not require students to provide proof of refugee status; students can begin studying much earlier, whilst applying for asylum. Students also do not need to provide proof of previous educational attainment, so students can begin studying at any time. Since it is providing mostly online content, running costs are lower than those for traditional higher education provision. As such, there is no tuition fee for the online component of the KOHE model. KOHE is inclusive because Kiron students can theoretically study from anywhere, and accepts students who may not yet be officially recognized as refugees. It has potentially unlimited student capacity,

Table 17.1 Main providers of online higher education to refugees (adapted from Ferede, 2016)

Initiative and date launched	Funding	Location(s) of operations	Curriculum/qualifications	Implementation and partners	Students enrolled
Jesuit Worldwide Learning (JWL), 2010	Private donor & Jesuit Refugee Service funds	Jordan, USA, Iraq, Malawi, Chad, Afghanistan, Kenya, Sri Lanka, Myanmar	Diploma of Liberal Studies & Community Service Learning Tracks (CSLTs)	Jesuit colleges and universities worldwide & Regis University in Denver, Colorado (accredits diploma)	1,960 since 2010
InZone, 2010	Privately funded (Foundation North & others)	Dadaab, Kakuma, and Nairobi, Kenya	Certificate in Community Interpreting (Dadaab) & Post-graduate continuing education degree in Humanitarian Interpreting (Kakuma)	Kenyatta University, University of Geneva, & UNIGE/InZone	314
Borderless Higher Education for Refugees, 2013	Public (CIDA) & private funding	Dadaab, Kenya	Teacher training certificates and diplomas; course completion credits can go toward full BA degree	Windle Trust Kenya, UNHCR, WUSC, (University Partners), Kenyatta University Moi University, UBC, & York University	290
Kepler Kiziba, 2015	Ikea Foundation	Kiziba, Rwanda	US degree in Business Communications or Health Management	Government of Rwanda (MIDIMAR), ADRA, UNHCR, & Southern New Hampshire University	25 per year
Kiron Open Higher Education (KOHE), 2015	Crowd funding & sponsors	Berlin, Germany but with three other focus countries (France, Turkey, & Jordan)	Bachelor's degree in Business & Economics, Computer Science, Engineering, Social Sciences	MOOC platforms including Coursera, edX, iversity, & openHPI 41 academic partners	2,300+ since 2015

since its courses are based online and there is no need for a physical space for its students to study. KOHE also offers support for its students in the form of volunteer study buddies, counseling services, language courses, study hubs, and career services. KOHE has been very successful in recruitment, with more than 2,300 students using its platform since 2015.

Limitations of the KOHE model

For students who wish to study at a traditional university, KOHE's solution may not be ideal, as students must wait for at least two years before they can be accepted at a partner institution. Students who wish to study with KOHE also need to have access to a computer and the internet. Accreditation is a further limitation for KOHE, as the work done by students online is not automatically accredited. Instead, KOHE relies on the agreements of the Lisbon Convention, whereby up to 50 percent of the credits of a degree can be acquired outside of the university that ultimately awards the degree. These externally earned credits can fall under the category of "recognition of prior learning," as long as it is determined that the prior learning is related to the degree content. However, this only applies to institutions within the European Union (EU) and other collaborating countries (de Bruin, 2016), so refugees based outside of a country signed up to the Convention may not be able to receive this recognition of their prior learning. The first two years of online learning are therefore reliant on the interpretation of the partner university as to whether they are appropriate to the course and rigorous enough to be counted as prior learning. KOHE relies on either certificates of completion from MOOC providers (such as Coursera and edX), or the willingness of the partner university to provide an examination that allows the student to prove he or she has mastered the relevant course content. The success of KOHE's students is therefore reliant on the flexibility of partner universities to accept a non-traditional route into higher education. In this respect, KOHE does have the advantage of support from the European Commission, which actively encourages nation-level government ministers responsible for higher education to increase the participation and completion rates of under-represented groups across Europe through ensuring the provision of alternative routes into higher education (European Commission, EACEA, & Eurydice, 2015).

Current and future challenges for KOHE

In the first two recruitment cycles since its inception, KOHE had similar retention rates to those of other MOOC providers, with approximately 10 percent of students completing courses on the Kiron platform (Greenaway, Hillers, & Rampelt, 2016). Since then, KOHE's support networks have become more active, and its retention rates are improving. That said, with KOHE's emphasis on MOOCs, achieving high retention rates will continue to be a challenge. Further challenges for KOHE include securing funding. It is currently crowd-funded, which could be difficult to sustain, with only some government funding. Since part of its founding ethos is to offer its services to students for free, KOHE requires consistent external funding sources. KOHE also relies on a large number of volunteers who work as study buddies and help with other organizational services. Retaining and recruiting volunteers will also be a challenge. The major challenge for KOHE, though, is in the transfer of its students to its partner universities. Since the MOOCs are not specifically tailored to the European Credit Transfer and Accumulation System (ECTS, the credits awarded by universities across the EU and other collaborating countries for the completion of courses within a higher education institution), it falls to the partner institution to run its own assessment of the value of the MOOCs the student has completed. This could be problematic for the student if the university decides that the prior study is not sufficient to enroll in the institution.

The case of Jesuit Worldwide Learning

Jesuit Worldwide Learning (JWL)[3] has a model of online higher education provision that is different from that of KOHE. JWL sets up small learning centers at select refugee sites where students can study (as of writing there are nine in total worldwide). At these centers, the students work to complete a liberal arts degree through online modules accredited by Regis University, or they follow Community Service Learning Tracks (CSLTs). The students are provided with access to computers to study for the courses. They are also given learning support by an on-site tutor, as well as access to other learning materials. As part of their study, the students collaborate with JWL students from other study centers in different parts of the world. JWL also provides places in its programs for non-refugee residents in the host community, recognizing that these individuals may also have limited access to higher education. The operation by JWL of many satellite campuses provides higher education access to some of the most impoverished parts of the world.

Strengths of the JWL model

JWL has much to recommend itself as a transferable and scalable model for providing access to online higher education to a highly disadvantaged demographic. The initiative is able to offer an accredited diploma course to its students, with a wide range of study tracks. Considering the number of degrees it has awarded, it has helped more refugee students than any other comparable organization. The students can either begin study for the degree directly, or take an academic and language skills course in advance to prepare them for the demands of the degree. The student community at each center, and the academic on-site support, prevent the students from feeling isolated. At the same time, the links to other JWL learning communities create opportunities for intercultural learning.

Limitations of the JWL model

Access to JWL is based on location. If a refugee is physically located at a place where JWL has a learning center, then there is access. In addition, despite courses being online, they are only accessible via the JWL learning centers. This excludes many refugees who are not at a location where there is a learning center. Since JWL provides the technology to the students, it has limited capacity based on its resources. The security of the site is also requisite for a learning center. In 2014, JWL had to close its learning site in Aleppo, Syria, because of the escalating conflict in and around the city. As the JWL model depends on these learning sites, the geopolitical fragility of specific locations can prevent it from successfully providing sustained access to higher education for its students.

Current and future challenges for the JWL model

The three pillars of JWL's project are sustainability, transferability, and scalability. In terms of transferability, the skills and qualifications that the students earn through JWL should be transferable to other contexts. The liberal arts degree provides skills and knowledge that are transferable to a professional context, such as writing, communication, and mathematics. At the same time, the CSLTs, which are co-developed with the refugees and members of the host community, are immediately applicable to the local context. However, in terms of sustainability and scalability, JWL faces challenges similar to those of KOHE, such as securing external funding, and recruiting and retaining volunteers. The scalability of JWL's model depends on the resources it has available (particularly financial support) in order to be set up at more locations, or to expand its existing learning centers.

Conclusion

This chapter has considered the current educational challenges faced by refugees worldwide, the factors that may limit the ability of refugee students to pursue higher education, and the potential challenges inherent in online education. It then explored the cases of KOHE and JWL, which offer innovative examples of what can be done to address the crucial need for refugee populations to gain access to higher education. Both initiatives have key strengths. They provide access and make real efforts to cater to the needs of their students, which can range from study support to access to technology. At the same time, both are constrained in what they can do, and have limitations on the access to online education they can effectively provide and the number of refugee students they can reach.

KOHE and JWL have shown that they are willing to use new technology and resources in order to meet the needs of refugees who wish to pursue higher education. These examples include breaking away from traditional higher education models of funding, and bringing the campus to the students. However, these two initiatives still rely on accreditation from traditional higher education providers, and their future is to some extent reliant on the support of these more established institutions. Nevertheless, KOHE and JWL are creating new paths and challenging existing frameworks of internationalization. They provide educational access to some of the most marginalized groups in the world. Through international collaboration and technological innovations, these and similar initiatives are transforming the lives of refugees, and encouraging a reevaluation of what we consider to be internationalization in higher education.

Notes

1 See initiatives such as NOKUT (www.universityworldnews.com/article.php?story= 20160401150619862) and recent conference tracks on refugees in higher education (www.eaie.org/blog/welcome-eaie-liverpool-2016/).
2 For more information on KOHE, see https://kiron.ngo
3 For more information on JWL, see www.jwl.org

References

Butler, D. (2015). Lost generation looms as refugees miss university. *Nature*, *525*(7570), 433–434.

Chung, L.-Y. (2015). Exploring the effectiveness of self-regulated learning in massive open online courses on non-native English speakers. *International Journal of Distance Education Technologies*, *13*(3), 61–73. doi:10.4018/IJDET.2015070105

Crea, T. M. (2016). Refugee higher education: contextual challenges and implications for program design, delivery, and accompaniment. *International Journal of Educational Development*, *46*, 12–22.

Crea, T. M., & McFarland, M. (2015). Higher education for refugees: lessons from a 4-year pilot project. *International Review of Education*, *61*(2), 235–245. doi:10.1007/s11159-015-9484-y

de Bruin, L. (2016). *The European Recognition Manual for Higher Education Institutions: Practical Guidelines for Credential Evaluators and Admissions Officers to Provide Fair and Flexible Recognition of Foreign Degrees and Studies Abroad*. The Hague, The Netherlands: EP-Nuffic. Retrieved from http://eurorecognition.eu/Manual/EAR HEI.pdf

European Commission, EACEA, & Eurydice. (2015). *The European Higher Education Area in 2015: Bologna Process Implementation Report*. Retrieved from http://eacea.ec.europa.eu/education/eurydice/documents/thematic_reports/182EN.pdf

Ferede, M. K. (2016). Virtually educated: the case for and conundrum of online higher education for refugees. *World Education Blog*. Retrieved from https://gemreportunesco.wordpress.com/2016/05/24/virtually-educated-the-case-for-and-conundrum-of-online-higher-education-for-refugees/

Gateley, E. D. (2015). A policy of vulnerability or agency? Refugee young people's opportunities in accessing further and higher education in the UK. *Compare: A Journal of Comparative and International Education*, *45*(1), 26–46.

Global Education Monitoring Report. (2016). *No More Excuses: Provide Education to All Forcibly Displaced People*. Paris, France: UNESCO. Retrieved from http://unesdoc.unesco.org/images/0024/002448/244847E.pdf

Greenaway, T., Hillers, L., & Rampelt, F. (2016). *Can MOOCs Be a Model for Providing Quality Higher Education to Refugees? Lessons From the First Experiment.* Paper presented at the European Conference on Education, Brighton, UK.

Hahn, J. (2014). *Commission Implementing Decision of 4.12.2014: On the 2014 Special Measure in Favour of Jordan for the Syria Crisis to be Financed From the General Budget of the European Union.* Retrieved from https://ec.europa.eu/neighbourhood-enlarge ment/sites/near/files/neighbourhood/pdf/key-documents/sm-2014-jordan-syria-crisis-financing-commission-decision-20141204.pdf

Hannah, J. (1999). Refugee students at college and university: improving access and support. *International Review of Education, 45*(2), 153–166.

Havergal, C. (2016). FutureLearn launches first MOOCs offering academic credits: Leeds and OU programmes signal significant change in online platform's pricing structure. *Times Higher Education.* Retrieved from www.timeshighereducation.com/news/futurelearn-launches-first-moocs-offering-academic-credits

Hirano, E. (2015). "I read, I don't understand": refugees coping with academic reading. *ELT Journal, 69*(2), 178–187.

Jordan, K. (2015). *MOOC Completion Rates: The Data.* Retrieved from www.katyjordan.com/MOOCproject.html

Kaprielian-Churchill, I. (1996). Refugees and education in Canadian schools. *International Review of Education, 42*(4), 349–365.

Khalil, H., & Ebner, M. (2014). *MOOCs Completion Rates and Possible Methods to Improve Retention – A Literature Review.* Paper presented at the World Conference on Educational Multimedia, Hypermedia and Telecommunications, Chesapeake, VA.

Moser-Mercer, B. (2014). *MOOCs in Fragile Contexts.* Paper presented at the European MOOCs Stakeholders Summit, École Polytechnique Fédérale de Lausanne, France.

Onah, D. F. O., Sinclair, J., & Boyatt, R. (2014). *Dropout Rates of Massive Open Online Courses: Behavioural Patterns.* Paper presented at the 6th International Conference on Education and New Learning Technologies, Barcelona, Spain.

Powell, L. Y. a. S. (2013). *MOOCs and Open Education: Implications for Higher Education: A White Paper.* Retrieved from http://publications.cetis.ac.uk/2013/667

Startnext. (2016). *Kiron University.* Retrieved from www.startnext.com/en/kironuniversity

Stevenson, J., & Willott, J. (2010). Refugees: home students with international needs. In E. Jones (Ed.), *Internationalisation and the Student Voice* (pp. 193–202). Abingdon, UK: Routledge.

UNHCR. (2014). *DAFI 2014 Annual Report.* Retrieved from www.unhcr.org/uk/568bd4a59.html

UNHCR. (2016). *Mid-Year Statistics.* Retrieved from http://popstats.unhcr.org/en/overview-_ga=1.1490737.1452783218

UNHCR. (2017). *Figures at a Glance.* Retrieved from www.unhcr.org/uk/figures-at-a-glance.html

Watenpaugh, K. D., Fricke, A. L., & King, J. R. (2014). *The War Follows Them: Syrian University Students and Scholars in Lebanon.* Retrieved from www.scholarrescuefund.org/sites/default/files/pdf-articles/the-war-follows-them-syrian-university-students-scholars-in-lebanon.pdf - search=war%20follows%20them

Watenpaugh, K. D., Fricke, A. L., King, J. R., Gratien, C., & Yilmaz, S. i. (2014). *We Will Stop Here and Go No Further: Syrian University Students and Scholars in Turkey.* Retrieved from www.iie.org/Research-and-Publications/Publications-and-Reports/ IIE-Bookstore/We-Will-Stop-Here-And-Go-No-Further-Syrian-University-Students- And-Scholars-In-Turkey

Welsh, D. H., & Dragusin, M. (2013). The new generation of massive open online course (MOOCS) and entrepreneurship education. *Small Business Institute Journal, 9*(1), 51–65.

Chapter 18

Internationalization, southern diplomacy, and national emancipation in Brazilian higher education

Susanne Ress

Internationalization is high on the agenda of national governments, international organizations, and institutions of higher education (Altbach, 2015). The paradigm and related policies have thus received widespread attention from scholars in the field of comparative and international education. Scholars commonly examine internationalization within frameworks of globalization, the global knowledge economy, corporatization of universities, ways to generate revenue, or student mobility (Altbach, Reisberg, & Rumbley, 2009; Robertson, 2009; Torres, 2011). Policy makers and education practitioners have even become accustomed to thinking about higher education institutions as objects of national pride when a university makes it into the top 100 of an international ranking scheme (Salmi, 2009). It has thus become a familiar gesture to associate a country's internationalization activities with a desired or actually achieved 'external' impression – the mark, so to speak, which national systems of higher education leave on the international scene of innovation and progress.

Meanwhile, comparative and international education scholars interested in policy borrowing and lending have shown that the reasons and rationales to adopt global paradigms, such as internationalization, are often driven by the innate circumstances of a national system (or subsystems, like education) – more specifically, by the desire to push for policy change domestically. Policy makers and others, who seek to influence policy processes, draw on global paradigms to supply the national system with additional meaning, which can serve as sources to legitimize policy change (Steiner-Khamsi, 2002). From this perspective, the question arises as to what 'internal' impressions internationalization leaves on the domestic scene.

This chapter explores some of the links between external and internal impressions by discussing the foreign affairs and domestic objectives of the internationalization of Brazilian higher education under the presidency of Luiz Inácio Lula da Silva (2003–2010). When Lula da Silva took office in 2003, he announced a foreign policy strategy that emphasized the building of stronger international ties between countries of the global south. His government did not intend to denounce the relationship with the 'West' all together, but it stressed that a stronger southern diplomacy would ultimately lead to a multipolar world in which peripheral and semi-peripheral countries like Brazil would be able to steer global politico-economic relations more effectively (Burges, 2005).

Burges (2005) took a unique approach to analyzing Brazilian foreign policy under the Lula da Silva government, making sense of it through a postcolonial lens. He argued that Lula da Silva continued the foreign policy of his predecessor Henrique Fernando Cardoso (1995–2003), who sought to reverse Brazil's economic dependency on countries of the northern hemisphere by emphasizing trade relations with southern partners, but that Lula da Silva went beyond mere politico-economic measures. Burges linked Lula da Silva's foreign policy to Frantz Fanon's anti-colonial text *Black Skin White Mask* (1967 [1952]), in which Fanon eloquently deciphers the psychological effects of colonization as cultural inferiority complex that manifests in the psyche of the colonized. According to Burges, Lula da Silva's foreign policy represented an attempt to transform the colonizer/colonized dichotomy and to instill in Brazilians a sense of national pride and emancipation.

Building on Burges' analysis (2005), this chapter argues that internationalization has provided the perfect platform to accomplish the simultaneous goals of promoting southern diplomacy internationally while reconfiguring national attitudes domestically. On the one hand, the Lula da Silva administration invested systematically in internationalization. It actively promoted academic dialogue, networks, programs, and projects to foster economic, political, and sociocultural relations with partnering countries in Africa, Asia, and Latin America (McCowan, 2016; Motter & Gandin, 2016). Through these south-south relations the government sought to increase Brazil's visibility and political leverage on the international stage (Abdenur, 2015). On the other hand, the government pursued domestic policies aimed at reducing socioeconomic inequalities and enhancing Brazilians' national self-confidence. It mobilized internationalization to reshape Brazilians' self-perception toward seeing Brazil as a confident and multicultural nation well able to generate solutions for its own problems and to build mutually beneficial ties between countries across the global south.

Internationalization and southern diplomacy

The Brazilian government employed internationalization as a 'soft power' tool (Nye, 2004) to foster diplomatic relations. Brazil's internationalization efforts in this regard can be grouped into three constellations: (1) with other emerging powers, (2) with Portuguese-language countries, and (3) with countries in Latin America. The following sections provide an overview of three modes of internationalization through which the government sought to deepen and diversify south-south relations.

The IBSA Forum

In 2003, the governments of India, South Africa, and Brazil created the India-Brazil-South Africa Forum (IBSA) as an international platform for diplomatic exchange. IBSA aims to address issues in a wide range of sectors through working groups and non-governmental forums, among them the IBSA Academic Forum. The Academic Forum facilitates trilateral cooperation between academic and research institutions, international student mobility, and high-level training programs for professionals in engineering, computer sciences, mathematical sciences, biotechnology, sustainable development, and higher education. The goal is to establish joint research projects, set up funding mechanisms, and publish research papers. The forum has established mobility funds and modest grants for researchers. Even as the forum has been criticized for the lack of significant results, it has initiated a high-profile southern diplomacy that allows representatives of the countries to mingle and become familiar with each other politically and culturally (Soule-Kohndou, 2013). Trans-regional coalitions like IBSA (and others, e.g., BRICS Forum, G20) have helped Brazil to gain global attention (Abdenur, 2015) and to usher in new modalities of economic trade relations (Burges, 2005).

The Community of Portuguese-Language Countries (CPLP)

Internationalization has also been an important component of the strategic collaboration with Portuguese-language in Africa and Asia including Angola, Mozambique, Guinea Bissau, Cape Verde, São Tomé e Príncipe, and East Timor. Similar to IBSA, for CPLP, higher education has been but one area of engagement and government interest centered on the exchange of knowledge, the training of professionals, and academic mobility. Universities have played an important double role. Unlike in north-south development relations, where professionals (e.g., state agency employees, NGO employees, bureaucrats, or technical experts and consultants) perform most of the development work (e.g., planning and implementing projects), in the case of Brazil, civil servants working for ministries and public agencies deliver the majority of development services including post-secondary training for professional development (Milani, 2015). Federal universities in particular have been crucial partners in the conceptualization and implementation of technical and scientific cooperation projects, for example, the agreement between the Federal University of Rio Grande do Sul and the University of Cape Verde to implement a graduate studies program (Ullrich & Carrion, 2014).

In addition, the Ministry of Education grants scholarships to foreign students – the Exchange Program for Undergraduate Students (*Programa de Estudantes-Convênio de Graduação*, PEC-G) and the Exchange Program for Graduate Students (*Programa de Estudantes-Convênio de Pós-Graduação*, PEC-PG) – that allow students to sustain themselves while attending public, tuition-free universities in Brazil. These scholarship programs, which have existed since the 1950s and 1960s, continue to be an important component of Brazil's southwards internationalization efforts. Between 2005 and 2009 these scholarships amounted to almost 10 percent of Brazilian investment in south-south cooperation in education (Ullrich & Carrion, 2014). Between 2004 and 2012, according to the

Ministry of Education, 5,319 foreign students enrolled in the undergraduate component of these government-funded scholarships (Ullrich & Carrion, 2014), many of whom came from African countries, African Countries of Portuguese Official Language (Países Africanos de Língua Oficial Portuguesa, PALOPs) and otherwise. By attracting and funding students from PALOP countries in the federal university system, Brazil accepted the responsibility – and showed a propensity for skill – as a regional leader that expands opportunities to those who may not have sufficient access to higher education otherwise.

Inter-regional universities

The Brazilian government's most distinct attempt to harness internationalization under the Lula da Silva administration was in the active creation of two inter-regional universities – the University of International Integration of Afro-Brazilian Lusophony in the state of Ceará (*Universidade da Integração Internacional da Lusofonia Afro-Brasileira*, UNILAB) and the Federal University of Latin-American Integration (*Universidade Federal da Integração Latino-Americana*, UNILA). These universities aim to transcend national borders through academic and cultural exchange between Brazil and countries that are viewed as regional partners in southern diplomacy (Neves, 2009; Robertson, 2010).

UNILA was founded in 2010 in the symbolic location of the trilateral border shared by Brazil, Paraguay, and Argentina, near the Iguaçu Falls. By 2015, the university enrolled 2,300 undergraduate students, 61 percent of whom were from Brazil. The remaining students came from Bolivia, Paraguay, Haiti, Ecuador, Uruguay, Argentina, and Colombia (McCowan, 2016). The first campus of UNILAB was established in 2011 in the equally symbolic location of Redenção, in the state of Ceará, which was the first town in Brazil to legally abolish slavery in 1883 (five years before the country as a whole). By 2015, UNILAB had three campuses, two in Ceará and one in Bahia. It enrolled 2,666 undergraduate students (on-campus, part- and full-time), 73 percent of whom were from Brazil. The remaining undergraduate students came from PALOPs and East Timor. It further enrolled 2,381 Brazilian students in several graduate and distance education courses. UNILAB employed 173 professors, 87 percent of them Brazilian, 13 percent non-Brazilian, two from each of the countries of Angola and Guinea Bissau, and one each from Peru, Cape Verde, Congo, Costa Rica, Gabon, Mozambique, and Portugal.

UNILA is a bilingual institution, with Portuguese and Spanish as languages of instruction. At UNILAB the language of instruction is Portuguese. Both universities are part of the Brazilian public higher education system, which means they are entirely funded by the Brazilian government and students pay no fees. In addition, both universities have been offering generous support packages to foreign students, including housing and monthly stipends for food, clothing, and other necessities. It remains to be seen whether these support packages can be sustained given the recent changes in Brazilian politics and the economic downturn (Waisbich, 2016).

Both universities offer undergraduate courses that are deemed relevant to the respective regions and the partnering countries, focusing on rural development, food security, engineering for sustainable energies, public administration, teacher education in the natural sciences, and health. Since they have been designed to promote inter-regional integration – MERCOSUR in the case of UNILA, and CPLP in the case of UNILAB – perhaps the most remarkable feature of the universities is the *currículo comum* (shared curriculum), which all students have to follow during their first year, regardless of their field of study. This curriculum comprises a number of courses that focus on the history, commonalities, and cultural diversity of the countries that belong to the respective regions. The objective is for students to learn about these countries and, at the same time, become familiar with each other, as well as foster mutual understanding and respect (McCowan, 2016; Ress, 2015).

McCowan (2016) describes UNILA and UNILAB as "radical alternative" universities in Brazil that counteract the increasing commodification and competition in higher education. UNILA focuses on the regional community and alternative approaches to knowledge production and dissemination (McCowan, 2016). Motter and Gandin (2016), who have explored UNILA's role in Brazil's new regionalism, conclude that "the regional vocation ascribed to UNILA reaffirms the paramount importance that Brazil has given to the integration of Latin America as a condition to fulfil its ambition as a regional leader and a 'global player'" (p. 273). Both McCowan (2016) and Motter & Gandin (2016) contend that the implementation of UNILA is not without challenges. The university faces legal and financial constraints, the latter due to Brazil's recent economic downturn. Similar issues have been reported for UNILAB (Ress, 2015).

Nonetheless, the strategic choice of location for both universities, their international student body, and the distinctive curriculum indicate that internationalization under the Lula da Silva administration was more than just a 'soft power' tool to build south-south alliances. UNILA and UNILAB were conceptualized to serve domestic needs as well. Drawing on insights from an ethnographic study conducted between 2012 and 2015, the following sections zoom in on UNILAB to show that the government also employed internationalization to reconfigure Brazilians' attitudes and enhance their national self-confidence. To put UNILAB in context, a brief description of higher education in Brazil is first required.

Higher education in Brazil

The Brazilian higher education system is unusual in its configuration. A stark divide between public and private institutions characterizes the sector. Public universities, which are either federal or state-run institutions, are free-of-charge but access is limited and gated through highly competitive entrance examinations. Private institutions, on the other hand, have ample space to enrol students, but charge tuition. Public universities rank among the most elite institutions in the country. They often focus on graduate education and have the highest research output. They are mostly located in large urban areas (e.g., São Paulo, Campinas). Private institutions absorb most of the undergraduate students and are often of lower quality, with some notable exceptions, e.g., well-established Catholic universities (Durham, 2004). In general, undergraduate enrollment has rapidly increased in recent years. In 2013 the net enrollment rate reached 46.45 percent according to UN data. However, scholars have argued that this expansion has been at the expense of the quality of education provided (Schwartzmann, 2009).

Historically, there has been an inverse status position between private and public institutions across the levels of education, and this public-private divide has contributed greatly to existing structures of socioeconomic inequality in Brazilian society. Low-income students often attend public primary and secondary schools whereas high-income students attend private schools at these levels. The quality of education in public schools is often lower than the quality in private schools. Therefore, students whose parents can afford private schools are generally better prepared and have a higher chance of success in the entrance examination to public universities. High-income students are therefore more likely to attend public, fee-free universities at the expense of low-income students, who are left to the less competitive but also less prestigious private institutions. Students who cannot afford fees are excluded from higher education altogether (Schwartzman, 2009). Furthermore, as a consequence of a long-standing pattern of racialized socioeconomic inequalities, non-white and indigenous students have often been excluded from higher education (Bailey & Peria, 2010). For instance, in 2006, 20 percent of white college-age students attended university, whereas less than 6 percent of their non-white peers were enrolled (Paixão & Carvano, 2008).

In response to and in collaboration with active social movements (e.g., *Movimento Negro* – the Black Movement), the Workers' Party government under Lula da Silva launched a number of reforms to combat these inequalities and to democratize access to public universities. In 2005, the government began giving tax incentives to private institutions through the *Program of University for All* (PROUNI) to open up slots for low-income students (Ceaser, 2005). In 2007, it implemented the *Program of Restructuring and Expansion of Federal Universities* (REUNI) to expand the federal university system, creating evening courses and opening new campuses (Paiva, 2013), including the inter-regional universities (McCowan, 2016). In 2012, the Supreme Court declared race-targeted quotas legal and, in 2013, the government made them mandatory for federal universities (Schwartzman & Paiva, 2014). In addition to policies aimed at expanding access for racially and socioeconomically marginalized students, the government also targeted popular attitudes. In 2003, as one of the first acts of his presidency, Lula da Silva sanctioned Law No. 10.639, which mandates the teaching of the history and culture of Africa and Afrodescendants at all levels of education, in order to enhance Brazilians' historical knowledge and to reduce prejudice against non-white people (Felipe & Teruya, 2012).

Internationalization and national emancipation

UNILAB is a product of the political objectives of strengthening southern diplomacy and enhancing Brazilian national emancipation simultaneously. It was created with funds from the REUNI program of higher education expansion. The university is located in the rural interior of Northeast Brazil, a region that has historically been under-resourced and lacking institutions of federal higher education. Additionally, the institution as a whole and the curriculum emphasize Brazilians' cultural affinity to African cultures rooted in the history of transatlantic slavery.

Many of UNILAB's students are non-traditional students, who did not previously have access to a public university. Only the most capable students and students with the necessary funds would leave the region to attend (public) universities in urban centres. At the same time, with the rather large influx of students, professors, and researchers, UNILAB attracted the interest of the academic community and significantly altered Redenção's demographic townscape. The Brazilian government, the university leadership, and many professors believe that UNILAB provided a way, through the mingling of locals with foreigners and non-local Brazilians, to connect Northeast Brazil with the world. UNILAB's dual purpose of fostering southern diplomacy through conviviality and enhancing students' national attitudes is also evident in the university curriculum.

The UNILAB curriculum

As mentioned earlier, UNILAB offers a set of common courses that all students follow in their first and second year of study. Two courses in particular – Society, History, and Culture in Lusophone Spaces (SHC) and Topics of Interculturality in Lusophone Spaces (TI) – teach about the histories, societies, cultures, and identities of Portuguese-language countries. The course descriptions show the courses' postcolonial orientation. SHC examines the world that Europeans found at the onset of colonization, which dates back to the 16th century. It discusses the colonial context and the trafficking of slaves, as well as the contribution of indigenous and black people in the construction of the Brazilian nation. It also covers the notion of Pan-Africanism, struggles for liberation, the affirmation of black identities, and the social conflicts in post-independence Brazil in 1822 and African countries during the 1970s. TI further explores the different temporalities of the colonial process, and the cultural practices, exchange, and conflicts that occurred during transatlantic slavery and colonialism, emphasizing cultural manifestations that arose from the process of occupation, struggle, and resistances.

The course descriptions include a list of readings, which feature well-known and less well-known postcolonial authors like Homi Bhabha, Amílcar Cabral, Stuart Hall, Maria Carrilho, and of course, Frantz Fanon. The reading list shows that UNILAB intends to provide a space of learning in which 'Europe' is displaced as the sole source of Brazilian modernity. The course curriculum aims to tackle what Madureira (2008) calls the "main goal" of postcolonial theory, which he describes as the reconsideration of the "history of slavery, racism and colonization from the standpoint of those who endured its effects" and to revise history from a position "oriented toward the South" (2008, p. 141). The descriptions conceive of colonized societies as spaces where everyday lives and cultures are substantially shaped by struggles against dominance. The course description displays an understanding of culture as something fluid, ever produced and reproduced in interactions between colonizers/slave traders and colonized/slaves (Young, 2003). It further emphasizes the multitude of cultural manifestations that resulted from colonial occupations and resistance(s) against it. Northeast Brazil, especially the rural interior where UNILAB is located, has long been entangled in the materialities and representations of center-periphery differences. Brazilian society traditionally perceived them as economically, socially, and culturally underdeveloped; in short, "backwards" (Weinstein, 2015). In light of this context, the curriculum represents an important and radical break with 'Eurocentric' understandings of Brazilian students' lives and cultures, which tended to dominate Brazilian teaching of history (Fernandes, 2005). It also represents a radically different approach to understanding their lives as historically linked to African societies, similar to Paul Gilroy's understanding of Black Atlantic 'routes' (1993), which clearly displays an international outlook on teaching.

The suggested contents of the common curriculum comply with Brazilian Law No. 10.639. The curriculum goes even further in that it acknowledges students' agency in shaping their own lives and experiences and encourages the use of course materials that elevate them to agents of their own histories. It seems that the descriptions were written in the hope that students would gain an understanding of the historical emergence of social relations in Brazil and elsewhere from a postcolonial/southern perspective and be able to compare and contrast these perspectives to the more common historical narrative of European intellectual, material, and overall imperial expansions. The curriculum thus clearly mirrors Lula da Silva's approach to southern diplomacy and national emancipation.

Conclusion

The IBSA Forum, bilateral engagements with CPLP countries, and the creation of inter-regional universities are in tune with current worldwide debates, which increasingly recognize the importance of internationalization for the global knowledge economy (Altbach, Reisberg, & Rumbley, 2009). The Brazilian government under the Lula da Silva presidency approached these global debates from a postcolonial perspective by combining them with an understanding of higher education as an institutional space responsive to domestic demands for development and equity (Ferreira, 2008). To that end, the Brazilian government designed internationalization initiatives that deliberately focus on and address the needs of developing and emerging regions and countries (Leite, 2010). It imagined these initiatives as beacons of Brazil's aspirations for international leadership across countries of the global south and a contribution to national emancipation as suggested by Burges (2005).

References

Abdenur, A. E. (2015). Organisation and politics in south-south cooperation: Brazil's technical cooperation in Africa. *Global Society, 29*(3), 321–338. doi:10.1080/136008 26.2015.1033384

Altbach, P. (2015). Perspectives on internationalizing higher education. *International Higher Education, 27*, 6–8.

Altbach, P. G., Reisberg, L., & Rumbley, L. (2009). *Trends in Global Higher Education: Tracking an Academic Revolution.* Chestnut Hill, MA: Boston College Center for International Higher Education.

Bailey, S. R., & Peria, M. (2010). Racial quotas and the culture war in Brazilian academia. *Sociology Compass, 4*(8), 592–604.

Burges, S. W. (2005). Auto-estima in Brazil: the logic of Lula da Silva's south-south foreign policy. *International Journal, 60*(4), 1133–1151.

Ceaser, M. (2005). Brazil offers incentives for private universities to give scholarships to needy students. *Chronicle of Higher Education*, 8 April, A39.

Durham, E. R. (2004). Higher education in Brazil – public and private. In C. Brock & S. Schwartzman (Eds.), *The Challenges of Education in Brazil* (pp. 147–178). Oxford, UK: Triangle Journals.

Fanon, F. (1952/1967). *Black Skin, White Masks.* New York: Grove Press. First published Paris: Editions du Seuil.

Felipe, D. A., & Teruya, T. K. (2012). Narrativas de docentes sobre a obrigatoriedade do ensino da história e cultura afro-brasileira [Narratives of professors about the mandated teaching of Afro-Brazilian history and culture]. *Educação, 35*(2), 208–216.

Fernandes, J. R. (2005). Ensino de história e diversidade cultural: desafios e possibilidades [Teaching history and cultural diversity: challenges and possibilities]. *Cadernos CEDES, 25*(67, September/October), 378–388.

Ferreira, R. (2008). A experiência do programa políticas da cor na educação brasileira: uma ação positiva pela democratização do ensino superior [The experiences of colour policies in Brazilian education: positive action for the democratization of higher education]. In IESALC-UNESCO, *Diversidad Cultural e Interculturalidad en Educación Superior: Experiencias en América Latina* (pp. 177–188). Caracas, Venezuela: Servicio de Información y Documentación.

Gilroy, P. (1993). *The Black Atlantic: Modernity and Double Consciousness.* Cambridge, MA: Harvard University Press.

Leite, D. (2010). Brazilian higher education from a post-colonial perspective. *Globalisation, Societies and Education, 8*(2), 219–233.

McCowan, T. (2016). Forging radical alternatives in higher education: the case of Brazil. *Other Education, 5*(2), 196–220.

Madureira, L. (2008). Is the difference in Portuguese colonialism the difference in Lusophone postcolonialism? *Ellipsis: The Journal of the American Portuguese Studies Association, 6*, 135–141.

Milani, C. R. (2015). *International Development Cooperation in the Education Sector: The Role of Brazil.* UNESCO Paper, Education for All Global Monitoring Report 2015. Paris: UNESCO.

Motter, P., & Gandin, L. A. (2016). Higher education and new regionalism in Latin America: the UNILA project. In S. Robertson, K. Olds, R. Dale, & Q. A. Dang (Eds.), *Global Regionalisms and Higher Education: Projects, Processes, Politics* (pp. 272–288). Cheltenham: Edward Elgar.

Neves, R. R. (2009). Território e integração [Territory and integration]. Doctoral thesis, Federal University of Rio de Janeiro, Brazil. Retrieved from www.ippur.ufrj.br/down load/pub/RafaelRust.pdf

Nye, J. S, Jr. (2004). Soft Power: The Means to Success in World Politics. New York: Public Affairs.

Paiva, A. R. (2013). Políticas públicas, mudanças e desafios no acesso ao ensino superior [Public policies, changes and challenges in access to higher education]. In A. R. Paiva (Ed.), *Ação Afirmativa em Questão: Brasil, Estados Unidos, África do Sul e França* [*Affirmative action in question: Brazil, United States, South Africa and France*]. Rio de Janeiro, Brazil: Pallas Editora.

Paixão, M., & Carvano, L. M. (2008). Relatório Anual das Desigualdades Raciais no Brasil 2007–2008 [Annual Report of Racial Inequality in Brazil 2007–2008]. Rio de Janeiro, Brazil: Garamond.

Robertson, S. (2009). Market multilateralism, the World Bank group, and the asymmetries of globalizing higher education: toward a critical political economy analysis. In R. Bassett & A. Maldonado (Eds.), *International Organizations and Higher Education Policy: Thinking Globally, Acting Locally.* London/New York: Routledge.

Robertson, S. (2010, January 3). Brazil's new Latin American and global integration university launched. *GlobalHigherEd.* Retrieved from http://globalhigherEd.wordpress. com/2010/01/03/new-latin-american-integration-universities-launched/

Ress, S. (2015). Solidarity, history and integration: a qualitative case study of Brazilian south-south cooperation in higher education, Doctoral dissertation, University of Wisconsin-Madison. Retrieved from ProQuest Dissertation and Theses (Accession Order No. wisc13144).

Salmi, J. (2009). The Challenge of Establishing World-Class Universities. Washington, DC: World Bank.

Schwartzman. S. (2009). Student quotas in Brazil: the policy debate. *International Higher Education, 56,* 11–12.

Schwartzman, L. F., & Paiva, A. R. (2014). Not just racial quotas: affirmative action in Brazilian higher education 10 years later. *British Journal of Sociology of Education, 37*(4), 548–566.

Soule-Kohndou, F. (2013). The India-Brazil/South Africa Forum a decade on: Mismatched partners or the rise of the South? GEG Working Paper 2013/88, November 2013. University of Oxford: The Global Economic Governance Programme.

Steiner-Khamsi, G. (2002) Reterritorializing Educational Import: explorations into the politics of educational borrowing, in A. Novoa & M. Lawn (Eds) *Fabricating Europe: the formation of an education space.* Boston: Kluwer.

Torres, C. A. (2011). Public universities and the neoliberal common sense: Seven iconoclastic theses. *International Studies in Sociology of Education, 21*(3), 177–197.

Ullrich, D. R., & Carrion, R. M. (2013). A cooperação brasileira na area da educaçãot no PALPOPs no period 2000–2012: principais atores e projetos [Brazilian cooperation in education with PALOPS, 2000–2012: main actors and projects]. *Sociais e Humanas,* *Santa Maria, 27*(1), 146–160.

UNILAB. (2010). *Diretrizes Gerais* [*Founding Document*]. Developed in July 2010 by the Commission of Implementation.

Waisbich, L. (2016, March). *Solidarity in Times of Fiscal Restrain? Reflections on Brazil as a Development Partner Since 2010.* Paper presented at the Rising Powers Young Researchers Conference, Institute for Development Studies, University of Sussex, Falmer, UK.

Weinstein, B. (2015). The Color of Modernity: São Paulo and the Making of Race and Nation in Brazil. Durham, NC: Duke University Press.

Young, R. (2003). *Postcolonialism.* Oxford/New York: Oxford University Press.

Chapter 19

Is there a gap to bridge between internationalization in secondary and higher education?

Adinda van Gaalen and Susanne Feiertag

Various developments – such as the internationalization of the economy, increasing immigration, and social segregation – have large impacts on Dutch and indeed European society, and will continue to do so in the long term. Against this backdrop, the internationalization of education at all levels is being accorded a crucial role in educating internationally and interculturally competent citizens. Ideally, these competencies are developed throughout a student's educational career, whereby each level adds to the other. However, do educational programs in higher education (HE) actually build on the previously developed international and intercultural knowledge of students?

To date little research has been undertaken on the link between internationalization in secondary education and HE in the Netherlands. Even though some studies do include both levels of education (European Commission, 2014; Scholtes, de Groot, & Visser, 2005), they rarely address the coherence between the two in terms of internationalization. And when they do, the focus tends to be on the internationalization of teacher training programs.

In this chapter we define secondary education programs as those leading to a diploma positioned at level 4 or 4+ of the European Qualifications Framework (EP-Nuffic, 2015). Given the growing international orientation of Dutch secondary education (Maassen van den Brink & van der Rest, 2016; Oonk, 2015), we may expect that, in the rather near future, a substantial number of students enrolling in HE will have previous knowledge of and/or experience with internationalization. HE institutions that actively respond to these developments in secondary education can benefit from an influx of internationally oriented students, as has been the case for university colleges in the Netherlands, according to de Wit (2015).

In 2015, there were 638 secondary schools in the Netherlands (Stamos, 2017b). Data for the 2015/2016 school year show a (provisional) number of 995,336 students participating in secondary education, of which 16 percent came from a non-Western immigrant background (Statistics Netherlands [CBS], 2017). Participation in secondary education in 2015/2016 had grown by 6 percent since 2010/2011 (Statistics Netherlands, 2017). Comparable data on the transition of secondary students into HE are publicly available only up to the 2013/2014 cohort.

In 2013, 3.9 percent of the total population of secondary students, then 940,400 students (Stamos, 2017a), continued their studies in research universities (Ministry of Education, Culture and Science, Dienst Uitvoering Onderwijs [DUO], & Statistics Netherlands [CBS], 2017b), while 6.7 percent continued on to the universities of applied sciences (Ministry of Education, Culture and Science, Dienst Uitvoering Onderwijs [DUO], & Statistics Netherlands [CBS], 2017a).

In this chapter we give a first impression of the current interest for and activities in cooperation on internationalization between secondary and higher education in the Netherlands. We describe the extent of internationalization in secondary education and then go on to sketch a general picture of internationalization in HE in the Netherlands. We analyze the most striking similarities and differences in internationalization between the sectors. Then we focus on the transition between the two sectors. Finally, we look into an ideal future for the transition between secondary and higher education in terms of internationalization. In this analysis, we deliberately exclude international schools in the Netherlands, as they form a separate group, which, in principle, are not open to Dutch students.

The chapter includes data retrieved from a number of sources. First, we analyzed literature and policy documents, and used national databases to provide an overview of the state of the art of internationalization in both secondary and higher education. We also drew selectively from two analyses of strategic documents of Dutch higher education institutions (HEIs) (van Gaalen, Hobbes, Roodenburg, & Gielesen, 2014; van Gaalen, Roodenburg, Hobbes, Huberts, & Gielesen, 2014). In addition, we include insights gained from interviews we held with experts from the secondary and higher education sectors and government officials. The interviews were conducted with nine individuals in total: three working in secondary education, two in HE, and four at government bodies involved in education. We selected respondents from one specialized HE institution in a small city and one internationally oriented secondary school located nearby, and from one comprehensive HE institution and one internationally oriented secondary school in the same large city. Finally, a survey was distributed among 48 members of two internationalization platforms in which all Dutch HEIs are represented – 71 percent of the survey respondents worked at universities of applied sciences (UAS), while 29 percent worked at research universities. Total responses received was 18 (i.e., a response rate of 38 percent), of which 15 (83 percent of all respondents) represented a university of applied sciences and 3 (17 percent of the respondents) represented a research university. Consequently, the survey should mainly be seen as a first attempt to obtain a provisional indication of perspectives from the Dutch HE community, as it does not provide a complete picture of knowledge and opinions within HE.

Internationalization in Dutch secondary education

A number of definitions of internationalization are in use in the secondary education sector (see, for instance, Maaskant, 2014; Maslowski, Naayer, Oonk, &

Van der Werf, 2011; Oonk, 2004). However, with a view to comparability and international recognizability, we have chosen to adapt the commonly used definition of internationalization for HE by Knight (2013) to the particular aims of internationalization in secondary education. This chapter refers to internationalization of secondary education as "the process of integrating an international, intercultural, European or global dimension into the purpose or delivery of secondary education."

The aims of internationalization in Dutch secondary education include the development of foreign language skills, intercultural skills, and an international orientation. In recent years there has been greater emphasis in secondary education on strategies for internationalization and for anchoring them in the curriculum (Europees Platform, 2015), as evidenced by grant programs such as VIOS and Erasmus+. VIOS is a Dutch government program financially supporting the internationalization of the curriculum. In addition, it supports the international mobility of students and staff, as does Erasmus+. Programs with an international focus have anchored internationalization in the curriculum for decades. As internationalization strategies for secondary schools are not usually published, in contrast to the strategies of HEIs in the Netherlands, it remains unclear what proportion of schools apply them and what these strategies entail.

What we do know is that sophisticated frames of reference are used for language skill development at the secondary level. The Common Framework for Europe Competence (CFEC) guides the approaches to developing intercultural skills, as well as to cultivating European and international orientations (EIO). Based on these frameworks, networks of schools have established international tracks (see Table 19.1 below).

Internationalization activities

Van Ruiten (2015) identified a trend whereby internationalization in secondary education is characterized by a wide variety of activities and foci. Our research shows that internationalization activities in government-funded Dutch secondary schools include, among other things, eTwinning and Erasmus+ mobility: 36 percent of government-funded schools participate in eTwinning (a form of collaboration between schools in Europe through the use of ICT), with 7 percent participating in Erasmus+ mobility (Kearney & Gras-Velázquez, 2015). Student competitions and guest lectures also take place, albeit in an unknown number of schools. In terms of educational content, all schools offer the opportunity to study a number of European languages (English, German, French, and/or Spanish), and around 19 percent of schools offer strengthened language education for German and/or French, including additional hours of language classes and more breadth and depth in language learning. Some schools also offer Chinese, Russian, or Arabic. In addition, 3 percent of schools offer global perspectives courses which aim to help students develop research, analytical, reasoning, cooperation, and evaluation skills related to global issues (Thijs & Resink, 2010).

Some of these activities form part of the curriculum, such as online international projects, but the majority are voluntary and, hence, often do not include all students. Secondary education staff most frequently mention student mobility and bilingual education as core internationalization elements (Maaskant, 2014). Our research, based on data from Nuffic and Alberts and Erens (2015), however, shows that these activities in reality are implemented by fewer schools than online international projects or foreign language courses.

Programs with an international focus

Dutch secondary education includes certain programs, or learning tracks, that involve a structural focus on internationalization. These are the most intensive forms of internationalization for students, as they are implemented throughout the curriculum in various forms and frequently include extracurricular activities. The three recognized international learning tracks currently in existence in the Netherlands are referred to as Elos – *grensverleggend onderwijs* (meaning 'education stretching borders'), TTO (*tweetalig onderwijs*, meaning 'bilingual education'), and UNESCO (United Nations Educational Scientific and Cultural Organization) tracks.

These tracks are partially complementary, but there is some overlap (see Table 19.1). Some schools and programs offer multiple tracks (TTO, Elos and UNESCO), which may be an indication of their complementary nature, a given school's commitment to internationalization, or a feeling of competitive advantage in attracting students in a country facing an increasingly smaller school-age population.

UNESCO schools form part of national and international networks of more than 9,000 schools worldwide. Similarly, schools offering the Elos track are joined in a network which was initially linked to other national networks of Elos schools in Europe. While the European network has become inactive, some of the national Elos networks have continued. Overall, however, unlike in HE, internationally networked secondary schools are scarce in the Netherlands.

Learning outcomes of internationalization in secondary education

In general, research on the impact of internationalization activities on students in secondary education is limited, fragmented, and sometimes contested. We are limited in what we know because, whereas foreign language competencies are tested in obligatory national exams, this is not the case for international and intercultural competencies. Our knowledge base is also fragmented, as current research mainly focuses on one type of program at a time, leaving out the context of the wider internationalization efforts in secondary education (Admiraal, Westhoff, & de Bot 2006; Maslowski et al. 2011; Oberon, 2010, 2012; Verspoor, Schuitenmaker-King, van Rein, de Bot, & Edelenbos, 2010; Weenink, 2005). Meanwhile, research on the impacts of secondary school internationalization is

Table 19.1 International tracks in Dutch secondary education

Characteristics	TTO track	Elos track	UNESCO track
Number of schools	130 (20%)	40 (6%)	24 (4%)
Number of students	33,000 (3%)	No data available	No data available
Frameworks	CLIL[1] & EIO[2]	CFEC[3] & EIO	UNESCO themes[4]
Activities	50% curriculum in foreign language international projects exchanges internationalization of the curriculum	enriched foreign language education international projects exchanges excursions internationalization of the curriculum	UNESCO-related activities UNESCO-flagship projects exchanges debates fundraising for charity
Acknowledgment	TTO label IB certificate[5]	Elos label	UNESCO label
Teaching language	English and German (2)	Dutch	Dutch

Sources: Nuffic and Netherlands National Commission for UNESCO (unpublished)

1 Content and Language Integrated Learning – "an additional language is used for the learning and teaching of both content and language" (Mehisto, Marsh, & Jesús Frigols, 2008, p. 9).
2 European and International Orientation (European Platform & Dutch Network of Bilingual Schools, 2012).
3 Common Framework for Europe Competence which provides indicators for the 'Europe Competence' of students and is used to structure and guide the development of EIO (European Elos Network, 2010).
4 UNESCO themes include peace and human rights, intercultural learning, world citizenship, and sustainability as a means of improving peace in the minds of men (Thij, van der Velde, Meershoek, van Dieren, & Arkesteijn, 2011).
5 Via a special agreement between TTO schools and the International Baccalaureate (IB) organization, a TTO student can obtain a certificate for English Language and Literature on top of their obligatory national exam.

contested, as variable results have been obtained for different subsets of TTO students (Verspoor et al., 2010; Verspoor, Xu, & de Bot, 2013).

However, there is some valuable research available that shows, for instance, that students with higher foreign language skills participate on average more often in international activities and obtain higher scores in the associated development of 'general skills' (Maslowski, Naayer, Oonk, & Van der Werf, 2009). Indeed, Warps and Nooij (2016) found that students who selected the foreign languages track (*taalprofiel* in Dutch), students in the TTO program, and students who had traveled abroad for school-sponsored activities were more likely to want to spend a period of their HE program in a foreign country. However, relatively little research exists about the long-term effects of international learning tracks at the secondary school level in the Netherlands in terms of students' future educational and professional careers.

Small-scale studies, which may not be representative of the whole sector, have been conducted on the education-related impact of student and teacher mobility and of the internationalization of curricula (see Beneker, van Dis, & van Middelkoop, 2014; Oberon, 2010, 2012). Oberon (2010) found that students were more positive about dealing with cultural differences after a period of study abroad than students in the control group. The effects of internationalization on students are often measured by self-evaluation, however, and this is not particularly strong evidence, as people tend to overrate their own abilities (Kruger & Dunning, 1999; Oonk, 2004).

In contrast, Maaskant (2014) found that 90 percent of staff members in Dutch secondary education believed that students automatically acquired international and intercultural competencies when participating in an international exchange experience. However, relevant higher education literature (such as Gregersen-Hermans, 2016) shows that it is anything but a matter of course that students develop intercultural competence by the mere fact of being in an intercultural setting. Instead, students need guidance to appropriately interpret and evaluate their own and others' values and practices. Both students and staff in secondary education may therefore be overestimating the impact of international activities in terms of the development or enhancement of intercultural competence.

Overview of internationalization in Dutch HE

In its vision on, and funding policy for, the internationalization of higher education, the Dutch government focuses strongly on attracting and retaining talented students from abroad, giving only fragmented support to the concept and practice of internationalization. This has led the Dutch Education Council to advise the Ministry of Education, Culture and Science to devote more attention to internationalization at home in its strategic HE and research agenda (Maassen van den Brink & van der Rest, 2015). Nearly 91 percent of the total of 56 HEIs in the Netherlands include internationalization in their strategic policies, with most of them focusing both on mobility and internationalization at home strategies (van Gaalen & Gielesen, 2016).

Internationalization at home

In our thinking, we are guided by the definition coined by Beelen and Jones (2015, p. 69) for internationalization at home: "the purposeful integration of international and intercultural dimensions into the formal and informal curriculum for all students, within domestic learning environments."

In a 2014 study for the Dutch Ministry of Education, van Gaalen et al. concluded that many Dutch HE institutions regard internationalization at home as relevant for the development of international and intercultural competencies among their students. A number of study programs include international content, a mix of students from different countries or online internationalization.

Some universities include internationalization in one or two programs only, or offer it on a voluntary basis, while others have integrated internationalization throughout their curricula. Common internationalization at home activities organized by Dutch HEIs include program components in foreign languages, the incorporation of international issues in the curriculum, and student participation in international projects. The international classroom concept offers "a learning environment where both domestic and mobile students and staff take part" (Teekens, 2003, p. 110), and is popular among Dutch HE institutions (van Gaalen, van Hobbes, et al., 2014; van Gaalen, Roodenburg, et al., 2014). The concept is in various stages of implementation around the country (van Gaalen, Roodenburg et al., 2014). Beelen (2012) states that universities of applied sciences in the Netherlands are ahead of research universities in articulating "graduate attributes" related to internationalization, but that a minority of the UAS student population actually acquires such competencies.

Jet Bussemaker, the Dutch Minister for Education, Culture and Science, emphasizes in her letter to Parliament (2014) the economic value of Dutch HE, and therefore the need for a strong position for Dutch science and HE abroad. In this vision, she values internationalization at home, because it enables every student to acquire international and intercultural knowledge and skills – for example, via the international classroom.

International mobility

Outgoing credit mobility, i.e., crossing a national border with the purpose of obtaining academic credit, is relatively strong in the Netherlands, with 23 percent of all graduates of the 2012–2013 cohort going abroad (Huberts, 2015). Large differences exist, however, between fields of study and between higher education institutions (EP-Nuffic, 2016).

The percentage of outgoing credit mobility is relatively high in the Netherlands, partly because of the above-average international orientation in some fields of study (for example, the green energy sector at both UAS and research universities, economics at the UAS, and the technical and health programs at research universities) and in some institutions (including universities of technology, and UAS in all fields of hospitality and art). These HEIs facilitate international experiences for their students to a large extent, which are offered as part of their studies (EP-Nuffic, 2016).

The Dutch HE sector offers around 311 English-taught bachelor programs (Dienst Uitvoering Onderwijs, 2017). These not only cater for Dutch students (e.g., from bilingual education), but also for a fairly large number of international students. In 2016, 55,740 international students (9.3 percent of all students) were registered for a bachelor program (EP-Nuffic, 2017), with the majority of these in English-taught study programs.

Foundation for cooperation

It is clear that there are a number of similarities between the secondary and higher education sectors in the Netherlands. These include the aims of internationalization (international and intercultural competence development) and activities such as student mobility, online international projects, and English-taught courses. In addition, internationalization is included in the strategies of almost all higher education institutions, and of a growing minority of secondary education institutions in the Netherlands. While bilingualism (Dutch-English) and intercultural competence are important in both secondary and higher education, the two sectors show a modest interest in one another's activities and achievements. Internationalization in secondary education is implemented in a variety of forms and degrees of intensity to accommodate unique settings, as is the case in higher education. HE staff overall state that they are aware of the forms and current extent of internationalization in secondary education.

Our research results point subtly towards two main outcomes from internationalization in secondary education from the perspective of higher education:

1   The development of interest among secondary school students in a career in an international working environment;
2   The development of foreign language skills, including advanced English language skills and basic intercultural and international skills.

In a promising development, our interviews indicate that HE staff feel Dutch secondary education sufficiently prepares students for the international dimension of HE. One respondent stated that students starting in HE "compared with five to ten years ago, . . . are more open to the international dimension." In addition to the internationalization activities of secondary institutions, this sense of 'openness' may also be due to a number of small-scale initiatives aimed at a smoother transition from secondary to higher education, such as alumni meetings or guest lessons provided by foreign students at secondary schools to prepare students for HE. Another example is regional cooperation between university colleges and secondary education, such as the Buurtalenproject (Buurtalen Limburg, n.d.).

Although based on our (admittedly limited) research, a more detailed matching of internationalization efforts between secondary and higher education does not seem to be a priority for HE institutions and (therefore) may not currently be feasible. Indeed, while structural and incidental coordination between secondary and higher education does take place, internationalization is very infrequently a subject of discussion. Two aspects seem to complicate cooperation between the two sectors on this topic:

1   There are few intake and monitoring activities to gauge the international and intercultural competencies of students entering HE. Examples that we did find were limited to a specific study program and tended to focus on motivation rather than on acquired competencies.

2   There is a real difference in focal points: internationalization of the curriculum, based on solid frameworks, has been implemented in a large number of secondary schools, whereas international mobility (outgoing credit and incoming degree mobility) is essential to the majority of higher education institutions.

Based on this explorative, and thereby limited, research, the impression at this stage is that there is limited foundation for cooperation at the present time. Although the secondary and higher education sectors share aims, further research is needed to determine in more detail the existing viewpoint(s) and the perceived or experienced obstacles.

An ideal future

HE and secondary education could dovetail their efforts to educate internationally competent students more effectively, if international and intercultural competencies for all schools in secondary education were defined. The Dutch Education Council (2016) has developed a model for the international competence of students, which has been proposed for a possible revision of the national curricula for primary and secondary education (PlatformOnderwijs2032, 2016). Inclusion of such standards in revised curricula could considerably increase the number of secondary school students graduating with basic or advanced international skills.

These competencies must be translated into testable secondary education learning outcomes and, indeed, tested. This will allow the HE sector to build upon these competencies from the outset. Coelen (2016) suggests that the appropriate levels of the educational system for delivering specific internationalization competencies should be identified in a national debate. An overarching internationalization vision for all education sectors, as suggested to the Dutch government by the Dutch Education Council (2016), could support connections across the various levels of education. This research shows a number of starting points for such a joint vision, including: curriculum internationalization, quality frameworks, and indeed measuring the outcomes of internationalization.

Furthermore, in an ideal scenario, bachelor's programs in all fields would provide active support to students in further developing their international and intercultural skills. This would help students to reap more benefits from their international competencies acquired in secondary education. In addition, higher education institutions could then increase efforts to get all students up to the desired level in terms of intercultural competence and English language skills.

Conclusions

There are a number of similarities between the Dutch secondary and higher sectors in terms of internationalization. The level of cooperation between the sectors, however, is limited. This is due, in large part, to a lack of insight into the nature and scope of international competencies brought by Dutch secondary education graduates into the higher education system, and a lack of knowledge as regards the internationalization needs and outcomes of both sectors.

Although the Dutch Council of Education advises coherence, we have not found proof of a sense of urgency among stakeholders. Both sectors focus their internationalization efforts on student mobility, albeit incoming mobility receives priority over outgoing mobility in higher education, whereas in secondary education incoming mobility is not a strategic aim. Internationalization of the curriculum, on the other hand, has a firm basis in secondary education, while the higher education sector shows a growing interest in this type of internationalization. Both in secondary and higher education institutions, quality frameworks for internationalization are being applied, but there is no deliberate link between them. If secondary and higher education leaders are interested in joining forces with respect to internationalization, more knowledge is needed on the scale and results (learning outcomes) of the various forms of internationalization, in particular in secondary education. There is a need for research that goes beyond the evaluation of programs in order to see the full scope of the accomplishments of internationalization in education, and to identify the aspects where secondary and higher education efforts can reinforce each other.

Note

We wish to thank Onno van Wilgenburg, Robert Coelen, Daan Huberts, Sandra Rincon, and Sjoerd Roodenburg for their valuable comments and suggestions for this chapter.

References

Admiraal, W., Westhoff, G. & de Bot, K. (2006). Evaluation of bilingual secondary education in the Netherlands: Students' language proficiency in English. *Educational Research and Evaluation, 12*(1), 75–93. doi:10.1080/13803610500392160

Alberts, R. V. J., & Erens, B. J. M. (2015). *Verslag van de Examencampagne 2015 Voortgezet Onderwijs.* Arnhem: CITO.

Beelen, J. (2012). The long wait: researching the implementation of internationalisation at home. In J. Beelen & H. de Wit (Eds.), *Internationalisation Revisited: New Dimensions in the Internationalisation of Higher Education* (pp. 9–20). Amsterdam: Centre for Applied Research on Economics and Management.

Beelen, J. & Jones, E. (2015). *Redefining internationalization at home.* In A. Curaj, L. Matei, R. Pricopie, J.,Salmi, & P. Scott (Eds.), *The European Higher Education Area: Between Critical Reflections and Future Policies* (pp. 59–72). Cham/Heidelberg/ New York/Dordrecht/London: Springer. doi:10.1007/978-3-319-20877-0_6

Beneker, T., van Dis, H., & van Middelkoop, D. (2014). World-mindedness of students and their geography education at international (IB-DP) and regular schools in the Netherlands. *International Journal of Development Education and Global Learning, 6*(3), 5–30.

Bussemaker, M., (2014). Letter to Parliament – Into the world: letter on the government's vision on the international dimension of higher education and VET. Retrieved from http://ecahe.eu/assets/uploads/2014/07/Dutch-government-vision-on-the-international-dimension-of-higher-education-and-VET.pdf

Buurtalen Limburg. (n.d.). *Buurtalen Limburg*. Retrieved August 17, 2017, from www.buurtalenlimburg.eu/

Coelen, R. (2016). Internationalisation throughout the education system. *University World News Global Edition*, 419. Retrieved from www.universityworldnews.com/arti cle.php?story=20160621203733208

Dienst Uitvoering Onderwijs (2017). *Centraal Register Opleidingen Hoger Onderwijs*. Retrieved from https://apps.duo.nl/MCROHO/pages/zoeken.jsf;jsessionid=k7aJc M8inZD4w7FwBrG5F09b.grnapj0057.lin.prd.duo.nl-instance7

Dutch Education Council (2016). *Internationalising with Ambition*. The Hague: Dutch Education Council. Retrieved from www.onderwijsraad.nl/english/ publications/2016/item7432

EP-Nuffic (2015). *The Dutch Education system Described*. Retrieved from www.epnuffic. nl/en/publications/find-a-publication/education-system-the-netherlands.pdf

EP-Nuffic. (2016). *Mobility Statistics. Credit Mobility. Outgoing Fields of Study*. Retrieved from www.nuffic.nl/en/internationalisation/mobility-statistics/cred-mobility

EP-Nuffic. (2017). *Mobility statistics. Total incoming degree mobility*. Retrieved from www. nuffic.nl/en/internationalisation/mobility-statistics/incoming-degree-mobility/ total-incoming-degree-mobility

European Commission (2014). *Erasmus+ Programme Annual Report 2014*. Brussels: European Commission.

European Elos Network (2010). *Common Framework for Europe Competence (CFEC)*. Retrieved from www.epnuffic.nl/en/files/documents/common-framework-for-europe-competence-cfec.pdf

European Platform & Dutch Network of Bilingual Schools (2012). *Standard for Bilingual Education in English – Havo/Vwo*. Haarlem: European Platform.

Europees Platform (2015). *Jaarverslag 2014*. The Hague: EP-Nuffic.

Gaalen, A. van, & Gielesen, R. (2016). Internationalisation at home: Dutch higher education policies. In E. Jones, R. Coelen, J. Beelen, J. & H. de Wit (Eds.), *Global and Local Internationalization* (pp. 149–154). Boston/Rotterdam: Sense Publishers.

Gaalen, A. van, Hobbes, H. J., Roodenburg, S., & Gielesen, R. (2014). *Studenten Internationaliseren in Eigen Land, Nederlands Instellingsbeleid*. The Hague: Nuffic.

Gaalen, A. van, Roodenburg, S., Hobbes, H. J., Huberts, D. & Gielesen, R. (2014). *Studenten Internationaliseren in Eigen Land, Deel II – De Praktijk*. The Hague: Nuffic.

Gregersen-Hermans, J. (2016). The Impact of Exposure to Diversity in the International University Environment and the Development of Intercultural Competence in Students. In A. Curaj, L. Matei, R. Pricopie, J. Salmi, & P. Scott (Eds.), *The European Higher Education Area: Between Critical Reflections and Future Policies* (pp. 73–92). Cham/Heidelberg/New York/Dordrecht/London: Springer. doi:10. 1007/978-3-319-20877-0_6

Huberts, D. (2015). *Internationalisering in Beeld*, 56. The Hague: EP-Nuffic. Retrieved from www.nuffic.nl/publicaties/vind-een-publicatie/internationalisering-in-beeld-2015.pdf

Kearney, C., & Gras-Velázquez, À. (2015). *eTwinning Ten Years On: Impact on Teachers' Practice, Skills, and Professional Development Opportunities, as Reported by eTwinners*. Brussels: Central Support Service of eTwinning – European Schoolnet. Retrieved form www.etwinning.net/

Knight, J. (2013). The changing landscape of higher education internationalisation – for better or worse? *Perspectives: Policy and Practice in Higher Education, 17*(3), 84–90.

Kruger, J., & Dunning, D. (1999). Unskilled and unaware of It: how difficulties in recognizing one's own incompetence lead to inflated self-assessments. *Journal of Personality and Social Psychology, 77*(6), 121–134.

Maaskant, E. (2014). *Internationalisering in het vo: Bevraagd en Bespiegeld. Onderzoeksrapport.* Haarlem: Europees Platform.

Maassen van den Brink, H., & van der Rest, A. (2015). *Advies Strategische Agenda Hoger Onderwijs en Onderzoek 2015–2025.* The Hague: Education Council.

Maassen van den Brink, H., & van der Rest, A. (2016). *Internationaliseren met Ambitie.* The Hague: Education Council.

Maslowski, R., Naayer, H., Oonk, G. H., & Van der Werf, M. P. C. (2009). *Effecten van Internationalisering in het Voortgezet Onderwijs: Een Analyse van de Implementatie en Effecten van Europese en Internationale Oriëntatie.* Groningen: GION, Gronings Instituut voor Onderzoek van Onderwijs, Opvoeding en Ontwikkeling, Rijksuniversiteit Groningen.

Maslowski, R., Naayer, H., Oonk, G. H., & Van der Werf, M. P. C. (2011). Implementation and effects of European and International Orientation at secondary schools in the Netherlands. In G. H. Oonk, R. Maslowski, & M. P. C. Van der Werf (Eds.), *Internationalisation in Secondary Education in Europe: A European and International Orientation in Schools Policies, Theories and Research* (pp. 271–294). Charlotte: Information Age Publishing Inc.

Mehisto, P., Marsh, D., & Jesús Frigols, M. (2008). *Uncovering CLIL. Content and Language Integrated Learning in Bilingual and Multilingual Education.* Oxford: Macmillan.

Ministry of Education, Culture and Science, Dienst Uitvoering Onderwijs (DUO), & Statistics Netherlands (CBS) (2017a). *Directe en Indirecte Instroom Hoger Beroepsonderwijs.* Retrieved from www.onderwijsincijfers.nl/kengetallen/hoger-beroepsonderwijs/deelnemers-hbo/directe-en-indirecte-instroom-hbo

Ministry of Education, Culture and Science, Dienst Uitvoering Onderwijs (DUO), & Statistics Netherlands (CBS) (2017b). *Directe en Indirecte Instroom Wetenschappelijk Onderwijs.* Retrieved from www.onderwijsincijfers.nl/kengetallen/wetenschappelijk-onderwijs/deelnemerswo/directe-en-indirecte-instroom-wo

Oberon (2010). *Het is Leerzaam, Leuk en je Ontwikkelt je Talenten Erdoor* (Expeditie Corlaer research report, 2009–2010). Utrecht: Oberon.

Oberon (2012). *De Opbrengsten van Expeditie Corlaer 2.* Utrecht: Oberon.

Oonk, G.H. (2004). *De Europese Integratie als Bron Voor Onderwijsinnovatie: Een Onderzoek Naar de Betekenis en de Resultaten van de Internationalisering in het Voortgezet Onderwijs in Nederland.* Alkmaar: Europees Platform voor het Nederlandse Onderwijs.

Oonk, G. H. (2015). *Startdossier Internationaliseringsagenda voor het Onderwijs 2015–2020.* Hannover: Leibniz Universität Hannover. Retrieved form www.onderwijsraad.nl/publicaties/2016/startdossier-internationaliseringsagenda-voor-het-onderwijs-2015-2020/item7420

PlatformOnderwijs2032 (2016). *OnsOnderwijs2032. Eindadvies.* The Hague: Platform OnsOnderwijs2032.

Ruiten, L. Van. (2015). *Internationalisering in het Primair en Voortgezet Onderwijs – Overbodige Luxe of Noodzakelijk Thema?* Brussels: Neth-ER.

Scholtes, E., de Groot, A. & Visser, F. (2005). *Varianten van Internationalisering in het Nederlandse Onderwijs*. Amersfoort: Twynstra Gudde.

Stamos.(2017a). *De Basistabel in Voortgezet Onderwijs. Leerlingen, Studentenaantallen.* Retrieved from www.stamos.nl/index.rfx?verb=showitem&item=5.27

Stamos. (2017b). *De Basistabel in Voortgezet Onderwijs. Scholen en Instellingen.* Retrieved from www.stamos.nl/index.rfx?verb=showitem&item=5.24

Statistics Netherlands (2017, April). *VO; Leerlingen, Onderwijssoort in Detail, Leerjaar.* Retrieved from http://statline.cbs.nl/statweb/publication/?vw=t&dm=slnl&pa=80040 ned&d1=0,3,6-8,14- 15,19-21,55,57-59,61-64,69-70,72-74,76-79,84&d2=0&d3= 0&d4=0-1,4&d5=l&d6=0&d7=7,(l-2)-l&hd=160216-1208&hdr=g4,g5,g1,g2,g3,g6 &stb=t

Teekens, H. (2003). The requirement to develop specific skills for teaching in an intercultural setting. *Journal of Studies in International Education, 7,* 108–119. doi:10.1177/1028315302250192 http://jsi.sagepub.com/content/7/1/108

Thijs, A., & Resink, F. (2010). *Leren van internationaal Onderwijs. Vier Internationale Onderwijsprogramma's voor het VO in Kaart Gebracht.* Enschede: SLO.

Thijs, A., Velde, J. van der, Meershoek, S., Dieren, S. van, & Arkesteijn, E. (2011). *Quality Framework for UNESCO Schools.* Enschede: SLO Netherlands Institute for Curriculum Development.

Verspoor, M. H., Schuitemaker-King, J., van Rein, E. M. J., de Bot, K. & Edelenbos, P. (2010). *Tweetalig Onderwijs: Vormgeving en Prestaties.* Research report. Groningen: University of Groningen.

Verspoor, M. H., Xu, X. & De Bot, C. J. L. (2013). *Verslag OTTO-2 aan Europees Platform.* Haarlem: Europees Platform.

Warps, J. & Nooij, J. (2016). *Gap Year, Buitenlandse Contacten en Belangstelling voor Buitenlandverblijf bij Startende Ho-Studenten.* Nijmegen: ResearchNed.

Weenink, D. (2005). Upper middle-class resources of power in the education area: Dutch elite schools in an age of globalisation. Dissertation, University of Amsterdam.

Wit, H. de (2015). School internationalisation: whose opportunity? *University World News,* 156. Retrieved from www.universityworldnews.com/article.php?story=201508 15164220756

Chapter 20

Future directions for internationalization in higher education

Ecological considerations for doctoral student research training

Louise Michelle Vital and Christina W. Yao

Despite the growth of internationalization in higher education, limited attention is given to U.S. higher education doctoral students' training for conducting international research. This chapter provides insight into the key issues related to doctoral student international research preparation, a topic that is underemphasized in research training. We present a theoretical approach to doctoral research training utilizing Bronfenbrenner's (1994) Ecological System Theory as a framework. From this framework, we have adapted an ecological model for doctoral researcher training, which we use to make recommendations for both individual and programmatic development in doctoral education.

An abundance of scholarship exists that emphasizes the role of internationalization in higher education (Altbach & Knight, 2007; Gopal, 2011; Harzing, Reiche, & Pudelko, 2013; Institute of International Education, 2015; Jung, Kooij, & Teichler, 2014; Knight, 2004; Mitchell & Nielsen, 2012; Rostan, Ceravolo, & Metcalfe, 2014); however, there is a dearth of literature related to international research preparation. In addition, limited attention is given to U.S. higher education doctoral students' training for conducting research in international contexts (Yao & Vital, 2016). This is surprising given the increased internationalization of academic activity in U.S. higher education institutions. Internationalization is a complex enterprise. To better understand its influence on doctoral education, we conducted a qualitative study on 22 doctoral students who represented 11 different higher education programs in the United States. We explored how students with expressed international interests perceived their preparation for conducting research in the global arena. Understanding internationalization from the student perspective has been under-researched and learning about the phenomenon from the voices of current doctoral students allowed us to consider how future researchers, scholars, and thought leaders of higher education contemplate new approaches to doctoral student researcher training.

Participants from our study shared their thoughts on their specific graduate programs and academic departments, provided feedback on their faculty, and discussed other factors that they believed helped or hindered their preparation to conduct international research. Several key issues related to international research preparation emerged, which could be loosely categorized into internal and external factors that influenced our participants' perceptions of their international research preparation. As a result of this study, we identify three overarching areas of key factors affecting doctoral student international research development: internal factors, programmatic priorities, and global perspectives. Doctoral students often must consider internal, or individualistic, factors that affect their overall international research development, which include reflecting on their personal identities and navigating interpersonal relationships. When asked about external factors, participants discussed some programmatic challenges that they faced. Specifically, many participants believed their doctoral curriculum had only a limited focus on global themes or lacked attention to these themes altogether. In addition, world events influenced participants' approach to international research, particularly due to constantly shifting geopolitical forces around the world. Thus, geopolitical influences are a critical component of the connected nature of doctoral student research development.

The three key issues identified above can be isolated components related to researcher training. However, we believe that the issues are distinct yet interconnected parts that affect research training for doctoral students. Drawing from the findings of our empirical study, we use the key issues to guide our recommendations for both individual and programmatic development. We apply Bronfenbrenner's (1994) ecological systems theory to our findings to frame our recommendations for a systematic and theoretical approach for future directions related to doctoral training. In the following section, we provide an overview of a framework that incorporates multiple components related to key issues in doctoral student training for international research.

Ecological framework

We used Bronfenbrenner's (1994) ecological systems theory as a way to organize the implications in a cohesive yet systematic way. Several other researchers have applied Bronfenbrenner's model to topics in higher education, such as mixed-race student identity development (Renn, 2003), academic advising for immigrant students (Stebleton, 2011), and ecology of peer culture (Renn & Arnold, 2003).

In his discussion on human development, Bronfenbrenner (1994) argued that "one must consider the entire ecological system in which growth occurs" (p. 37). His ecological systems theory offers a model that includes the five systems from which one receives support and guidance for human growth (see Figure 20.1). These systems begin with the individual at the center, followed by the five structures that move further away from the individual, which are categorized as the microsystem, the mesosystem, the exosystem, the macrosystem, and the chronosystem. The ecological model takes into consideration that "human development takes place through processes of progressively more complex

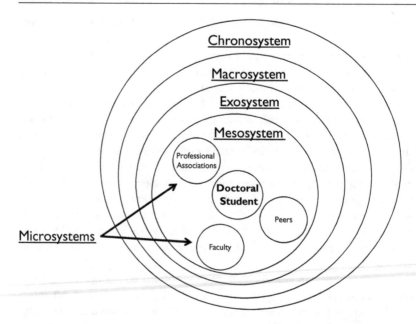

Figure 20.1 Applying Bronfenbrenner's (1994) ecological model to doctoral research training

reciprocal interaction" with the individual and stimuli in the immediate environment (Bronfenbrenner, 1994, p. 38). Also, effective human development requires that the interaction should occur over time and on a consistent basis. In addition, Bronfenbrenner stressed that development occurs as a combination of "the characteristics of the developing person; of the environment in which the processes are taking place; and the nature of the developmental outcomes under consideration" (p. 38).

At the center of the model is the individual, which in this case is the doctoral student. The doctoral student arrives in their new environment, bringing with them prior knowledge and perspectives. When considering the model, the focus is entirely on the student, who is surrounded by different levels of environmental systems that influence and shape their doctoral experiences. By examining research preparation with the student as the nexus, we can examine the challenges and support they experience in their graduate programs. We can then determine the appropriate interventions and resources necessary for international research preparation.

Ecological considerations for doctoral research training

In the ecological model, the environment has a large role in influencing an individual's development. Likewise, in our study, participants are influenced by and situated in various dimensions of their environment: their programs, their institutions, the nation, and the global community. By conceptualizing scholar development in this way, we can discuss the various factors that influenced the international research training of the participants in our study. In this section, we offer Bronfenbrenner's (1994) definition of the five components of the model and describe how we have framed the various systems in the context of our own research on this student population. In addition, we offer practical recommendations, at both the individual and external (mostly programmatic) level, within each of the five components to provide a systematic and comprehensive approach to doctoral researcher training. We provide some examples of how and what to implement in response to each component; however, we do recognize that successful practice must take contextual factors into consideration, including differing departmental structures, teaching delivery (e.g., virtual, face-to-face, etc.), and student interests.

Microsystem

The microsystem is the environment that is the most immediate to the individual. Bronfenbrenner (1994) described this system as "a pattern of activities, social roles, and interpersonal relations experienced by the developing person" (p. 39), in which the interactions become progressively more complex. For doctoral students, the microsystem refers to the individual agents that affect the development of doctoral students, including their peers, faculty, advisors, and potentially professional associations with which they may be affiliated.

Individual

As they matriculate through their doctoral programs, students with international interests should prioritize interactions with various members of their institutional environment and participate in activities to create the set of experiences they believe necessary for their successful international research development. By doing so, students can supplement their doctoral education in ways that their programs may not have the capacity to do. We recommend that doctoral students use their own initiative to determine which key experiences should form the totality of their graduate education and then map out how they will go about realizing these experiences. Examples of this include students considering departments that offer brown-bag discussions, guest lectures, webinars, or other learning opportunities that mirror their research interest. In addition, students should consider attending conferences that offer sessions related to international research, which allows for additional collaborations and/or mentorship opportunities. Class projects could include partnering with peers who have similar interests in international research as a way to infuse additional international perspectives in their required coursework. Overall, students can be strategic with their microsystems as they capitalize on opportunities to enhance their international scholarly development.

External

We recognize that academic departments and specific graduate programs are constrained by the limitations of their resources, both financial and in relation to personnel. We also understand that students may have international interests that are beyond the scope and capabilities of their doctoral programs. With this understanding, program faculty as one part of the microsystem should consider all the ways in which they can support the international research development and progress of their doctoral students. We recommend that, in the initial student/ advisor meeting, faculty are clear about the importance of students contributing to their own learning beyond the classroom. In these meetings during the first semester of a student's program, no assumption should be made about any pre-existing information the student may have, particularly with first-generation college students. Furthermore, faculty advisors should introduce students to other key faculty that a student should know, highlight the myriad curricular and co-curricular offerings within the university, and encourage students to form peer-mentoring relationships with students who share similar international research interests. In addition, faculty could encourage students to advance such peer interaction through class projects as well as encourage students to join professional associations that fit their career interests in international education.

Mesosystem

The mesosystem can be described as a network of microsystems (Bronfenbrenner, 1994). This system "comprises the linkages and processes taking place between two or more settings containing the developing person" (p. 40). In this case, the mesosystem would include connections between the doctoral student, peers, and the faculty. In this system, linkages between microsystems directly influence the individual. Here, doctoral student international research development is based on the interactive nature of graduate education via connections with peers and faculty in the classroom setting. Furthermore, doctoral students experience the linkages between institutional agendas (comprising one microsystem) to prioritize global perspectives at the department level (yet another microsystem) to be more competitive in the global knowledge community.

Individual

Given the interconnectedness of the global academic community, students have several avenues through which to engage with others and also to extend their learning beyond the classroom. Utilizing their coursework as a foundation, we recommend that students wanting to infuse international perspectives in their graduate training should seek out opportunities that allow for short- or long-term opportunities to conduct research with faculty members, both inside and outside of their home department or institution. In addition, students can participate in knowledge communities or special interest groups that are a component of academic associations. In doing so, doctoral students may create an additional network, or mesosystem, beyond their home institution. There are also benefits in participating in international engagement opportunities sponsored by professional organizations or other higher education institutions, which again could form an additional network of support for doctoral students, particularly those from smaller programs. Investing time and effort into these kinds of opportunities, in various academic and practical environments, can ensure that students are shaping their graduate experiences in ways that can advance their international research development.

External

We recommend that faculty think about ways to guide students to connect different microsystems. For example, conference attendance is not only an opportunity to share research or best practice projects, but also a place to form valuable relationships and learn from peers, thought leaders, and practitioners in the field. Most academic and professional associations are attuned to the shifts in national priorities and set the agenda for national conversations at the conference level based on key and emerging issues affecting their affiliated institutions and members. Thus, we recommend that doctoral programs emphasize to students the importance of actively participating in the annual proceedings of their discipline-specific or scholarly interest-based associations. Faculty can help students to create linkages between the knowledge gained from the classroom (one microsystem) and gleaned externally from conferences (another microsystem), with the understanding that the interactions between these two environments (i.e., doctoral programs and professional associations) influence students' development as international researchers.

Exosystem

The exosystem is the next environmental level that one experiences in human development. According to Bronfenbrenner (1994), the exosystem "comprises the linkages and processes taking place between two or more settings, at least one of which does not contain the developing person" (p. 40). Examples of the exosystem could be faculty members who conduct international research projects and later incorporate the realities of conducting research outside of one's home country into doctoral research coursework. Another example can be a doctoral program attempting to meet national priorities related to providing quality training in higher education by embedding international perspectives within it. In both examples, doctoral students are impacted by changes in the environment due to decisions that have been made outside of their immediate milieu or control.

Individual

Recognizing that there are forces beyond one's control can prove to be a challenge for students, particularly when said forces influence the doctoral experience. Over the course of a student's doctoral program, they may experience the departure of a key faculty member, the elimination of a course they deem necessary to their education, diminished availability of funding, and, most critically, governmental or bureaucratic decisions that block them from conducting field research in a given country. These factors can directly or indirectly influence a doctoral student's trajectory. Thus, we recommend that students develop a 'progress to degree' plan that is reflective of the fluid nature of the large, complex organization in which their doctoral program is situated. Furthermore, their plan should allow room for changes that, while disruptive, do not completely derail their progress. Also, students should consider how to capitalize on the networks established with different microsystems and how those networks could be a source of support during times of ambiguity.

External

One of the challenges that program faculty face is making decisions that benefit their student population, while still meeting institutional and departmental priorities. These challenges are increasingly common, particularly considering financial constraints affecting higher education. How then are faculty to make large-scale program changes that positively influence the doctoral experiences of students who have diverse scholarly interests? We recommend that program faculty utilize the information gleaned from advising conversations, as well as emerging trends indicated by academic associations, to both support the priorities and mission of their departments but also to minimize the impact on students. It is up to the academic department and the faculty to ensure that they are maintaining the mission and priorities of the department, particularly in times of disruption, such as leadership change or financial setbacks. The program faculty serve as a buffer. When external changes present difficulties, they should ensure that students' research development still advances, so that students do not lose the valuable experience and training necessary for their effective development.

Macrosystem

Bronfenbrenner (1994) indicated that the macrosystem can be thought of as a "societal blueprint for a particular culture or subculture" (p. 40). Furthermore, the macrosystem

> consists of the overarching patterns of micro-, meso-, and exosystems characteristic of a given culture or subculture, with reference to the belief systems, bodies of knowledge, material resource, customs, life-styles, opportunity structures, hazards, and life course options that are embedded in each of these broader systems.
>
> (Bronfenbrenner, 1994, p. 40)

When considering macrosystems and their influences on doctoral education, epistemology is an example of how doctoral students are influenced by their environment, or doctoral space. Epistemological knowledge in the U.S. context (i.e., how U.S.-located students know things) is often based on Western or U.S.-centric training. The nature of their knowledge or "bodies of knowledge" represents the culture they are situated in, in this case their graduate programs within specific academic departments, housed in a specific college or school, and as a component of the doctoral institution.

Individual

Students have the responsibility to reflect on how they may be demonstrating methodological nationalism, a concept in which researchers focus only on the boundaries of their nation-state (Chernilo, 2006; Shahjahan & Kezar, 2013), in their approach to international research. In doing so, doctoral students can avoid the neo-colonial aspects of international research. We recommend that students engage in reflective processes, such as journaling or writing reflective memos, throughout all aspects of the research process. For example, we suggest that students start with writing a reflexivity statement that includes their awareness of their own epistemological and ontological stance. In doing so, the student may be more aware of the dangers of methodological nationalism inherent in their own research perspectives.

External

How U.S.-trained students produce knowledge, interrogate different knowledge claims, and the scope of their knowledge is framed within the U.S. national context. However, to engage in effective international research, students must be trained to recognize the inherent bias that exists within their doctoral training. Socialization is often considered a positive and much desired aspect of doctoral education; however, what are the implications of subjecting students to particular academic norms? Thus, doctoral programs must examine the core beliefs that undergird the curriculum to better reflect on how these programs reproduce U.S.-based epistemological knowledge. We recommend that programs include research training on multiple epistemologies, including indigenous and global perspectives that are often excluded from traditional research discourse. In addition, methodological nationalism must be addressed in courses. Finally, and most importantly, faculty must model good research practices, in relation to how their own epistemology affects their approach to international research. Seeing such transparency in action can be more valuable to students than any learning provided in textbooks and articles.

Chronosystem

The chronosystem considers the growth of the human, not only over the life course but also across historical time (Bronfenbrenner, 1994). Thus, "a chronosystem encompasses change or consistency over time not only in the characteristics of the person but also of the environment in which that person lives" (1994, p. 40). With respect to the historical level, change over time in the environment of a doctoral student could include a major global political or humanitarian event that influences the doctoral experience, including funding priorities or interest in current events for research. The chronosystem can also refer to colonial aspects of research that persist due to U.S.- or Western-centric research that does not take into account other notions of research or knowledge.

Individual

We recognize that research training is not static, particularly for novice researchers. Rather, we argue that there is a temporal dimension of research training that continues beyond doctoral education. On an individual level, the change over time can reflect all of the development the student received prior to becoming a graduate student, all of the support they received while a doctoral student due to events in the microsystem, and who the individual is once they graduate, representing the training and socialization they received from their institution. As such, we recommend that students continue to engage in workshops and training beyond their doctoral education, with an emphasis on exploring international dimensions. We further encourage researchers to continue to reflect on how past experiences (personal and professional) may shape their researcher perspective. In addition, regarding the temporal dimension of higher education, constant attention must be given to current political events that are happening around the globe because those events affect both the research process as well as research participants.

External

We suggest to doctoral programs and faculty that there be engagement with current events and issues that are happening globally. For example, political refugees from regions in conflict are arriving on college campuses in the United States. How can doctoral programs incorporate conversations about worldwide responses to political issues as well as encourage sensitivity from students as they research this population? How do programs address safety issues with doctoral students who may undertake research in locations around the world where violent conflicts may be pervasive? Thus, in the research preparation process, doctoral programs and faculty must take into consideration the temporal dimension as well as the current political climate.

Most importantly, faculty must discuss research in a humanizing way, rather than emphasizing unbiased and sterile research. The reality is that research involves the human condition. As such, people must be recognized as human beings and, especially those who are living through conflict and strife, deserving of dignity and respect, rather than just being viewed as research participants.

We must continue to underscore the human element of international research and ensure that the next generation of researchers does not view people just as interview participants or survey variables.

Conclusion

In this chapter, we have provided insight into the key issues related to international research preparation. Drawing from the rich data we collected from our participants, we presented a theoretical approach to doctoral research training utilizing Bronfenbrenner's (1994) ecological system theory as a framework. Our individually and externally focused recommendations are consistent with the perceptions of our study's participants, who shared several internal and external factors that they perceived helped and hindered their international researcher development. Although our ecological model is not intended to be a final checklist for international research development, we believe that it serves as a starting point for individuals to approach doctoral student research development in a systematic and holistic way. More importantly, our model serves as a first step towards clarifying good practice in doctoral student international research development, a subject that is currently under-studied in higher education. From our point of view, it is critical that the conversation on internationalization includes doctoral students, who will be our future scholars, practitioners, and thought leaders. They will be the future voice of our profession, and thus, considerations for 'how' they are trained to conduct research in international contexts is of vital importance.

References

Altbach, P. G., & Knight, J. (2007). The internationalization of higher education: motivations and realities. *Journal of Studies in International Education, 11*(3–4), 290–305.

Bronfenbrenner, U. (1994) Ecological models of human development. In *International Encyclopedia of Education*, Vol. 3, 2nd ed. (pp. 1643–1647). Oxford: Elsevier. Reprinted in M. Gauvain & M. Cole (Eds.), *Readings on the Development of Children*, 2nd ed. (1993, pp. 37–43). New York: Freeman.

Chernilo, D. (2006). Social theory's methodological nationalism myth and reality. *European Journal of Social Theory, 9*(1), 5–22.

Gopal, A. (2011). Internationalization of higher education: preparing faculty to teach cross-culturally. *International Journal of Teaching and Learning in Higher Education, 23*(3), 373–381.

Harzing, A. W., Reiche B. S., & Pudelko, M. (2013) Challenges in international survey research: a review with illustrations and suggested solutions for best practice. *European Journal of International Management, 7*(1), 112–134.

Institute of International Education. (2015). *Top 25 Places of Origin of International Students, 2013/14–2014/15*. Retrieved from www.iie.org/opendoors

Jung, J., Kooij, R., & Teichler, U. (2014). Internationalization and the new generation of academics. In F. Huang, M. Finkelstein, & M. Rostan (Eds)., *The Internationalization of the Academy* (pp. 207–236). Netherlands: Springer.

Knight, J. (2004). Internationalization remodeled: definition, approaches, and rationales. *Journal of Studies in International Education, 8*(1), 5–31.

Mitchell, D. E., & Nielsen, S. Y. (2012). Internationalization and globalization in higher education. In H. Cuadra-Montiel (Ed.), *Globalization – Education and Management Agendas* (pp. 3–22). Rijeka, Croatia: InTech.

Renn, K. A. (2003). Understanding the identities of mixed-race college students through a developmental ecology lens. *Journal of College Student Development, 44*(3), 383–403.

Renn, K. A., & Arnold, K. D. (2003). Reconceptualizing research on college student peer culture. *Journal of Higher Education, 74*(3), 261–291.

Rostan, M., Ceravolo, F. A., & Metcalfe, A. S. (2014). The internationalization of research. In F. Huang, M. Finkelstein, & M. Rostan (Eds.), *The Internationalization of the Academy: Changes, Realities, and Prospects* (pp. 119–143). Netherlands: Springer.

Shahjahan, R. A., & Kezar, A. J. (2013). Beyond the "national container": addressing methodological nationalism in higher education research. *Educational Researcher, 42*(1), 20–29.

Stebleton, M. J. (2011). Understanding immigrant college students: applying a developmental ecology framework to the practice of academic advising. *NACADA Journal, 31*(1), 42–54.

Yao, C. W., & Vital, L. M. (2016). "I don't think I'm prepared": perceptions of U.S. higher education doctoral students on international research preparation. *Journal for the Study of Postsecondary and Tertiary Education, 1*, 197–214.

Conclusion

Chapter 21

Perspectives on internationalization from and for a new generation

Laura E. Rumbley and Douglas Proctor

From the inception of this book project, purposeful steps were taken to shape its focus around what we opted to term 'next generation' perspectives on internationalization. Dictionary definitions of the term 'generation' typically hinge on two main notions. On the one hand, a generation speaks to the idea of individuals of or pertaining to a group of contemporaries, or a cohort, living or undergoing an experience at the same time. The term 'generation' may also relate to the idea of creating something, i.e., bringing something new into being.

Both of these meanings resonate most authentically with our original aim for this volume and for what we see as its ultimate output. In terms of the notion of a generational cohort, of course not all of the authors whose work has been featured in this publication fall closely enough within a similar age range to be classified as a pertaining to one specific generation. But, true to our original intent, their scholarly work in relation to the internationalization of higher education has come of age largely within the past decade. Collectively, they stand on the shoulders of the first generation of scholars who initially recognized that the phenomenon of internationalization deserved scholarly attention. From our perspective, the connections across these generations are vital. Indeed, in the Preface to this volume, Jane Knight and Hans de Wit reflect on the past, present, and future of internationalization in higher education. They highlight the work that they, and others, have undertaken over the last twenty years to define what internationalization means, on the one hand, and to lay the foundations of a new field of investigation and research, on the other. If the contributions to this volume have highlighted one thing, it is the influence that these two scholars have had on the next generation of international education and internationalization researchers and practitioners – barely a single chapter in this volume fails to make reference to the definitions of internationalization proposed and re-worked over time by Knight and de Wit.

With such strong roots in a body of literature from these two leading scholars, we could be led to believe that there is a homogeneity of focus in relation to internationalization research. However, the next generation authors in this volume dispel this supposition and – in their multidisciplinary, multisectoral, and multinational approaches to the topic – they clearly demonstrate the second key definition of the word 'generation,' which turns on the idea of creating something new and novel. Indeed, they have continued to highlight the growing maturity of research in this field, as it gradually asserts its position as an established, and truly interdisciplinary, field of study.

Testament to the growing status and acceptance of the field is the operation of major specialist research centers in the United States and the United Kingdom, with other strong sites of academic expertise in Japan, Canada, Italy, Australia, and other countries. Nevertheless, despite these advances, analysis of global trends in internationalization research has highlighted that this research tends to focus on a narrow range of key topics in a limited number of predominantly English-speaking countries (Proctor, 2016). This is in spite of the fact that research into the internationalization of higher education is conducted around the world (Rumbley et al., 2014), and that new perspectives are actively being sought from outside the dominant English-speaking paradigms (de Wit, Gacel-Avila, Jones, & Jooste, 2017).

In seeking to present alternative perspectives on the internationalization of higher education, this volume has deliberately sought to widen the horizons of international education research through its focus on new contexts and new topics, but also on new modes for exploring and understanding the field. While some of the chapters in the volume could readily be assigned under more than one of these headings, the editors have worked closely with chapter authors to frame their contributions accordingly. In this light, the new contexts explored in the volume include evolving political and economic contexts (for example, in the United States and the Republic of Ireland), a specific disciplinary and organizational context (i.e., schools of education), less frequently referenced geographic contexts (such as Siberia), and new perspectives on potential alignment in policy context (focusing on indigenization in Canada). In relation to new modes of research, cases are put forward for alternative methods, such as systematic topic modeling and the increased availability of big data to support analysis. Other authors in this section question the origins of Western understandings of internationalization, or propose new ways of understanding how international knowledge is retained and transmitted amongst academic staff. New topics brought to the fore in the volume include the alignment between international education and refugee education, the potential disconnect between internationalization policy and practice in secondary and tertiary education, and a call for the publicness of higher education to be rearticulated in a global world.

The contributions to this volume certainly focus on the international dimensions of higher education more broadly, rather than on the process of internationalization alone, further highlighting the breadth and depth of the field. Reflecting back on the Preface, a number of these chapters also seek to address some of the key concerns that have been raised in relation to the future directions of internationalization itself. In their Preface, Jane Knight and Hans de Wit point to the potential disconnect between the global and the local, which the chapters from Saito, Knutson, and Ota and Horiuchi each approach from a different perspective. Likewise, the chapters on doctoral student research training (Vital & Yao) and Chinese social science journals (Li) throw some light on the international dimensions of research and graduate education.

Where, then, are there research gaps that still need to be addressed? In their Preface, Jane Knight and Hans de Wit reflect on the framing of internationalization as soft power (rather than as knowledge diplomacy) and question whether soft power provided an appropriate framework given its relation to competition between nation-states. On a related note, they bemoan the increasing reliance on economic and political rationales (over social or cultural rationales) to drive internationalization thinking and practice within governments and institutions. While neither of these concerns has been fully addressed by the contributors to this volume, the editors are alert to other avenues for the exploration of these research gaps – for example, through the burgeoning communities of scholars focusing on the internationalization of the curriculum in North America, Europe, and Australia. From our perspective, other continuing research gaps of note relate to faculty and staff perspectives on internationalization, the social and community impact of staff and student mobility (abroad and at home), and the influence of new commercial modes of international education service delivery (in particular, the increased outsourcing of core services).

In line with the aspiration of the editors to present new perspectives from next generation voices, a large number of the chapters have been authored or co-authored by advanced graduate research students or early career scholars and practitioners. Alongside existing communication methods – from blogs, to industry magazines and occasional papers, to peer-reviewed journals – the editors believe there is a distinct need to broker new pathways to publication and dissemination for both early career scholars and practitioners. We continue to advocate for this through our work for the International Education Association of Australia (IEAA), the European Association for International Education (EAIE), and the Association for International Education Administrators (AIEA). However, we are delighted that this volume has afforded one such opportunity to a group of next generation thinkers and actors in the field.

We would, however, sound a note of caution in relation to what some might see as a homogenization of professional training in international education. With the development of professional master's courses in internationalization and international education in many U.S. colleges, if not more widely, we may risk encouraging new practitioners in international education to consider these academic pathways as the only valid route into a professional career in this field. Yet, as we know from own personal experience, let alone from the pathways of other scholar-practitioners (Streitwieser & Ogden, 2016), the career paths into international education are (at present) as varied and as disparate as the focus of internationalization research is broad and multifaceted.

We believe that the varied pathways that scholars and practitioners follow into the field bring significant richness to our institutions and to the governments and other agencies which support and nurture internationalization. As such, we hope that the next generation of researchers, scholars, and practitioners will continue to be drawn from a wide pool, and that this breadth of experience will continue to foster diversity of opinion and approach to the future agenda for the internationalization of higher education. Fostering synergies between diverse perspectives on internationalization is perhaps the most crucial concern that we identify for the future. To this end, "intelligent internationalization" (Rumbley, 2015) issues a call for deeper, more frequent, and more meaningful engagement among internationalization's most central stakeholders (i.e., institutional and systemic leaders, policymakers, scholars, and – crucially – practitioners). Meanwhile, bridging – indeed, fundamentally undoing – the longstanding disconnect between the world's cultural, political, and academic centers and peripheries (Altbach, 2004) continues to demand our urgent attention.

As we move toward the start of the third decade of the 21st century, we see an ongoing need for internationalization to be understood in relation to evolving contexts, innovative modes of making meaning, and emerging topics, in line with the way that we have chosen to frame the analysis in this volume. We will also need subsequent generations of reflective thinkers and inventive actors who will help us move this important conversation forward in ways that advance the agendas of higher education institutions and systems in a dynamic and equitable fashion. We already know that ambitious global and regional agendas – such as the African Union's Agenda 2063 and the Sustainable Development Goals of the United Nations – will require major contributions from the higher education sector to achieve the aspirations for ecological stability, societal wellbeing, and human dignity that are at the heart of these major international initiatives. There is enormous forward momentum in pursuit of the brighter global future envisioned by many, but there are also a multitude of serious barriers to success. Still, we believe it is fair to assert that the internationalization of higher education – understood broadly as a set of phenomena that ultimately seek to bridge the barriers that stand in the way of maximally meaningful living, learning, and knowledge creation in a globalized context – has a key role to play in the future success of initiatives designed to enhance educational, economic, political, social, and cultural realities at local, national, and global levels.

This is a very tall order. Can the internationalization of higher education really meet such expectations? Only time – and the careful analysis of subsequent generations – can give us an answer to that crucial question. In the meantime, our job is to ensure that what we understand as internationalization – as a field of study, a professional arena, a fundamental consideration for policymaking – continues to evolve in meaningful interplay with the challenges and opportunities of our time. Each new generation of higher education scholars and practitioners is thus called upon to bring forward their best efforts – creatively, critically, and, ultimately, constructively – to the enterprise of advancing our understanding of internationalization's inner workings and impacts to the farthest frontier.

References

Altbach, P. G. (2004). Globalization and the university: myths and realities in an unequal world. *Tertiary Education and Management, 10*, 3–25.

de Wit, H., Gacel-Avila, J., Jones, E., & Jooste, N. (Eds.). (2017). *The Globalization of Internationalization: Emerging Voices and Perspectives.* New York/London: Routledge.

Proctor, D. (2016). The changing landscape of international education research. *International Higher Education, 84*(Winter 2016), 19–21.

Rumbley, L. E. (2015, Spring). "Intelligent internationalization": a 21st century imperative. *International Higher Education, 80*, 16–17.

Rumbley, L. E., Altbach, P. G., Stanfield, D. A., Shimmi, Y., de Gayardon, A., & Chan, R. Y. (2014). *Higher Education: A Worldwide Inventory of Research Centers, Academic Programs, and Journals and Publications* (3rd ed.). Bonn, Germany: Lemmens.

Streitwieser, B., & Ogden, A. C. (2016). *International Higher Education's Scholar-Practitioners: Bridging Research and Practice.* Oxford: Symposium Books.

Index

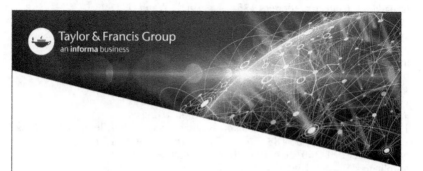